ARE YOU OUT OF YOUR MIND ... YET?

How to set your human-self free to fully experience its Spirit-Nature

To Patrick

with much appreciation

Peter

Printed in the United States of America

ISBN-13:   978-1732756007 (PB PUBLISHING)

ISBN-10:   1732756007

Contents

Are you out of your mind ... yet?

How to set your Human-self free to fully experience its Spirit-Nature

Preface

Would you like to experience all that your unique human experience is offering you?

Would you like to get out of your mind's constraints?

The point of my sharing this story below, is to show you the power of the Experience Ability we all have, which is our mind drama anti-virus. This simple ability literally dissolves drama and allows you access to the lessons that your experiences are giving you. From there, you can apply what you learned. It is this application that is needed, to change the experience and continue to move forward ... or stay still ... or just simply know what that next step is.

In my story, you will see that there was no hour-long process or even fifteen or five minutes of it. There was no body tapping or affirmations to make or chants to perform or breathe work to carry out. Having previously experienced the power in all these other processes, I was able to appreciate the simplicity of this Divinely given ability "we" already have at our disposal. The simple power of this method is that there is none of those physical or mental convulsions that you and I have probably both, spent thousands of dollars being trained in how to do. I'm not saying that you wasted your money doing those trainings, as I have also spent thousands and I know they work within the parameter of existence they were created from. I have found though, that all those processes, systems, techniques etc. all work ... but only when they get you to that one last place of "Experiencing".

My intention here, is to show you there is another simple, extremely effective tool available that is an *ability* we ALL have got already ... and we don't have to learn anything. This ability is naturally inherited when we come here for this human experience. The parameter of existence that created this method though, comes from the same creator that designed the playground called our "Human Reality", in which we get to experience Being Human.

The bargain price you have already paid for this tool owever, was simply your decision to come here and BE HUMAN.

Let me demonstrate the power of this ability and its potential to free us from our mind's dramas and limitations.

Some time ago, I went to the Winn Dixie grocery store and was feeling low and a little discouraged. Actually, I wasn't a little discouraged, I was a lot discouraged. I had just returned to the USA after spending four months in my beloved Australia. After 4 years away, it was an incredible opportunity to see my daughters and grand-daughters again. Having single parented my three daughters through their teenage years and even though they were now in their 20's; being away from them for such a long time was extremely stressful. From our reunion, I learned that it was the same for them also.

Unfortunately, from not working while I was in Australia, my finances were depleted, creating incredible hardships for me now being back in America. Dropping so deeply into my mind's poverty drama and being separated from my family again, I was spiraling down a black hole of "what's wrong with my life" after returning to the USA. I had come back to no work, with only a small handful of faithful clients from my conscious bodyworks practice willing to pick up where we had left off. My bank account had turned into a home for moths, while overdue car, telephone and insurance payments ensured these new occupants would not get crowded out with any excess cash and coin. To top it all off, my personal relationship had ended after months of intense drama and disconnection.

The good news was that I had a roof over my head, even though there was a back-rent owing on it also. The not so good news was that I was still sharing this roof with my ex-partner, as we tried to part ways amicably. Although the intense drama was less than what we had been experiencing while in Australia—I was still living on a floor of egg shells and breathing the thick fog of disconnection and withheld disappointments. To say my mind drama was running my life would be a gross understatement. I was struggling to feel my ownership for the suffering I was creating to both myself and my ex-partner. My mind was blaming her for the drama I was creating, so I could blame her for it all. It was the ultimate "avoid all ownership" shell game of self-deception that my mind excels in.

At that point, I was trapped deep in my mind, as its drama virus rapidly overwhelmed my *experiencing* anti-virus. I struggled to get out of my mind. Drama had infected every thought, deed and action. Suffering had become the norm, as a dark cloud blocked the warm nurturing rays of passion and joy that once shone their light of inspiration into my life's purpose.

I was going out of my mind trying to get ... out of my mind.

In one of my meditations, I asked the Divine what's he-her-it doing, and why have I been left this low down the prosperity and happiness ladder. Of course, at that time, I was so deep down my *mind's shaft* that even God couldn't hear me ... or was it that I couldn't hear him. The writing of this book had slowed to a snail's pace. My intention to always help empower others though, was still high and for the greater good. Although my passion is to empower all who share this third rock from the sun, my motivational energy to share this passion was being sucked into the black hole of my mind's lust for drama. My heart yearned to share its Love with one and all. I was straining to hold my focus on what's right and keep in sight my intention to not wallow in self-pity. In this moment though, self-pity and giving up was starting to look good compared to the incessant mental anguish of trying to get out of my single-minded focus on my lack of resources. I knew within my Spirit that the familiarity of this mental focus was attracting my experiences of lack. I felt powerless to stop its depressing spiral though.

So, why did I need to go down so low once more, to yet another restart? How many restarts must I endure before I reach that everlasting joy; the joy that all those spiritual salesmen keep telling me is my right and what I deserve and just sitting there for the taking? At this stage of my game of life, I had lost count of all my restarts and now, in my mind's black hole, I was choosing to selectively forget. Couldn't we just keep going up to where I've always known my passionate purpose would take me?

Well I mustn't have been as deep in my mind's shaft as I thought, for I got a message from my Higher Guidance that would break the fever of my drama virus. This message came in a most unsuspecting way and from the least likely person I could ever have imagined.

As I'm walking to the store, a fairly well dressed, clean African American man was sitting on the rail, right at the entrance to the store. When I arrived within shouting distance, he locked eyes on me and yelled," You must be a preacher? You are going to preach to the people and the Lord is going to raise you up."

My mind's judgmental identity jumped in to set free yet again, its disqualifying version of its virus; to judge and label and pull me deep within its caverns of discredit and invalidation. "He's a nut with too many cheap wines under his belt," I thought. He's no doubt full of wine already and obviously not seeing straight at all for that matter. I gave him a smile and a wave and a good ole Aussie "you betchya mate" with a wink and patronizing nod. I made sure not to stop though and just kept walking straight through the door. I asked myself, "How did he know my passion, my dreams and my life purpose,"? How did he know my intention was to speak to many, of self-empowering things—things that connect one to their Spirit and the higher realms of Being Human? I tried to dismiss it as just a crazy man's delusion, but the message had already hit its mark and the coincidence was well beyond invalidation. As I came out of the store, he was there again. He jumped off his rail this time, to shake my hand and reaffirm his past statements. With a gesture that resembled picking up two shopping bags he said, "You won't be just picked up by God." He then stretched out both arms and slowly raised them to heaven saying, "You will be raised up to God and you will preach to the people." This time I had to stop and set this apparently, poor delusional soul straight.

I said," That may be the case mate, but right now, God isn't paying too well, and I need a raise in wages, not stature." What I overlooked was his intuitive knowing that I needed to raise my spirits before either wages or stature would change. He looked me in the eye again and said with a smirk and a wink, "You will preach ... you will preach to many people ... you are a *very* good man." He had captured my attention and wasn't letting go until the message was acknowledged and driven deep into my heart. I could feel there was a message here, somewhere behind my mind's *drama* of mental judgments. I could feel his conviction in the belief he just stated—as it distracted my mind for a brief moment. Here was an opportunity to inject my drama anti-virus of experiencing with Awareness and I grabbed it with both hands. I began to bring my Awareness deep within me again and simply *feel* what was really going on *within* me—without the mind drowning out my experience by screaming its judgments, definitions and descriptions at me and everyone else, as it so incessantly does.

The simple act of feeling with my Awareness or rather, deliberately experiencing—effortlessly drew me out of the dungeons of my mind.

As my mind began to quiet, my Spirit saw its opportunity to speak. I *felt* the subtle and familiar assurance of my Spirit delivering its intuitive *feeling* message. I looked back at my Winn Dixie Messenger square in the eyes as deep as I could, back into his Soul, back through those dark sparkling eyes he had firmly locked onto me with. As I shook his hand, I said with my most grateful and loving Aussie tone, "Thank you mate, you have no idea how big a message you just gave me." He smiled at me again and I noticed his hand was warm soft and incredibly comforting. This was nothing like my mind drama had judged it would be. It was almost uncomfortably comfortable as it helped dissolve the last of my ego mind judgments of him, once and for all.

As I began to feel more, I realized this was Love I was feeling from him—and unconditional at that. I was out of my mind and free of its drama virus at last. It seemed like time had stopped and the busy noise of the store had disappeared as we held our loving gaze into each other's eyes. I have never seen this man before, or since, but the Love I felt from him was greater than any I have known from some of the most well-travelled Spiritual students or teachers. I could feel the genuine Love this being naturally expresses in our world. I really appreciated the message behind the fact that he had no titles or fancy qualifications to say or prove that he was either ordained or enlightened. He was though most definitely able to share a level of real genuine Love that surpassed many of the other spiritual celebrities I had met.

It was the simple power of his Love that jolted me out of my mind and empowered me to embody my Awareness again and feel my true essence once more.

I walked away shaking my head, with a smile I couldn't wipe off my face and a chuckle steadily growing into an uplifting laughter. I had received the first part of the message that my Spirit had been trying to send me—the virtues of trust, faith and patience. I KNOW it is all coming and yet I still allow my mind drama to weave it's not-so merry way back in, infecting me with its sabotage and dismantling my trust and belief ... in myself. The more I went into my mind and let it infect, the more my passion and courage for this life mission was slowly dying an agonizing death—taking with it my self-confidence. Eventually, I've no doubt my desire for this human life would follow. From being "in my mind", my life had started to go sideways and my mental drama of what's wrong was steadily increasing.

By being "in my mind", I was disconnecting myself from the intuitive guiding light of my Spirit's higher intention for my human experience.

When I arrived home from the store, I knew I had to apply what I've learned from my Experience Embodying work and what I'm writing about. My Winn Dixie messenger was right, and it was time to practice what I preach ... to myself. I set my intention and dropped deeper into feel, to experience more and more of the lesson this moment was presenting to me. As I quickly immersed myself further into my Awareness, revealing the real experience I was having, I was able to *feel* more clearly how my mind drama had once again been concentrated on what's wrong. Feeling deeply into the experience I was having in that moment, connected me with the victim identity suit, the one my mind had selected for me to wear—the one I had been creating this debilitating experience through.

I could feel how the virus had seeped deep within me once more and at the same time, dragged me even deeper into my mind's caverns of limitations. Although it was much subtler this time, I could feel the strands of attachment I had to the *need* for money to create this work. It wasn't that I DIDN'T need money to bring it into the world ... that was an obvious truth. Now though, I was able to feel the *attachment* I had on the need, which was creating my suffering. I could feel my resistance creating my need for an experience other than the experience of lack, the one I was avoiding in this moment. My attention energy had become fixed on having a lack of resources. I could *feel* the old adage show up—energy flows where attention goes. I got my "Ah Ha" moment of integration.

Through a lack of Awareness, this fixed attention was what was actually attracting and creating the experience of lack that I was having right now.

This was my mind's drama virus subversively blocking my movement forward. These were the belief structures that motivated my sabotaging actions. Another "Ah Ha" as I realized, it was not really my mind blocking me—it was my resistance that was fueling my mind to create its highly effective drama. I was trying to be some place other than where I was at—right then and there; in that present moment. I was deep in my mind's wants and desire and at the same time resisting my present moment life experience. I wanted a different experience to the one my mind was resisting—the one of restarting with a fresh canvas. This experience was the one my Spirit intended, but my mind was in conflict through its dynamic of resisting and attaching. The fresh canvas presented to me now, was to appreciate all of Life's lessons that I was now completing and embody the virtues that reveal their self to me, before beginning along the new path of experiences Life was laying out ahead of me. A little more Awareness *feel* and my resistance to this integration also dissolved. As I started to fully experience this, I could feel yet another aspect of the lesson my Winn Dixie messenger experience was presenting me.

The minds drama is relentless, but our ability to feel and fully experience Life's lessons, is the most powerful and freeing asset we ALL have.

It is this inherited ability we all come here with, that allows us to integrate and handle *ALL* manner of experiences that BEing human can deliver. I recognized again the simple and natural power of deliberately experiencing my Life, by being able to *feel* my way through it. I gained a new appreciation for the fact that it was this simple yet powerful ability, that was rapidly shifting me out of the overwhelm and discharging the constraints of my mind's drama. It was undoing in seconds and minutes, the constraints of my drama that had been building in me over the past months. I realized how covertly my mind had shackled my Spirit's intuition and disempowered my ability to experience and integrate my life lessons. I became present with the power of this simple ability we all have, this ability that enables us to fully experience Life and how easily *experiencing* dissolved my drama in a matter of moments.

There was no process or mental gymnastics to complete ... just plain ole "deliberate experiencing".

I noticed that my mental drama had stopped completely now. I didn't have to *quiet the mind*, for it quieted on its own, once it again had my Spirit's Awareness to guide and direct it to higher perspectives. My mind was quiet again, but more importantly, it was working with me, not against me. There was no more endless chatter about what's wrong—just calm descriptions of what I was experiencing, now in this moment, along with an increasing flow of positive feeling potentials for my future. I noticed how incredibly calm and relaxed my whole being had become, nothing like the turmoil of my minds previous drama filled days, weeks and months. I also recognized how effortlessly this whole process had turned around completely ... in moments. My Awareness of

EVERYTHING around me was now most intensely acute again. Things just looked and felt brighter somehow—both internally and externally.

My "Ah Ha" moment was not any perceived earth-shattering mental experience, but rather a powerful "matter of fact" experience of a knowing Spirit.

Tears of gratitude and love for me, my Winn Dixie messenger and the Divine began to flow unabated. This IS my restart. This is my final beginning. This is why I love Being Human, and this ability that we all have is what my life purpose has led me to this point for—to share with the world the knowledge of the power of Awareness to deliberately experience and discharge Life. A deep grounding anchored me in this moment, as a realization revealed to me that this simple Awareness knowledge that dissolves the drama virus of not just my own experiences, but maybe ... the drama of the world as well.

A couple of people became concerned for me after hearing my previous drama story and even called to see that I was OK and not on the edge of doing something crazy.

The edge would be that delusional state the drama virus can take one to.

I'm sure many suicides and addictions can be contributed to being immersed in the mind's infection from its drama virus.

I was not on that edge because I was ... out of my mind.

I was "in feel" with my life again.

I would never be on that edge, as long as I knew how to inject the Mind Drama Anti-virus of deliberate experiencing into my life; of feeling with my Awareness.

As long as I had the courage to feel what was really going on behind the illusion of my mind's drama, I would never be taken to that edge ... or push my-self over it.

There is no need to get to some quiet space and free the mind and center myself or chant or any techniques or process to be done. The mind naturally quieted all by itself. This is a simple present moment method of experiencing that is always available to every single human being on the planet—in every present moment. This is a natural ability granted to us all, to easily and effortlessly integrate the lessons of our human experiences. Through my conscious bodywork, I have found that this simple yet powerful ability of experiencing with Awareness, is also the key ingredient to health and wellness. Many times, I and my client on the table experienced *in-the-moment* healings from just this simple application of this experiencing with Awareness ability.

This is true experiencing, which is simply feeling with your Awareness— without definitions, judgments or descriptions of what you are experiencing.

This experiential book is my way of sharing with you the one common denominator that sets us all free from our mind's incessant and debilitating drama, along with its inherent ill-health, dis-ease and sickness. This denominator is the same one we all have and all those who have come before us have had. Even the enlightened masters have at some time in their lives, fallen victim to this drama virus. Ultimately it spurred them on to discover the anti-virus that allowed their amazing teachings to come into being.

If you wish to free yourself from the chains of your minds drama, then by the end of this book you can experientially know the power of experiencing through your Awareness. You can come to know the power you hold within you to discharge the Drama virus of your mind, along with how to use it in your everyday life. You will discover *your* keys, the ones that unshackle the drama handcuffs imprisoning your purpose for being here— setting free your dreams of all that you intended coming here to BE.

By the end of this book, you will have had *your own personal experience* of this Awareness ability that sits within you. You will be able to reconnect to that passionate, purposeful Life once again—the one you intuitively know you came here to live. This is the life you have maybe always wanted to live but felt trapped by the life you were told and indoctrinated into believing you should live.

If you have felt that there is a greater, more powerful aspect of yourself that knows the higher intentions of your Path, then by the end of this book, you can be reconnected to your intuitive guidance. This guidance is the one that knows NOT what you *should* be doing but, what is right ... for you ... to BE what your Spirit Self intended for the human you came here to BE. This inner knowing of what the next step is and the right decision to make—the one that is in perfect alignment with your personal Life Path, comes from that part of you that is beyond the limitations of your mind's drama. It is this inner knowing that is not only beyond the minds drama, but it dissolves the resistances to being human.

Are you ready to get ... out of your mind ... yet—and fully experience the latent potential of the rest of your Life?

Are you out of your mind … yet?

How to set your Human-self free to fully experience its Spirit-Nature

Introduction

True Freedom … is the willingness to experience anything … free of <u>*influence*</u> *… from both inner and outer originations.*

How free can I BE, if I am under the *influence* of something? How free can I be to make clear decisions about my life, if I am under the *influence* of beliefs indoctrinated into me to live a certain way. How free am I to live my life, if I am under the *influence* of "peer pressure"? If we have no *awareness* of the effect of indoctrinated beliefs, peer-pressure or any of the intricate myriad of influences that play upon us in our everyday existence as human BEing's on this emerald third rock from the sun, then how can we know if we are operating free of manipulation? How can we do anything about influence, if we have no idea of what aspect of our BEing Self is being influenced or manipulated? How can we BE free of influence from both our inner and external worlds, if we have no understanding or cognition of the intricate and complex makeup that is … the Human we are BEing?

Are we truly free if we are being influenced in any way at all?

If you allow the intricacies to reveal their selves throughout this book study and let them stimulate your remembrances—without over intellectualizing them by trying to understand it all immediately, you will naturally and effortlessly expand your capacity to bring in more information and have new experiences of your most authentic Self. There is an expansive spiritual experience of your Spirit Self lying just beyond your Souls material intellects *concept of mind*. This *concept of mind,* which has been embraced by the intellectual component of your Soul, is the one that traps you in your materialistic viewpoints and continues to push out the intuitive guidance of your Spirit. This Intellectual Soul component uses this *concept of mind* as a substitute for your true Spirit Self; to justify staying disconnected from its higher guidance.

That is why this book is titled, "Are you out of your mind … yet?" As you journey through the pages of this spiritual landscape and allow your remembrances to reveal the intricacies that lie within the true form that is your BEing, you will naturally and effortlessly begin to free your Self from the chains of this *concept of mind*. This concept is a covertly false indoctrination of an aspect of your human self that is believed to be elusive, unmanageable and rampantly working against your greater good. This *concept of mind* has become this present intellectually materialistic age's scapegoat. It has become the excuse for anything and everything unexplainable about our human-Being-self, particularly those unvirtuous elements that one doesn't want to take ownership of. It has become a widely used practice these days to shelve responsibilities with statements like, "I just can't control my mind" and "I need more mind control" or "I can't think straight" etc. Ironically, all the mind control courses and workshops to tap into the *power of the mind* etc., are all based on the material world and using "IT ", to get what you want and live the life you've always wanted or entitled to. This however, simply doesn't ensure happiness, freedom or fulfillment. Yet, the real state of true happiness and freedom that comes from a truly spiritually rich life, is only achieved—as the enlightened Masters and Teachers tell us—from that place of "no mind". I would suggest that the Masters used the term "no mind" for our benefit, so that we could more easily relate to what they were *experiencing*. In fact, they had become Masters by intimately and *experientially* knowing all the relationships of all the *intricacies* of the Human BEing Self. It was through Self-knowledge of the intricate make up of BEing human, that they became free from the deceptions and constraints of ... *the concept of mind*.

The intricacies of BEing Human can be overwhelming to say the least. Maybe that's why the Divine gives us re-incarnation, because it is far too intricate and often paradoxically complicated for us to master being human in just one lifetime. When sharing this work with new students, the inevitable question asked by most of them is, "why do we need to know all of this intricate stuff about being human? It seems like we are just making it all too complicated. Surely the 'KISS' adage of *Keep It Simple Stupid,* is more helpful and a better guideline on the path to any form of enlightened Self-Awareness. Surely that is better than getting bogged down in the complicated intellectualizing of our Human Nature?". Of course, this viewpoint does have some justification. Understanding however, that "intricate" and "complicated" are two different experiences is pivotal to clarity and understanding. Just because something is intricate, doesn't mean that it is intrinsically complicated. Knowing this can set one on a simplified self-empowerment path toward mastery of the intricacies of human BEing-ness. This path can expose all manner of debilitating influences that inhibit our TRUE freedom to BE.

Just because something *is* intricate or complicated, doesn't mean that it must come from over-intellectualizing, although this can definitely be the case for some people. If we look to the dictionary for an example, we can clarify this a little further.

com•pli•cat•ed

adj.

1. composed of elaborately <u>interconnected</u> parts; complex: *complicated apparatu.*

2. difficult to analyze, understand, or explain: *a complicated problem.*

3. A <u>confusing</u> relationship of parts.

in·tri·cate

(ĭn'trĭ-kĭt)

adj.

1. Having <u>many</u> complexly arranged elements; elaborate: *an intricate pattern; an intricate procedure*

2. Difficult to understand, analyze, or solve for having many interconnected elements.

3. Obscure; complex; puzzling

in·tel·lec·tu·al·ize

(ĭn'tl-ĕk'cho□o-ə-līz')

tr.v. **in·tel·lec·tu·al·ized, in·tel·lec·tu·al·iz·ing, in·tel·lec·tu·al·iz·es**

1. To furnish a rational structure or meaning for.

2. To avoid psychological insight into (an emotional problem) by performing an intellectual analysis.

3. to make intellectual; analyze intellectually or rationally.

4. to ignore <u>the</u> emotional or psychological significance of (an action, feeling, etc.) by an   excessively intellectual or abstract explanation.

From this, we can see that although intricate and complicated can be interwoven, they are still different. In a nutshell, intricate is an *elaborate system of connections* of the *many parts* that make up a whole. Complicated is, although still about connections of parts etc., has a far more confusing and difficult to understand *structural* element to it. Having said this, we would, no doubt be accurate in saying, BEing human is both intricate and complicated. The confusing aspect only comes about when some of the intricate parts are not known—along with their relationship to each other, as well as to the whole in which they are parts thereof. There are many intricate parts, both external and internal, both physical and spiritual, that make it possible for us to BE Human. Some can never be explained successfully through this present human intellect. There is also no doubt that the intricate structure of BEing Human is immensely complex in its form, of both physical and non-physical spiritual elements.

The confusion created via doubt when we start to explore the complexities of our human existence however, comes about simply from one or more of the intricate parts ... simply not being known. Consequently, this creates a gap in the stream of information; from which doubt and confusion result. I have a saying that "Nothing is impossible. If you can know all the parts that make up the whole, and you can know the correct sequence that they go in, then you can create anything."

Everything has a relationship to something else.

The correct sequence or position that a specific part needs to have in relation to the whole that it exists in, is a part of the *relationship* that part has with the whole. Another part of the *relationship* is the effect or influence that part exerts on the whole. Yet another part of the *relationship*, is the *resultant* function of the whole, because of the position and influence of the part within it. Although these elements are not necessarily all there are that make up a *relationship*, as we see here; all the parts have an *influence* on how the whole functions and is made up. This *influential force* is what plays out in what we are calling, *relationship*. So, if a relationship is dis-functional or dis-harmonious, then if we know all the parts and their position or sequence, then we can potentially harmonize it again and improve (or heal) the function of the whole. By knowing which element is out of sequence, or which is the wrong part that is asserting a detrimental influence and adversely affecting the functioning of the whole, we can make real changes that bring the whole ... back into harmony with its Self. All of this applies directly to the parts of our Body Soul and Spirit that make up the whole that is the Human-Being that you are.

The real power to effect changes within my Human BEing-ness, is in intimately knowing the intricacies of my Human BEing-ness and their relationships together.

So, when my students would ask why we need to know all this stuff about our consciousness, I would reply with a couple of questions. "How can you change something, or the effect of something on you ... if you don't know where the influence is coming from, let alone what part of your Self is actually being affected by such influence? How can you be *free of influence*, if you have no idea what the influence is, where it is coming from, or what part of your BEing Self is actually under the influence? Self-Knowledge, holds the power to change, harmonize and heal one's self."

To know thy Self ... is to know God.

Throughout the exploration within this book, you will be led through the intricacies of our human existence and evolution. There will be many elements and components revealed, of not just your human self, but the intricacies and complex natures of your Soul and Spirit Self's as well. These newly revealed components, or parts of the intricate structure of your Human BEing, will for some, be revelations of a knowing that they already have deep within their Soul, yet for so long have doubted and denied. Generally, this can happen because of the overlay of their own *unknown* indoctrinations. For others, this information will seem confusing, complicated and even overwhelming.

If you stay connected with the facts above and remember that confusing and complicated, simply come about from missing information (integral parts and their relationships), then you may be able to allow the rest of the information within these pages to reveal their self and fill-in the greater picture of the BEing that is your True Self. This True Self is that spiritual aspect of you that has been continually trying to present its Self to your Soul and BE embodied in your Human.

A picture is a great analogy for the intricate relationships of the parts that make up our human BEing-ness. Like all pictures, this one starts out with an outline, a sketching of the whole, a Divine concept if you will. If I can serve my purpose correctly for you with the information and exercises within these pages, we will be able to fill in the shades, tones and colorings of the different forms together. As the WHOLE picture of what you truly BE begins to form into vibrant and colorful life, you will awaken latent Soul forces that can transform your present existence and spiritualize your human-self.

If you look deeply into a master painter's artwork, you can't help fall into awe at the way forms are created through not just the shape the element takes, but the relationship of colors, tones, shadings and strokes that are brought together to create the form we see as a completed whole. The position of the tree within the landscape and where its shadows fall, or its lights reflected, shows us the relationship the tree has to the landscape it exists in. Ultimately, this all helps determine the perspective we receive of the picture as a whole, and how we bring it into our Soul as an experience. If we explore this more deeply, all the different relationships of colors, tones, shades and strokes etc., that lie within the total landscape; we may see where the right separation of color creates a certain effect or influence, and yet another blending of the colors creates yet another influence. To explore the depths of these *intricacies* within the total landscape we call a picture, to bring them into the light of our own Awareness and make all the intricate parts *known*, naturally draws one deeper and deeper into awe at the skillful artistry that brought such a masterpiece into existence.

The more intricacies we can make known to us of the whole landscape we call this picture, the more *intimate* we become with it. If you notice your Souls reaction to all of these painted stimulants and influences, you might notice the Soul becoming harmonized within its self, being calmed yet inspired, excited yet grounded, in the presence of its own relationship with the picture. The same applies again to the way our human-Being-self is put together and the relationship of the parts within us to each other. If we can come to intimately know all the parts and relationships etc., of our physical, but more importantly our spiritual nature, then we can harmonize and heal not just our physical, but our Soul and Spirit as well.

To not be present and explore these intricacies of the picture, leaves one disconnected and dis-associated from it, blind to any influence being emanated by it. The picture would just be another picture of another landscape, and the intellect would immediately pull up a reference point memory of a landscape in real life, to invalidate or discredit not only the masterpiece, but the master himself who painted it.

We are each the master artist of the masterpiece we call ...

I AM ... HUMAN.

To know thy Self, is to know the intricacies of the whole BEing that is you. This BEing is not just a human, but a co-creating Body Soul and Spirit Being, imbued with abilities, organs and functions, specifically designed to *experience*, not just the physical material world, but also the non-physical spiritual world from which ... everything originates.

To stay with the picture analogy,

- The Spiritual Realm is the canvass we are created upon.

- Your Spirit Self is the master artist.

- Your Soul self is the paint.

- Your Body-self human is the final *picture creation*, through which experience manifests as both an inner and outer expression, of Soul and Spirit.

Determining the *quality* of the masterpiece you create of your Self, *requires* knowing the intricacies that make up the whole BEing. If you are trying to create a sunset scene and you don't know what yellow and red are, or how they go together to make orange, then your sunset would be a gross misrepresentation of the true sunset experience you're wishing to convey. If your human of Body and Soul are the colors of red and yellow and you don't know how to mix them correctly, or what their relationship together is that brings about the burnt orange of a sunset experience, then how can you possibly bring about a true experience of a sunset. If you don't know the difference between your Human and Spirit-Self's, then how can you know the difference between a true experience of your Spirit or the biased over emotional event of your human? If your

Body and Soul are not in a correct relationship to each other, then the human creation expressed, will inevitably be one of chaos within a broken and disjointed form. Paint is only paint, it is the strokes of the Spirit master artist that puts them in correct relationship together; from which they may then create a beautiful physical form that can bring inspiration into our material world.

It is your Spirit-Self that carries these Cosmic wisdoms of correct relationships. The correct relationships between the canvas of the Spiritual Realm, the master artist of the Spirit Self, the Soul components of the paints and the Body creation that is the final physical expression of all these elements, need to be intimately known to be able to create a human picture that harmonizes with reality. The parts of Body Soul and Spirit and their relationships together, MUST be known intimately ... before one can become a true master creator of the destiny of their own Human BEing.

This study work is most definitely intricate and complex. I won't lie or pretend that this is simple, even though simplicity lies at the heart of these spiritual intricacies. Some of the terminology will no doubt seem foreign to you. It can be difficult to comprehend, but only to an Intellect that has cut itself off from its spiritual source. It can be confusing, only because there are elements not yet known or received, or rather more accurately, have not been re-awakened within you ... yet. In truth, there is nothing here that you as a fellow human Being here now in this stage of our evolution, don't have knowledge of within you. These pages of words are designed to help you awaken the wisdom that lies within. Although yes, we are all here to still learn some things, we have however evolved to the point that the onus is on US to now apply *all* that we have learned, from our many previous incarnations. You are the culmination of wisdoms from all your previous lives that have brought you to this here and now. When something makes sense to you within these pages, it's not because you just learned something new, it's because you just *remembered* something you had already learned in previous incarnations. The wisdom we acquired through our lifetimes is accumulative.

The learning of something *new,* comes about when you *apply* what you have remembered, to your present life. Everything we have learned and integrated through previous lives, comes with us into the one we live presently.

> *Know that when you get an "Ah Ha !!" moment within this book exploration, it is because you just remembered something you have already known.*
>
> *It is this awakened remembrance and the actions you take from it, that now gives you the opportunity to learn something new.*

As the intricacies of your whole BEing Self reveal their true nature and relationship throughout these pages, you will come to intimately remember and know the elements of your Human and Spirit Self's that have, for so long been strategically hidden behind the deception that is ... the *concept of mind.*

There are certain Beings that don't want us to intimately know the truth of these intricate elements of our Body Soul and especially Spirit; which make up our true Human BEing Self. These Beings are the ones who gave us the confusing and complicated *concept of mind* in the first place, to keep us all in the dark about our true nature and the personal power and freedom that lies in experientially knowing our true relationship to the Spiritual World. The only power and influence that these Beings hold over you, lies in your self-imposed ignorance of the intricacies of your Authentic Spirit-Self and the power that you have available when you embody it in your Human-Soul-self. All of this lies in the relationships pulsating within your whole BEing Self, of your Body Soul and Spirit.

To experientially know the influences of both inner and external originations, frees me to choose and act only from and for, the highest good of both Self and others.

So, enjoy your journey into the depths of your True BEing Self.

BE excited for the remembrances that will be triggered back into your present incarnation, from which you can then bring new and empowering experiences into your life's future.

BE prepared to embody a new expansive and empowering sense of freedom, beyond the limits of your materialistic indoctrinated beliefs of what freedom is meant to be in this day and age.

Are you ready to slip into something more comfortable, to allow your Soul to wrap its human self in the warm, cozy, nurturing cloak of your empowered Spirit Self, that Highest-True-Self that you are, that is capable of embodying your human with a true sense of freedom?

Are you ready to get ... out of your mind?

Are you out of your mind ... yet?

How to set your Human-self free to fully experience its Spirit-Nature

Chapter 1

The Power in Story Telling

For thousands of years the family histories, ancestral linage, historical events, general knowledge, skills and practices of the ancient Hawaiian culture, were conveyed without any written words to describe them. Many other cultures throughout the history of Human Life on this planet have done the same. From healing and spirituality, to agriculture fishing and construction of buildings and boats—no matter how intricate or complex, not a single word was written. The essential power and understanding of the message weren't lost or diminished in any way by being conveyed in this time honored, non-written practice. Even though this knowledge was verbally passed down over thousands of years, the context survived ... intact.

All knowledge from our original civilizations was originally transferred through story and speech.

The ancient Hawaiians knew that it was possible to influence outcomes by the correct use of the power in the spoken word, along with the tone and context through which the message was delivered. Their sacred chants were constructed in this way to heal, to influence the weather, to invoke prosperity and success in their ventures and to generally create favorable outcomes for their communities in everyday living. They had a profound and abiding respect and understanding of how to use this power. They understood that the words are just the content, the mental drama of what they are trying to convey or describe to the other. They knew that the content of the spoken word would be understood by the reasoning, rational Uhane as they know it or lower-self as I have labeled it. The context or *"inner feeling"* of the message would be received and understood by the experience of the Spirit High-Self. If one could *feel* the message being delivered instead of trying to mentally understand it, they would gain a far deeper comprehension of the message being delivered.

~ 23 ~

The experiential transmission is the feeling behind the words and is interwoven throughout the story being told—it "lives" in the space between the words.

The original Hawaiians, although at that time not having any comprehension of what a written word is, understood conceptually that if a written document was created, then the context and feeling of the message could be lost. They intimately knew the intellects propensity for drama and because of that, they understood that one would only get what one could mentally understand. This original culture knew that the essence and true experience—*the feeling* that was being conveyed, was what was important and could be lost through the ridged written word.

They understood and respected the minds ability to create drama from anything—even Spiritual teachings.

I have noticed in our western intellectual societies that the mind, especially likes to focus a lot of attention on creating drama around Spiritual teachings. For the original Kanaka Maoli or natives of Lahui, the Hawaiian Nation, it was just too complicated and confusing to write. Resources would be wasted, unnecessary energy would be lost, and confusion would ensue, so there didn't seem any benefit in it.

It was far simpler and much more fun to express through story, song, chant and speech, along with more power and energy conveyed to each other. This was done in each present moment and done directly to the person for whom the message was intended. They knew that it was easier to capture the minds attention by tricking it, through staying in feel and having fun. This was also a much easier way to stay connected to the other person and vice versa. The ancient Hawaiian's level of connection to the other person from this feeling form of communication was such that, they could *feel* what each other were saying as they followed the story. Actually, the intention of both parties at the start of any communication with another person was to first *feel* what that person was saying and talking about—then hear what they were saying second.

Our extraordinarily dramatic western mind is at the other end of this paradigm. We are constantly trained to "listen to me … listen to what I'm saying" not "feel me…feel what I am saying."

It was only when the white man came with his insatiable need for mental understanding, which brought with it generations of bigotry persecution and arrogance, that the first Hawaiian dictionary was attempted. The white man's arrogance was so great that they even banned the Hawaiian language for many years at first. The drama of the white mind couldn't comprehend what the Kanaka Maoli indigenous Hawaiian was saying. The white settlers *fear drama* was so extreme that they even banned all Kanaka Maoli from naming their children with traditional names. All natives had to have a white European name as well, just so the white settlers would know who they were talking to and about.

As the whites began to research the language, they discovered that most of the words in Hawaiian had multiple meanings. In one *context* a word would mean this, and in another context, the same word would mean something completely different. Some words had as many as 20 or more meanings and were complicated further by how other words were used with it and the *context* of how the words were delivered. To listen to the true Hawaiian language is to hear a musical form of tone communication that softens and subdues one's Soul. This tone form was far beyond the comprehension of the rigid western minds ability to translate—let alone understand. From these realizations, you can imagine the drama generated by the fixed minds of the western missionary of the time.

Their mind drama became so extreme that they couldn't comprehend this ancient form of communication at all. The concept of *feeling* the meaning of any story, whether for entertainment or education was incomprehensible to the drama created by the majority of western thinking intellectual minds. Eventually the white man's mind drama became so intense, that they just gave up trying to work it out. They just took the presumably easy path of banning all Hawaiian language from being spoken at all. It became illegal for the Kanaka Maoli to speak their ancient native language or practice their cultural ways. This so-called western civilized intellectual mind, effectively brought to the edge of extinction, an ancient cultural way of living and communicating at an intense intimacy and connection rarely experienced, even in todays perceived "more evolved" reality. This very same ancient cultural way had been at the heart of a society who lived for over thirteen thousand years without war or any major disease or plagues.

The power of the intellectual mind's "drama" is so great that it can shut down a whole civilization's way of living and communicating.

The way the Kanaka Maoli conveyed their knowledge so effectively and understood each other was to tell stories. They would tell real stories that had to be followed by feeling the story as if the listener were there. As well, the storyteller would deliberately *feel* the story as it was told, to help the listener connect to the story and *feel* it directly. This form of communication was so suppressed and outlawed by the white authorities that the Kanaka Maoli had to make their knowledge secret, to protect it from the destructive intentions of the western white man's incessant mind drama of control. Unfortunately, nearly 75% of the true Hawaiian cultural ways were lost or *mis-interpreted* out of their original form.

My intention for this book is to convey its message through the communication principles of those ancient Hawaiians—to reawaken your Spirit through the context of story. Any discussion about the mind, which is the partial topic of this book, can and will always be a very intellectually complex subject to try to talk about—but there is another way—a short cut through the minds maze of mis-understanding dramas.

When the mind gets involved with anything, the conversation is likely to become more and more complicated.

From what we have just read, can you see the complications that can be created by conveying the true essence and meaning of any message purely by the written word? Words aren't context, they are content. As essential as the written word is to write a book and to transmit a particular message or teaching—the words themselves can become the very limitation or obstacle to conveying the true essence of the message to the other. This is only a limitation when we try to understand the message by only using our minds limited intellectual resources.

Our ancient enlightened teachers knew all too well this fact also. They would often write, speak and teach with analogies, parables or in riddle. They purposely set out to confuse the student's mind, so the student could *feel* the context of the message, versus mentally distorting it through the drama of the student's mind interpretations.

A student's level of non-attachment to the mind would determine how much of the teacher's essential context was experientially understood and how much was mentally interpreted.

There was no right or wrong from the teacher to the student about this. The teachers knew that any *new* understanding gained at whatever level of consciousness the student was at, would naturally change the student's viewpoint. This change of viewpoint would then create the platform for the student to attain his next level of understanding. Therefore, we can read the same book, paragraph, phrase or sentence many times over a period of time and with each reading, get a different viewpoint of understanding. The words haven't changed; my understanding of the words changes. My understanding changes because my viewpoint changes. My viewpoint changes because what I read and understood from the previous time, changes how I view it the next time I read it. Each time this happens, my level of consciousness changes. Each time my level of consciousness changes, my ability to feel and experience more, changes with it also. It is the evolution of my consciousness, one small shift—one viewpoint at a time. This process can be accelerated simply by reading or studying "in-feel", that is, feeling for the context and essence of the message. Ironically, to *feel* the message of any information whether it is written or any other form of subtle transference such as light, vibration or energetic—one must get *out of their mind*. The mind cannot *feel* or *experience* anything.

Story telling automatically conveys the contextual "feeling" of what is being said and thus experientially delivers the meaning, bypassing the mind's propensity to dramatize and distort.

Now our western world has taken this paradigm to the opposite extreme. The latest wave from the drama of our mental west is to not get involved with our story or our drama and let it go—don't talk about it. Unfortunately, I feel this concept also indoctrinates the wrong message. Ultimately it will compound our disconnection from the context within the spoken word. We have been so entrained to release and get rid of our stuff and the so-called baggage in our life, that we can't feel the disconnection we have created from the context of our life—from our life's *Story*. To not be involved in my story is impossible—my story is the human experience I have had and am having in every moment of my life here.

Our experiences are the only thing that we truly have and in fact, are the only thing that we do take with us when we leave this Human reality.

Can you see the drama created in your life when you are always trying to get rid of and not own your Life story—the one you are living in every present moment of your existence here? This is why so many of our planets human population have become so reluctant to take responsibility and ownership for their life. Something to clarify at this point and which we will talk about in more detail further on in this book, is that our story is not the *events* of our Life, but rather it is the *experiences* we have IN those events of our life.

If we are "non-attached" to our story—then we can be experientially involved in it—without being mentally trapped by it.

From the drama of our intellectual thinking mind, we have effectively been indoctrinated to take the written word as gospel. If it is written and if my perception is that it resonates with me, then it is the truth, the whole truth and nothing but the truth. Look at the newspapers, what's written in them and how much we rely on them for our daily drama fix ... Oops, I'm sorry, I meant information. Actually, I did mean *Drama Fix*. We seem to have come to a place where news is only news when it is dramatic.

If it is spoken, we are taught to treat it with caution and doubt—after all, it might not be the truth. The person speaking those words may have, or probably has a hidden agenda and is only out to get me. This indoctrinated pattern goes back to those early days of parental deceptions when our parents said one thing and did another. Add to this that those same parents were most likely *feeling* something completely different to both their speech and actions. You can still see this happening today as the virus of our mind's drama blinds us to this indoctrinated way of false communication.

Isn't it fascinating that the more we have developed our mind and intellect, the more drama we seem to be experiencing and the less we are able to effectively communicate with each other?

Our lack of trust in our ability to *feel,* disconnects us further from the speaker and the context of what's being spoken. Look at how we feel about politicians and governmental departments. Those that live within these realities are continually taught to mistrust the spoken word, along with the speaker of those words. They believe only the exact written word. If we are outside of these departments and their *definitions* of the written word, we experience the drama of confusion, misrepresentation and all too often, deception.

You can see how this form of communication actually creates, confusion and disconnection from each other, rather than clarity and connection. This is the perfect breeding ground for the mind's drama virus to replicate and multiply. Facebook is a great present-day example of this disconnect through the written word, because it is all done through type. I can't tell you the number of times I have ended up in facebook-drama through miss-interpretations of what I was saying, especially when we have been discussing life ownership issues.

Legal documents are another great example. Legal documents are so lengthy, because within the mentally created legal system, the written word is taken so literally, that it has now become a weapon. Look at what some environmental studies have told us, only to find out years later the truth that was hidden and the real damage that was caused. Look at what we have learned from the tobacco industry's multi-million-dollar lobbies to have us believe something other than the real facts about smoking. Put the CEO's on the witness stand and watch them squirm from their mental drama of trying to avoid *speaking* the truth. They are quick to give you a lengthy document written in complicated dramatic language and terminologies designed to cover and confuse, all to justify winning their case by any means.

We could say the use; or rather miss-use of the written word by the intellectual world, has become a weapon of mass destruction as well as, mass deception?

The literal meaning of contracts, agreements and statements struggle to convey the context. When they do, in an attempt to cover all contextual implications, some governmental and legal documents can be hundreds or even thousands of pages long; trying to cover the context—and still not get it all. A clever, ambitious lawyer can win the case by finding one contextual discrepancy that invalidates the other thousand or so pages. It is an unfortunate testament to the disconnection and mistrust we have for and from each other, that a lawyer is such an integral part of the operations on this planet. The drama of our Intellectual-Mind is forever trying to understand everything and so, translates what it hears or reads into a form that it can comprehend and rationally describe and understand. An experience is something you *feel*—not something you can necessarily describe in full detail.

Our description is only a translation of the experience, not the experience itself.

The Intellectual-Mind, reasons and rationalizes, but it can't feel.

In this book, I am intentionally attempting through story, to invoke ancient communication principles to simplify the experience for you, the reader. I do this so the true context in between the words and their meaning can be received by you as an *experiential knowing*, rather than just an intellectual understanding or "knowing about". Your own unique belief structure that makes up *your* human reality, will determine what the particular message in *any* story is for you. The literal written words on the page won't give you that entire message. There is no standard meaning in these stories that are absolutely 100% the same for all of us.

I have a saying that, we are all the same ... just different.

For you to connect with the context; real life stories like my Winn Dixie Messenger, have been interlaced throughout this book. Feel for the context behind the words as you follow along with the story. See if you can *feel* the *experience* being transmitted through the story and its relationship to the stories of *your* life. By doing this, your consciousness will automatically give you the meaning and message of which is unique to your life situation—of the consciousness concepts I am sharing through the story. By *feeling* for the context while you are reading, you will intuitively know what the story is giving you to take notice of. You don't have to relate to the whole story. When you *feel* for the context, you will *know* and naturally get the parts that are for you—right now. When you feel an extra charge or a particular piece in the story grabs your attention, respect it and know that your Spirit is giving you a "heads-up". It is your Spirit giving you a tap on the shoulder to deepen your feel and awareness for the message being presented to you in that moment of the story. Your intuitive answers of what these stories mean to you come from the *feeling* within the *context* of these stories, not the *content* of the written words.

Feeling for context transcends all race creeds, translations, interpretations, language, religions or differences—and especially the drama of the mind.

Be alert to feel the context of these stories, so that you may get the message and learn the lesson that your Soul seeks from what you are reading.

The Soul experiences by context and the mind rationalizes by content.

The balanced blending of these two creates an experiential understanding that will integrate as your *knowing*. It is far simpler to *feel* the context of the message than it is to mentally try to *understand* the written content. The words in this book can be your gospel truth, only to the extent that their context resonates with you. These words are an expression of my experience as a Spirit having this Soulful human experience. If at your core they resonate with you, then follow along with them. If they do not, then put the book down and come back to it at another time. If they still don't resonate for you after time, then pass them to another without your interpretation of them. Allow and empower the other person with the opportunity to explore for themselves.

The Intellectual-Mind will always look for and make complications—its intrinsic nature is to reason and rationalize. There is nothing to be gained from trying to stop the mind doing what it was designed to do. The Intellectual-Mind also likes to make things wrong, so don't expect all of these words to make perfect sense. This is just your mind wanting to invalidate what it doesn't understand or know about, so it can maintain the continued existence of its Superior Identity. Your experience could be a simple *knowing* or a complicated mental *knowing* "about it". Let yourself feel the context of the stories and this will free you from the drama of your mind's incessant need for mental clarity.

Ironically, mental clarity is a natural by-product of a simple experiential knowing.

In attempting to simplify our human experience we will first need to identify the components of Self that create the effects from the complicated patterns that already exist and what effect they have on our ability to truly experience anything. We will also need to recognize the difference that simply experiencing anything makes to our life. Yes—life can be so complicated sometimes. Actually, I think some of us would say life *IS* complicated *ALL* the time. The complicated lifestyles of this western world have become so intrinsically woven into the way we are, that most of us have become numb to its effects on us.

The mind will want to dramatize what the Spirit—purely by experiencing, always simplifies.

So, relax into the stories and concepts given here. Don't look for the message but *feel* for it instead. Let the message reveal its self to you, rather than trying to mentally unearth it from beneath the avalanche of mental drama created by your Intellectual Mind. Don't try to understand it all. Allow yourself to have the *experience* that this book and the information it conveys is offering to you. Allow yourself to feel, and awaken your natural and inbuilt Drama anti-virus, so you can embody the Awareness of your Spirit; from which you may experience the unlimited depth of your Soul, as you get ... *out of your mind.*

Chapter 2

In the Mind

Some years ago, after my marriage had broken apart and single parenting my three gorgeous teenage daughters had become the norm for me, I began to pick up my spiritual practice again with meditation and spiritual study etc. Although I had never given up my spiritual life completely, I had put its development on-hold, because of the discomfort it created for my then wife. Her rigid catholic upbringing struggled with the freer flowing path of my Spirit driven study and practice. Through the inherent moral values of family coming first; of which were embodied in me through my parents, I chose to put my overt devotion to my spiritual path to the side, for the sake of marital harmony. Slowly, once our marriage had broken apart, I began to feel my spiritual passion revive from the extreme trauma my mind had been creating, because of my life being turned upside down from my marriage dissolving over the previous five years. Obviously, continuing my practice during the breakup trauma would have been somewhat helpful, but my minds spiral into its drama black hole, blocked all inner vision of a spiritual way out. All that I had held dearest to me was crumbling down around me, like an old building shaken to oblivion in the continual upheaval of a raging mental earthquake. Of course, in those moments it was not a physical earthquake, but the two-opposing heart-quakes of my then wife and myself. The resultant conflict between these heart-quakes were destroying the safe and comfortable abode of family structure we had both been building throughout the previous twenty plus years together. In the aftermath of my heart-quake, I would try to drown out my minds incessant dialogue of doom and gloom, through immersion in anything spiritual I could get my hands and heart around.

From a spiritual awakening I had when I was fourteen years old, up until about twenty-four, I was obsessed with spiritual books and practices. My awakening had shown me my spiritual potential for this life and from then on, I couldn't get enough of it all, as I would read books cover to cover and the very next day start the next. Strangely, the more I read, it seemed like the more I remembered stuff that was not in the books, as spiritual thoughts and concepts flowed freely through me, like a dam had burst wide open and the raging waters of knowledge saturating everything in its path, flooding every cell in my body and transforming the forces within my passionate Soul. If my addiction had been for food, I would have been grotesquely obese. Any spiritual program or course that The Divine Orchestration would feel appropriate to send my way, was swallowed up. I was like a kid let loose in the spiritual candy store and my appetite was insatiable. Of course, in hindsight I can see now the scope of the huge gift I had been given, but in those moments of spiritual gorging, my whole sight was on the next insight, the next exaltation of concept, the next super-sensory experience. An insight I did have through that period, was that my mind was also totally immersed in all of these spiritual concepts and exercises. This seemed to stimulate it to higher thoughts, along with what seemed to bring an excited heightened Awareness into my whole life as well. My mind actually seemed much more acute and sharpened by the experiences I was having ... whether human or spiritual. I struggled with this realization for a long while, because a lot of the information around me at that time was more about getting out of the mind and letting it go, because it was a hindrance to spiritual development. On the one hand, I could completely agree with this viewpoint, as I recall now the extreme drama created specifically by my mind throughout my family heart-quakes. On the other hand, I was, in those moments of spiritual obsession, experiencing a powerful and dynamic mind, of which the experiences I was having with it on this dam-busting spiritual flood, were extremely helpful and supportive, if not _essential_ to the progress I was achieving.

My mind's quality of function and calm acuity dramatically improve, the more I harmonize my life by engaging in spiritual pursuits.

Unfortunately, my wife didn't have the same obsession with anything spiritual as I did. As we married reasonably early at the age of nineteen, there was in the beginning, a three-year period of some rather testing moments. I couldn't understand why she got upset with me going to another room and sit in front of a lighted candle, losing my self/mind in the flame for over an hour at a time. I guess it heavily challenged her staunch catholic upbringing and indoctrinations of potential evil influences coming from any practice other than Diocese approved. Fortunately, we were still young then and without children, so our conflicts were reasonably short lived. However, after three years of this intermittent conflict and the pressures of our new first born, I succumbed to her fears and icy cold disconnections until submission and stopped my overt practices. I basically at this point became a closet spiritualist. Although I kept reading and silently practice my techniques during the day, I could feel my drive and passion for continuing the *intensity* of my practices waning dramatically and rapidly. My mind had gradually slumped back into mental justifications for ending practices, rather than passionately inspired to seek out more practices to experience and learn from. This barren badland of spiritual drought lasted for the next fifteen years; the drought only broken by the occasional passionate spiritual debate between myself and a handful of my closest like-minded friends.

My mind shrunk back into the problematic state I had read about, when my Soul was starved of its spiritual stimulation.

Although our marriage was generally one of many years of loving moments of deep connections and my daughters were by no means starved of love and attention like my spiritual ambitions were, the minds virus of both my wife and I eventually took its toll on the whole family. Between her not practicing any of her catholic upbringing, nor me for years now suppressing my spiritual necessity for higher development, our minds had no higher Spirit guidance to follow any longer. Our Spirits were pushed completely out the door of our Life's bus. Now left with only the survival mentality of a shrunken misguided mind, lost to the materialistic intellectual doctrines of society's needs and desires, the inevitable happened. After nineteen years of marriage, the last five of which were suffered by both of us in mental conflicts and struggling pretenses of affection, our relationship finally broke apart as dramatically and traumatically, as the Titanic's back-breaking collide with that infamous unseen iceberg. Our iceberg was the hard-cold force of our pretending to not see the ever-growing mental iceberg of the extent of our own *blame-game* of separation and discontent.

My saving grace was my love for my daughters, which grounded the strength of my Spirits Will pressing in on my consciousness, to not give up my daughters to go live with their mother. She was spiraling into depressing non-ownership, compensating with substance abuse to relieve or block out the pain of her own self-denial. Within the following year after the inevitable of her leaving us, I gradually stabilized our home environment as best I could. With my still ill but recovering Soul, I was able to re-establish my spiritual practices and meditations. As my spiritual passion began to reignite the flame of my Souls need for growth, the Divine once again started to send me what I needed to pick up the development once more of my still knowing spiritual journey toward my Life's destiny. This was like my rebirth, my re-awakening if you will and my Soul-mind responded yet again to my Spirit's heightened Awareness of Life's enthusiasm for me to learn and evolve.

No matter how dead my mind's identities may "think" it has become, the re-stimulation of my Souls Consciousness through grounded Spirit guidance, can resurrects my mind back to its highest design and function for use toward my highest good.

It wasn't long before the Divine would send me my next quantum leap back to my Spirit's loving guidance. Of course, by this stage I am again soaking up everything I can and so, jumped right into this organization boots and all. What was interesting with this Divine gift, was that the organization the Divine sent to me, would have no tolerance to any mention of Soul, Spirit or God or such. This organizations whole focus was the power of the mind and its workings of beliefs, identities etc. Although their lofty mission statement professed to create an enlightened planetary civilization, the inner sanctum of its student masters and trainers etc., were completely indoctrinated into believing that this enlightened planetary civilization could only be achieved when everyone was living within their "organizational family" as the result of their training. The very first manipulating invitation given to any and all new potential students, was that they would not be indoctrinated with any more belief systems, but that the organization has the technology to free them from any and all existing belief structures that limit the new student from living the life they deserve. Seriously, I wish I had a buck for every time I have heard this subtle manipulation to influence one's lower natured Spirit-less mind into buying what these spiritual salesmen are selling. Of course, they were quite deliberate in their indoctrination of you that _their_ system wasn't a belief system, even though the common rhetorical premise for their exercises to work, was stated as _everything_ is a belief system. Through my ten-year involvement with them; along with many thousands of dollars for the privilege, I have come to fortunately experience myself out of this organizations subtle indoctrinations of what I can now see as, potential dis-empowerment and entrapment into their system ... for Life. Now don't get me wrong about this self-development system. The profound gains I received from my involvement in this organization; because they were enormous, were actually pivotal in my empowerment to get out of their system. Remember I said that this organization's teachings are all around the mind and not Spirit.

> *I can't learn anything about something, without getting totally involved and experientially immersed in the thing I wish to learn.*

> *Wisdom is gained from experience, which results in a deep and fully integrated KNOWING of that thing.*

So, as you get to the end of the last of the first three courses of this organization and of course, you have parted with quite a few thousand dollars again, there is an initiation at the very end of the third weekend course that is worth mentioning here. It is worth mentioning, because of the experience I achieved from this initiation and the insight into the mind through such experience. What revealed itself to me ... about me and the minds functions etc. ... is appreciated beyond words of gratitude. The intimate experiential detail of belief structures, identities, entities, resistances and so much more, have been so instrumental in my understanding of what has been revealed since leaving there, particularly through the addition of what my Spirit reveals about it all. I would say that this system helped me to pull the lid of the container of Human Consciousness. From there, I was able to explore the component parts of what _they_ called the mind of our human-self, more clearly as individual segments. It was much later that the Divine again sent me to Rudolph Steiner's work where I was able to take the greatest quantum leap into the most intricate detail of the components of consciousness; of which we will discuss and explore through the later chapters of this book. It is the experience of the initiation that has relevance now to our study of the mind.

We must understand that this weekend course was quite intense in respect to deep self-ownership of all the darker and lower nature if you will, of our human identities. Discovering that I am not my identities, and that when I thought I was acting from my own determinations, was actually a react triggered by an identity, can be quite unsettling to say the least. Trust me, there were more than one occasion that I was dragged to the alter of self-denial, to sacrifice the comfort zones of my pretending identity. From this particular course, I coined the phrase, "Vulnerable and Courageous". This was my catch-cry every time I came up against my resistances to ownership. Vulnerable enough to feel what I was experiencing, and courageous enough to own it all. It was also my saving grace many times, as well as many times since, that invoked the strength of my

Soul forces to smash through the false veils of what my Spirit-less minds resistances were trying to hide from.

To break through resistances that create the pains of self-denial, I must be vulnerable enough to allow my-self to FEEL the experience I AM having ... and courageous enough to take full responsibility for all that I have created.

So, on this last course, you get to enter the deliberate experiential world of feeling through this particular initiation. This initiation is not a mental excursion, but an experiential one of feeling into one's consciousness, guided by specific questions etc. that you would experience to completion. From their process or exercise as they call it, you get to discharge any attachment energy that keeps these belief structures active and effective on your Consciousness. You are guided through this process by your "master" in a quiet room devoid as much as possible by any external stimuli. Although they don't share the expected result of this initiation with you, my experience of it is that by dismantling several constraining mental structures, you are able to get to an *experience* of your "feeling/experiential nature". Of course, they dare not call this your Spirit or BEing-Self nature, as this would open a far greater can of experiential worms than they could handle with their mind-based exercises. Heaven forbid that it be known that it was the forces of your Soul and Spirit that brought about the results and not their exercises, the ones they would have you give up your power to. Ironically, there is a statement from its creator that says, "when you assign any result of insight to something outside of your Self, you weaken your ability to access those insights for yourself." Now this IS a great truth, but the irony of that statement, is that they continually give praise and power to the exercises and their creator—which is assigning your results to the exercise—which is outside of yourself. I would call this subtle covert dis-empowerment. Don't get me wrong here, remember I said I was in boots and all, so I was giving up my power just as readily as the next ... until the real power of Spirit Awareness revealed its Self to me.

I give up my power to create or change, whenever I attribute experiences within me, to anything outside of myself.

Attributing the result of this initiation to the initiation process, would be giving up my power to the process, which weakens my ability to achieve the result again for my-self. I feel this is the subtle and covert dis-empowerment device this organization used to keep its students entrapped in their system. I can't say whether this was done deliberately or not, but the results really speak for their self. I'm sure there are many other organizations and systems doing the same also. Fortunately, I was given this insight from Spirit early in my journey through this organization, so I was able to feel deeply into the dynamic of my Spirit for the wisdom of the results I was getting with their exercises. I see also now why there was so much conflict and turmoil for me when trying to _feel_ from consciousness, when in fact our ability to feel/experience comes from our Spirit, not our consciousness. This is how the _embodying-experience_ work that came through my Conscious Bodywork practice; of which we will explore later, was able to reveal its self to me.

The result of my initiation was one of a distinction between my consciousness minds ability to create sensations and my Spirits nature to _feel and experience_ on a super-sensory level. By the end of the initiation, I was in a state of what I would call deep Awareness ... which I must add is an ability of Spirit, not the mind. At the end, the student would go for a short walk before coming back into the classroom with the other hundred plus students. On my walk, I had the most profound experience I had ever had up till that time, of deeply and fully experiencing Nature's _field_. At that time, I called it the usual generic term of "energy", of which we all use when our mind can't experience or define something. Now, I know it as the dynamic inter-relationship of the spiritual forces, of which the BEing of Nature is. On this occasion, when I walked out into Nature, my experience was most surely super-sensory in nature. I could see, feel and experience deeply, the forces flowing and moving. It was the forces responsible for the manifestation of the physical world I was walking in with my body. Nature was not rigid or solid to me from this super-sensory space, but fluid, mobile and highly energized. Literally, everything in my reality was no longer solid and material, but fluid and energetic in nature. I remember being extremely Aware of my mind in that moment also, as it was silently in harmony with what I was experiencing, with my Spirits Awareness seemingly embodied throughout my consciousness and of course ... my mind. My mind was calm, quiet and obedient to every Awareness sensation coming into it. Oddly enough, my mind didn't have its usual tendency to describe and categorize everything that was now coming to it from this ecstatic stream of spiritual existence. My mind didn't seem perturbed or shocked or concerned with what it was receiving. It felt like it was actually home and comfortable within my Spirits input and intimate relationship with Earth's spiritual environment.

> **When human consciousness surrenders its stance of separation and disconnect, Spirit Self is allowed to enter consciousness, making my human ... Consciously Aware.**

I find the mind an absolutely fascinating study, yet a deceptive distracting one. What makes it so fascinating for me is the fact that nobody seems to be able to put a definitive finger on exactly what the mind is and most intriguing; where does it come from? Even more enticing and enchanting is ... how do we control it and what was it designed to be used for? Throughout the ages, many Masters of the Mind, have given us fantastically helpful insights and techniques for going _beyond our mind_ or getting _out of our mind_ or getting the _mind out of the way_, but still none that I have found, gives a comprehensibly understandable depiction of the mind in its full and glorious construction. I feel a lot of the present-day definitions of the mind etc. are much more intellectually conceptual in nature rather than experiential. I have found the teachings of Rudolph Steiner most interesting on this topic, as he has practically no mention of mind as an aspect, tool or element of consciousness or spirit to speak of. From his spiritual science approach, the extensive and intimate detail he shares places importance on the _collective_ ... of elements and aspects that make up the Body Soul and Spirit of our human existence, with very little if any, reference to the mind as an aspect or evolving spiritual element.

What if what you know of _your_ mind, is actually not you at all?

What if the mind is actually not a single organism, but is the result of a collective?

What if your mind is not an organism at all, but simply your Souls Consciousness expression of its _collective nature_, within this human reality?

What if your mind is more like a type of organ for your Consciousness to express its self in the here and now of your present human physical existence?

Have you noticed how much your mind _appears_ to be the "you" that thinks, directs, decides, conceptualizes, extrapolates, contemplates, judges, blames, emotionalizes, plans, organizes, denies, complains, interprets, sympathizes etc. etc. etc. This is an awful amount of stuff and so much more again going on—and all coming from within this one space you call "you"? With all of this going on, it's no wonder the most asked and yet misunderstood question of our time is, "who I am?". The complexity of all of these functions and abilities etc. seem to be beyond comprehension for our poor ole mind and to think or try to understand it all quite often blows our mind, or drives us "_out of our mind_" ... right? If this is the case, then how could we say that these are all _creations_ of our mind. If it blows my mind trying to _understand_ the nature, structure, function and purpose of all of these _creations of my mind_ ... then how could the mind actually be the creator of them? If my mind isn't the creator of all of these attributes and abilities etc. then where do they come from and who or what created them? Also, why does my mind seem to be the instigator and creator of it all? Let's take a look at a few standard definitions from our wonderful world of Wikipedia to get a feel for what our human consciousness world has come up with.

- In popular usage, _mind_ is frequently synonymous with _thought_: the private conversation with us that we carry on "inside our heads." Thus we "make up our minds," "change our minds" or are "of two minds" about something. One of the key attributes of the mind in this sense is that it is a private sphere to which no one but the owner has access. No one else can "know our mind." They can only interpret what we consciously or unconsciously communicate.

So, all of these depictions seem to point toward our mind as an element of self, or even of self itself, the you that you are with all its thinking and emotions etc. On first glance at thought for example, we could put the mind as the originator of our thoughts simple because they seem to come from within our mind. If we explore just this one aspect of thought with our Awareness and not our mind and _feel_ for the _experience_ of thought and not the intellectual interpretation, we can see that the _origination_ of thought doesn't really come _from_ our mind at all. Thought itself isn't originated in our mind, but our mind does seem to be more of the organizer of the thoughts. On meditation, I have found that what I perceived as _my thoughts_, come from another place within the greater inner me. I have found my mind isn't originating thought, but rather is the final organizer of the thoughts into a suitable expression, of which I can then use to relate and project into the human world reality I am co-existing in with you. The thoughts themselves seem to come from a deeper or different space of a collective consciousness.

My mind is not the originator of thoughts, but the presenter of thoughts.

It's like the news reports we see on television, where the information in the report is collected by reporters and formulated through editing and qualifying within the newsroom, then those thoughts are finally delivered to the world through the presenter on the screen we all see and relate to. Even in this analogy of the newsroom, the origination of the thoughts that get to the screen; originate *outside* of not just the reporter or the newsroom, but outside the television station as a collective and from the human world reality itself. It is through the collection of the thoughts by the reporter that first brings them from the world and into the newsroom reality. The true original context however, hasn't actually originated within the newsroom, but in the *world reality* outside of the newsroom. The last two sentences of our Wiki depictions is interesting as an example of how a viewpoint of the origination of thought can be misconstrued as coming from our mind.

"No one else can "know my mind." They can only interpret what I consciously or unconsciously communicate."

Because our mind seems so personal, so private, so individual and separate from the world around us, a concept of the thoughts we hold so dear within our mind not coming from our self, seems far too foreign to entertain as a truth. This of course, is only too foreign or far-fetched for the mind its self to contemplate—simply because the mind is a presenter of thoughts and as such is not capable of the processes of contemplation or extrapolation. These later processes are actually functions of a higher state of consciousness than that of the mind. The mind if you like is that final interpreter that your communications into the world … pass through to be delivered into the world.

From Awareness insight, gained through true meditation of thought, I can get a sense of the subtle realm of which truly original thought can come from.

Let's look at another Wiki depiction.

- A **mind** is the set of cognitive faculties that enables consciousness, perception, thinking, judgement, and memory—a characteristic of humans that almost certainly also applies to other organisms.

I find this one quite contradictory and confusing. If the mind is a set of faculties that enables these functions, then is it the mind that created these functions also? Specifically, is it the mind then that creates consciousness it's-self, for it to come about? Maybe the mind didn't create consciousness, because no doubt consciousness is an extremely high order of creation, yet it seems by this depiction that it is the deciding factor that enables consciousness to exist in this present human form? To me, this would put the mind ahead of consciousness as an evolutionary state of BEing. The mind would need to be far more evolved than consciousness to be able to facilitate consciousness existence. If we then look at the mind *enabling* the other faculties of perception, thinking, judgement, and memory etc.; which are all actual *functions* of our human consciousness, then the mind is placed yet again above consciousness. I feel that when we accept these depictions and *enabling* functions of the mind above our own consciousness, we have then placed the mind above, not just the consciousness of the human-self that we are, here on this planet, but also above our eternal experiential Higher-Self of Spiritual origination. From this we might as well say that the mind is created above the spiritual nature of your true BEing-Self and your BEing-Self is thus held at the mercy of your mind or must be subservient to the mind.

Now although this may quite often seem to be the case; that we certainly appear to be at the mercy of the mind, as confused and subservient puppets to its apparently incessant whimsical ways, we must come to see the deception in these kinds of viewpoints. Many Masters who have set the way before us, to help accelerate our evolution through their enlightenment, point to the need for us to master our mind and see the falseness in its deceptions of self. Maybe the mastery they refer to is not mastery of mind but is really mastery of consciousness. Maybe their description of mind was given because our consciousness wasn't sufficiently developed to understand the components of consciousness itself, and so packaged up the collective components and called it mind for ease of communication?

Let's look at some more Wiki.

- Another question concerns which types of beings are capable of having minds, for example whether mind is exclusive to humans, possessed also by some or all animals, by all living things, or whether mind can also be a property of some types of man-made machines.
- Whatever its relation to the physical body it is generally agreed that mind is that which enables a being to have subjective awareness and intentionality towards their environment, to perceive and respond to stimuli with some kind of agency, and to have consciousness, including thinking and feeling.

Once again, we see here another reference to the mind being not just the facilitator of consciousness, but also now as our ability to perceive and respond to external and environmental stimuli and even subjective Awareness. I have to say, according to all of these standard definitions, our mind is the be-all of existence and consciousness or even the "self" that you are is only capable of existence because of the mind. This is why I feel, these definitions come from the limitations of our intellectually based analysis of the mind, rather than true experiential Awareness of the spiritual nature of the mind's construction. I must admit however, that it is much easier to package it all up in a *concept of mind* and simply right off all deeper truths of our Being's construction, functions and place within the dynamics of our human existence. This is much easier than to dismantle the complex consciousness nature of our <u>whole</u> human existence and study our human BEing as a collective of Body Soul and Spirit components.

The problem with the simplified version though, is that I never actually get to master the individual components that make up the whole, as long as I only look at the whole and not its parts.

A correlating analogy could be that of the alcoholic who can never master his addiction to substance, if he is unable to firstly identify the addiction, and then be able to identify the components of his addiction. Only from there is he able to become master over them. If an addict of any kind, can't identify the triggers, inabilities, processes, responses and reacts etc., then how can he know what actions etc. to take to stop the specific triggers etc.? The triggers etc. are what set off within him the uncontrollable thoughts feelings and actions etc., which manifest the physical condition of the addiction in the individual's world reality. To find the cause of the triggers, one first needs to identify the triggers ... then ... what part of self is home to the triggers being stimulated. We could analyze these triggers as psychology does, which is done through intellectualizing, but this doesn't always uncover the subtle spirit based *experiential* triggers, let alone the aspect of consciousness they come from.

I can't find the components of consciousness that make up the collective I falsely call mind, without accepting the possibility that the mind is simply a concept and indeed ... a collective.

To find these components; which are aspects of your human consciousness self, you have to invoke the power of Awareness to experience the inherent *ability*, of your Spirit BEing-Self. I have a saying from experience that, "if you are looking for an experiential aspect of consciousness and you can't find it ... it's because you are in it". Generally, in consciousness we can't see what we are in, until we step out, until we can *observe* the thing and become <u>Aware</u> of it. If I am trying to see something that is within my human-self's consciousness, then I need to observe my consciousness through my Spirit-Self's ability to experience or feel, with Awareness. Consciousness is conscious of its self as separate from its environment, but it isn't naturally Aware ... it's only conscious.

And yet another Wiki depiction.

- A lengthy tradition of inquiries in philosophy, religion, psychology and cognitive science has sought to develop an understanding of what a mind is and what its distinguishing properties are. The main question regarding the nature of mind is its relation to the physical brain and nervous system – a question which is often framed as the mind–body problem, which considers whether mind is somehow separate from physical existence (dualism and idealism), or the mind is identical with the brain or some activity of the brain, deriving from and/or reducible to physical phenomena such as neuronal activity (physicalism).

I feel this one is closest to a truth of the mind's existence. Within the understanding of spiritual science, it is known that the nervous system, which of course includes the brain, is associated with the Ego as its manifestation in the physical world through the physical body. Our current nervous system and brain came into being when we evolved sufficiently into "I Consciousness" to be able to obtain the Ego. This Ego is not understood or experienced the same as is commonly depicted in todays Intellectualized Spirituality. In spiritual science it is not seen as being a negative hindrance or problem for our human existence and its evolution back to Spirit. On the contrary, per spiritual science, the Ego is actual the house or body for our Spirit. Through this body, it is possible for our _experiential_ Spirit-Self to be grounded into our human-self. Ultimately, through this spiritualization of our human-self, we enable the expansion and evolution of our current human consciousness. It's through the Ego-Body that higher thinking is obtained. It is actually through the Ego that the quality of our thinking can be improved within the lower consciousness nature of our human. There is a hint of truth in the above definition where it poses the possibility of the mind being identical to the brain. In ancient Hawaiian philosophies, it is known that there is an identical etheric body to that of the physical body. It is through this identical etheric body that the Kahuna of healing is able to create their mind-blowing feats of bone mending and tissue repair. There is much truth to be revealed yet about the true nature of our Ego-Body. We will explore this further in later chapters. Could our mind however, actually be our consciousness-Body's brain?

If my brain is the link between consciousness and the physical body, then could it be possible that the mind, is the equivalent link between my Spirit within the Ego-Body and my physical world?

And for our last look at more Wiki standards.

- The concept of mind is understood in many different ways by many different cultural and religious traditions. Some see mind as a property exclusive to humans whereas others ascribe properties of mind to non-living entities (e.g. pan-psychism and animism), to animals and to deities. Some of the earliest recorded speculations linked mind (sometimes described as identical with soul or spirit) to theories concerning both life after death, and cosmological and natural order, for example in the doctrines of Zoroaster, the Buddha, Plato, Aristotle, and other ancient Greek, Indian and, later, Islamic and medieval European philosophers.

- Important philosophers of mind include Mulla Sadra, Plato, Descartes, Leibniz, Kant, Martin Heidegger, John Searle, Daniel Dennett, Thomas Nagel, David Chalmers and many others. The description and definition is also a part of psychology where psychologists such as Sigmund Freud and William James have developed influential theories about the nature of the human mind. In the late 20th and early 21st centuries the field of cognitive science emerged and developed many varied approaches to the description of mind and its related phenomena. The possibility of non-human minds is also explored in the field of artificial intelligence, which works closely in relation with cybernetics and information theory to understand the ways in which human mental phenomena can be replicated by non-biological machines.

Here we are yet again with even more ambiguous depictions and definitions for mind. Clearly, I feel it shows just how much our Intellectual Soul has taken what it can't explain (let alone experience) and package it up in a form that just cries out as unexplainable. Interesting really how we do that, or rather our arrogant intellectual identity does, that rather than admit something is out of its scope of understanding, in this case being consciousness itself, then it will put a label on it that is so ambiguous that no human consciousness can come up with a definitive definition of it. I feel the fact that the emergence into artificial intelligence is also embracing the mind concept for its technology, says a lot to the fact that the mind is not an organ in itself, or even an attribute of consciousness. Could the mind merely be a function or process of thought correlation and presentation? Maybe there is something other than "the mind" that has a far greater potential in the linking of our non-linear Spirit to the linear world reality of our human existence.

A greater question still remains however which is, is this process I call mind simply a process of my Body Soul or Spirit, or is the mind the resultant process of a collective of all three? Even further, is it possible, that if my mind is simply a process or aspect of any _one_ of these Body Soul or Spirit components of the Self that makes up the you that you are as this human BEing, then, is it possible that each component is also a collective of specific Consciousness and Spiritual elements also? Is it possible that there are even more specific elements that make up the whole of each component we call Body Soul or Spirit? The works of Rudolph Steiner's Anthroposophy has some great detail of these different components and collectives that make up our human-self, along with their dynamic natures also. Without diminishing or devaluing any of Anthroposophies teachings; for which I hold a highest esteem, I will attempt throughout the following chapters to give you a simplified experiential account of these differences and the way they manifest the Life of our human-self we exist as.

As I said previously, to master anything, we need to know the components and functions of the parts that make up the whole of what it is we wish to master. To master our mind is not possible by mindlessly following someone else's mind process.

To get my true Self out of my mind, I must fully immerse this Self, my higher experiential BEing-Self, into the deceptions of the mind's domain, to find the components of dynamic structure, from which the mind is perceived to manifest from.

So, let us leave the perception of mind we might have at this present time, at the front door for a while. Let's see if we can explore this all further from a more *feeling* and *experiential* space of allowing higher information to reveal itself to us, rather than trying to intellectually understand it all. Many Masters before us have shared the deceptions of mind and their pitfalls, but now let's entertain the possibility that the current *concept of mind* itself ... is a deception also. I would like to suggest the possibility that the deception of this current *concept of mind*, is actually a self-deception of consciousness, which stems from its own evolution into the solid and dense form of existence that is our present "I Consciousness" of separation. At this level, we have as a humanity, become conscious, that is, conscious of self, separate from our surrounding physical and spiritual environment. However, we have as yet, only become a physically conscious human, yet not become a fully, spiritually experiential human-BEing. The current *concept of mind* is our human consciousness way of describing what it can't experience, what it can't as yet, feel ... what it can't fully embody of the spiritual realm of which consciousness its-self has manifest from. Consciousness can sense this spiritual realm but can't experience it ... yet.

For the purpose of this book study, our present importance is to get out of the current *concept of our mind*, out of its trap in lower conceptual thinking, and raise our Consciousness Soul into the higher realm of our Spirit-Self. From here you can free your human-self from its lower-mind based nature and bring in the higher thinking of your Spirit, that facilitates the transfer of concepts into percepts, where they become fully experiential events. Through the higher-mind nature of your Spirit BEing-Self, you can access your true ability to feel and experience Life fully through Awareness. To access this higher nature, we need to find and understand the components that make up the structure of our consciousness and its use, as we are using it in this present time. To *change* the way we function—we need to *know* the way we function, along with all the parts that create that function.

So, let's explore together further and see if we can find all of those illusive aspects and components within Body Soul and Spirit, that make up the human-self you exist as.

Are you ready to get out of your mind's drama of not being able to fully and joyously experience life, but merely dramatize the human-ness of it?

Chapter 3

Being Human

We are all the same, just different.

What does it mean to be human? What is being human really about and what does it take to accept and master being human? I'm sure there are many more questions we could ask about this subject. Most of us would never ask these questions. Why would we ask these questions anyhow? It's generally such an effort just to *be* human, forget about understanding it—right?

My first intention for this book was to share a viewpoint about the minds role in the simple power of being human, along with the gift that being human offers us all. One viewpoint I had was that all the complicated self-help processes and techniques to understand and improve "being human" were mostly unnecessary. By experience, I have found that the simplicity of the *human experience* is all that we need to know, and deliberate *experiencing* is all that we need to BE doing.

I began to find all the processes to improve my life, enlighten my soul, remove limitations, create prosperity and unlock my potentials etc. etc., were fast becoming the very limitations to being at peace within myself ... as a human with my Spirit having this human experience. All of these processes were actually preventing me from truly, fully experiencing my life with real joy of my Self, along with all these things in my everyday life.

Processing my life was fixing my attention on what was wrong with this human form of existence, rather than allowing me to deepen my love for it and experience of it.

I came to find, that the processes were only managing aspects of being human rather than empowering me to integrate my whole human experience of which life, was continually presenting to me.

The loudly proclaimed "miracle" processes that promised to make my life less complicated were actually making being human more complicated.

The fact is—being human is multi-faceted and in its structure quite complex. Trying to understand and master all of these complexities was literally driving me out of my mind. Being human is an almost infinite mixture of influences, circumstances, alternatives, coincidences, interpretations, misinterpretations, viewpoints, situations, beliefs, energies, identities, judgments, frailties etc, etc.—and the list goes on. At any moment in the space between our human events that we call time, one or all of these aspects can come into play and dramatically change my perception of the reality I am experiencing. My human experience at any given time is a direct result of the influences of these different aspects ... all coming together. I know at my core that the design of these influences and their effect on me is created specific to my Spirit's Life intention to grow and evolve through this life time here. This uniquely personal design of these combinations determines the parameter of human events and the experiences I will have within these events. It is this design that gives me the optimal opportunities I need, for my personal growth and expansion. Our personalized design is what makes each one of us uniquely individual.

There is a system on our planet now called "The Human Design" that I believe, has given us to date, a very comprehensive and as accurate as possible *breakdowns* of our *human design*. This design gives us the makeup of our personal Human vehicle for this lifetime, and although this vehicle is obviously not just our physical body, it still doesn't refer directly to our Soul as well. This Human Design system is created from a combination of Astrology, the I-Ching, Kabbalah, the Hindu Chakra System as well as aspects of Quantum Physics. The fact that this particular system is a collection of four already elaborate systems of human understanding, is testament to the intricacies that make up our human structure and shows clearly that we are not just here as a Soul in a human body.

The "human" element of my existence here on Planet earth, is actually a combination of Body and Soul forces.

I'm sure most of you would have at some stage in your life heard talk of the Body Soul and Spirit elements of your existence. As we will discuss further in the next chapter, the *human* element of "Being human", is a combination of the Body and Soul elements, while the *Being* element is our Spirit. Therefore, I have always felt that there is not one system of human understanding on our planet at this time that covers all parameters of human potential and makeup of both Human and Being. This statement also applies to this Human Design system. I am mentioning the Human Design system here as an example, because I have found it to be yet another helpful tool in finding an understanding into the *human* element of Being Human. At first glance of this Human Design system, one can be slightly overwhelmed by the number of centers, gates, channels and profiles etc., that are either turned on or off, are defined or undefined and opened or closed. Although my mind loves detail and unraveling complexities, it was at first, stopped in its tracks trying to grasp the functions of all these interactions. I was only able to comprehend and appreciate the accuracy of this system, when I dropped into *feel* and connected this Human Design system, with my *experience* of being human, with how this system actually correlates within human Life. Eventually, I came to understand that when we can intimately know the true structure of our human-self, and integrate our human design, we can use it more deliberately and we can grow ourselves **out of it**. This system helps give us insight into the design we each have chosen for this particular lifetime.

I have not simply chosen this design—I am actually the co-architect of my own unique human design for this lifetime.

This design actually facilitates our particularly unique range of human events to experience. It is aptly labeled "Human Design" because it gives us an insight into the design of our own unique human vehicle for this lifetime. It is this human vehicle that allows us to create and experience the infinite individuality of human events I would call my life. From our interaction with other human designs, we are able to create an incredibly wide parameter of human events to experience and learn from. With this system, maybe for the first time in the history of "I Consciousness" human experience on this planet, we are able to understand more clearly why our human experiences are limited and created within a certain parameter of possibilities and potentials. Although other systems such as astrology, can give us an understanding of our blueprint for this lifetime, the "Human Design System" provides a greater clarity and detail of that blueprint. We are also able to see how our reactions and energy is affected by others, along with the reason some affect us certain ways and more than others.

Contrary to my indoctrinations of being an unlimited human being, I am to a very definite degree, bound by the defined parameters of my own unique "human design".

Have you ever been curious or even mildly amazed by the fact that, there is not one other person amongst the almost seven billion other residences on this emerald green third rock from the sun, that is exactly like you? There may be a few that are similar, and some may even understand you, but none are exactly the same.

Even identical twins still have character differences between them. It is these differences between us all, which enables us to swim in the sea of continual change that being human creates. No matter how much we may try to deaden our awareness to the changes going on around and within us, change is inevitably rolling through us. Shift and change from our interactions with each other and our environment, goes on relentlessly. These shifts and changes continually influence every aspect of our life and Being. They mysteriously seem to be guiding us toward an end goal or higher intention for this life time that most of us have no idea even exists.

Have you ever wondered how, just when you needed something to change or assistance to come your way, that a set of synchronistic events just seemed to show up? Is it possible that these fortuitous circumstances just happened to be in the neighborhood, just when I needed to have their influence on my life? Who or what is it that could create such an amazing sequence of happenings, connections and interactions? What powerful influence could possibly bring about exactly what I needed, to trigger the change I needed, let alone the one I asked for?

When I first came to live in Sarasota Florida, it was a culmination of such powerful influences coinciding, that presented me with exactly what I needed to stabilize my life there. Even the circumstances of my second marriage which brought me to America were powerful shifts and changes that transported me to the opposite side of the planet. Those same forces guided me to the eventual discovery of this work. All of these were a series of seemingly coincidences, that had me swept over to the other side of the planet, far away from my comfort zone of very close and supportive family and friends in Australia. It is this unique sequence of influences, connections and experiences which I call our Divine Orchestration, that eventually brought me to this point in time and writing this book.

Time and time again people asked me why on Earth I would come to live in America, when Australia is such a beautiful country with an easy-going culture and life style. I asked myself that very same question numerous times throughout those first two extremely hard years being here. I was half a planet away from the love and support of my gorgeous daughters, my family and friends. In Australia, I was debt free with a successful and fulfilling landscaping business and conscious bodywork practice and yet, in America, I had lost everything and was penniless, having to do a complete restart of my life. Regret was a heavy weight on my heart throughout that period. I couldn't make sense of why I would come here and loose everything and have to start again. To the question from others of "what brought me to America" my reply was simply, "I married an American girl and the consciousness work we were both passionate about was located in Orlando Florida, so we lived just two hours away with her mother in St. Augustine."

Although this was true, I have since come to realize my Spirit had a higher agenda for our connection. Our human design facilitated the necessary energetic and chemical reactions between my then wife and myself, to bring about the seemingly irrational and dramatic life changes for us both at that time. These changes were necessary to create this complete change in my life that would facilitate the grounding of this work that I'm writing about here now. Unfortunately, our designs were not apparently compatible enough to sustain a long-term relationship though. Maybe it wasn't that our designs weren't compatible enough, but rather that we had simply completed our higher intended experience together.

According to the Human Design system, when I come in contact with someone that has an open gate which is opposing mine on the same channel, our interaction together opens both gates and activates that connecting energy channel between the two relevant centers within each of us. Having the same channels open, creates an attraction impulse between the two of us. From this reaction, we both now have a shift in our human make up that will facilitate specific feelings and actions etc. that may seem spontaneous, out of character or even downright irrational. This can explain why after meeting someone for the first time, we might feel like we have known that person all our lives. A muse can be someone that triggers a gate to open and inspires you to act in a new or improved way.

Someone once suggested that my American wife was my ferryman, who brought me to America. I believe there is some truth in this, as our marriage didn't last long and even seemed to deteriorate rapidly after coming to the USA. It was almost as if the Universe had decided that once I was in America, there was no need for the marriage or relationship. I know now, that it was definitely Divine Orchestration that was providing that influence for dramatic change of which brings about the experience stream I should have. However, although this is true and Divine Orchestration brings about the experience stream, it is always me, my True Self that makes the final decisions that determine my final outcomes within that stream. It was the choices and decisions I made throughout the human events of our marriage, that contributed to ending our marriage relationship just 2 years after arriving in the USA. Although at the time my conscious intention was to not break up, the events that unfolded certainly manifested quite a shocking breakup reality. The shock was that in such a short time, all the money I had raised from selling everything in Australia to start a business and new Life in America … was gone. I had an old car that was eventually gifted to me by my then mother-in-law, and I was travelling from one side of Florida to the other every week. I was just making enough money to keep the phone connected, enough fuel in the car to get from coast to coast for work and occasional food in the belly. What was amazing also, was that my previous life in Australia with all its comfort zones and safe reference points, apparently needed to be dismantled entirely for me to eventually experience and explore the intricacies of human reality. As it turned out, it wasn't just the dismantling of my Australia comfort zones, but my American ones as well. After months of back and forwards from one side of Florida to the other, my then wife told me she didn't want to do this anymore and I had to move out. This is what ultimately brought me to live in Sarasota. Always being an upside to ever down in Life, it was the dismantling of all of these structures that allowed the true power of deliberate experiencing to reveal itself to me. It was this deliberate experiencing; which I now refer to as our *experience ability*, that dissolved the associated mind-drama of being homeless, penniless, stranded and alone, half a planet away from the love and support of my daughters, family and friends.

The relationship that was ending at the time of my previous Winn Dixie Messenger story; which was some four years after landing in America, is another good example of this Divine Orchestration and the Human design system at work. It was by chance that we met when she rented the second house on a beautiful property by a stream in Sarasota I was living in at that time. That first fateful meeting was life changing … for both of us. Just prior to our meeting, I had created an intention to start writing seriously about my work. To that point in time, I was writing short stories and nice poems etc., but I couldn't say I was a really writing, let alone a writer.

At that same time, I had become weary from the constant drain of my attention on being alone now. My mind was full of "being lonely drama" from my American marriage breakup and I had decided it was time to integrate my sexual disempowerment and was now ready to have a truly empowering Spiritually sexual relationship. A word of caution here, when you are "in-feel", be careful and very clear what you ask for. Just two weeks earlier I had completed a whole afternoon exploration and *experiencing* of all my beliefs etc. about these issues. I had come to a very clear space about both issues and felt ready to apply what I had learned into my life.

She is a writer and had set an intention for herself just one month prior to our meeting, to integrate her spirituality into an intimate relationship. From the human design viewpoint, we were made for each other. From some more detached and aware outsider's viewpoints, we were doomed to a dramatic ride at the least. A friend much later shared with me this same viewpoint about us. As being human will relentlessly facilitate the way things turn out—both viewpoints became valid.

She was and still is no doubt a very sensual woman and loved exploring and expanding the intimate physical human connections of two people. Her powerful sexuality triggered every disempowering cord of my sexual hangman's noose, which tied me to the lower desires of my human need for procreation and physical pleasure—along with my need for approval and companionship of course. I could feel the culmination of all my previous experiences of sexual disempowerment showing up for integration in this one fiery and tumultuous relationship. There was no doubt that she had triggered my Human Design gates and centers of intimate physical connection to open. A flow of almost overwhelming sexual energy had taken the reins of my human-ness and was riding me hard toward the last hurdle of my sexual empowerment.

> *To integrate and apply empowerment, I must first experience dis-*
> *empowerment. My opportunity to be empowered comes through*
> *overcoming the experience of being dis-empowered.*

From my spiritual practice with the Experience Ability and consequent heightened Awareness, I could *feel* this would be a drama filled experience into the resisted emotions of my human-ness. My gates were open, my emotional horse had bolted, and my intuition was waving its Stetson in the air as it shouted, "keep going!". My mind of course ... was scared to death and constantly coming up with reasons and rationalities why I should stop now and dismount this stampeding course of action. My intuition prevailed though and took hold of the reins to my experiences once more. It began stimulating more frequent and highly charged sexual experiences to bolt from the attempted confines of my minds fear corral of control. From the stimulation of these moments, writing had now become a passionate expression also. I began to put to paper my suppressed sexual emotions as they were wildly set free by my newfound sensual cowgirl.

I cannot presume to know or accurately state what the deepest aspect of her experiences were for her, but I can say without a doubt that her gates and channels had been flung opened too. In alignment with her intention to integrate more spirituality in her sexual relationship, we attended the very next self-evolvement course together. She embarked down some first-time experiences of spiritual ownership and expanded awareness of herself, that she may well have never thought existed. I was one of the facilitators on this course, so we both had taken a big bite into the experience of lovers/teacher/student relationship as well, even before we had begun integrating our intimate/personal relationship. Actually, we hadn't even had time to define accurately *what* that intimate relationship meant or looked like. We were both still riding our sexual broncos, holding tight the reins to maintain some kind of delusional control of an obviously out of control stampede of our most human emotions. I feel the consciousness course was an attempt to balance the effects of our new human design— as lights, camera, action was set in play from the flood of energy coming from our gates, channels and centers, that were now opening up.

Now the depth of ownership that this particular course takes one to—can be daunting to say the least. Although my sensual cowgirl had been thrown a couple of times throughout the course, she courageously climbed back on and rode it through to completion, without too many scars and bruises. I was proud of her and felt this would be a great neutralizing ground for us both to nurture a new experience of real Spiritual integrity within our intimate relationship together. I understood my challenge would be to leave my teacher identity in the classroom, as this became the focus of my integration on the course also. There was already some mind-drama from my teacher identity's pretentious and relentless intention to empower her to get "it". Drama arose of course, when this same identity was expecting some personal recognition for *her* empowerment. I could feel my superior teacher identity wanting to take her reins. I knew that to apply what I had learned from the lessons its dominance was presenting to me, a high level of intentional Awareness would be needed. I am always fascinated by the way our human-ness can create exactly the right "event" for us to *experience*, one that offers us exactly what we need to integrate something.

To experience equality in my intimate personal relationship, I realized I must embrace my vulnerability and integrate my asserted superior identity.

Another course or two, along with many deep sharing's and ownerships, intermingled with occasional assertions of right and wrong of course, and the inevitable happened— we moved in together. If accelerated integration was the intention for us coming together, then the intense experiences we were now beginning to have, were fueled by the interactions of our gates now being thrown open wide... 24 hours a day. The combination of our Spirits intention coupled with the experiences created by our human designs, were just the right recipe for a rapidly changing, mind-drama filled adventure ride to the destination of our higher intentions.

Confirmation of my sexual disempowerment integration started to come along many times. It came in the form of many opportunities to apply my self–empowerment and not succumb to the sexual manipulations of my sensual cowgirl. These encounters would come in the form of enticing sexual intimacy in the bedroom to compensate for the lack of open intimacy in our everyday life together. Succumbing to the mind created emotions of my very human element of self, were my moments of sexual dis-empowerment, and at the same time my opportunity to step into the final sexual freedom coming from my self-empowerment. I guess the bottom line for me was, that I was looking for our deepest intimacy to be in the everyday moments of our life, and the bedroom encounters would then become an expression of that deep intimacy.

I felt her bottom line may well have been reversed, with the deep intimacy to be expressed in our bedroom encounters, but our everyday moments to be a show for the world, rather than a true expression of open intimacy. Unless both parties involved in an intimate personal relationship are aware and prepared to be intimately honest with their-self first; manipulations and blame of the other are inevitable. In my case, at the time of our breakup and for some months prior, I felt we were both in this mode of avoidance of self-honesty and as such, the inevitable aggressive separation happened.

It has always amazed me how two people can be so intimate, caring and connected with each other and yet, our human-ness needs to create such drama and blame to separate. Why is it so hard to accept the inevitable change that comes from separation when our experience together has been completed? When explored more deeply and honestly, we may well find that it is the suppressed and resisted judgments and expectations of previous times together; when experiences were incomplete, and honesty not embraced as we swim in the cesspool of blame and manipulations; which bring about our inevitable dramatic and often traumatic end to relationships. All of this to simply justify *resisting* a lack of control of change in the present moment and staying *attached* to trying to create some form of delusional perception of control.

Attachment to the past will always have me resist being present with the experience being presented to me in this present moment.

I believe if it wasn't for understanding that my human design is not me, but merely the vehicle for *my* experiences, then our whirlwind eighteen months of intense growth, could have been an overdramatized eighty days of attack, blame and suffering. True to the nature of this human experience we had created for each other, our breakup was also as dramatic and intense as the bronco ride to get there. If I had been stuck in my human identity; in the human-ness of my reactive emotions judgements and projections, then I am sure our relationship would have ended in the eighty days, but without any integration of what either of us was intending. After our breakup, another dear friend asked me why I would stay or even enter into such an experience, knowing that it was to be so eventful. I tried to explain to her that by intending to *experience* being human and to learn from those experiences, I was intending to not resist the experiences being presented. By staying "in feel" and connected to my Spirit's intuitive guidance, I knew that this experience held a key to set me free from my sexual dis-empowerment and connect me to my ability to write. This could not happen if I avoided or ran away from the experience of dis-empowerment being presented to me in that present moment ... just because one of my minds identities was afraid of being hurt.

One of the functions of my mind is to create my human identities, which facilitate my human events together. My identities are not my experiencing "True-Self", they are the transient creations of my "human-self".

An early confirmation of our connection by Divine Orchestration, came in the form of her having a *knowing* that we were meant to create something together also. The ending confirmation for me, was my freedom from sexual dis-empowerment; my neutral lack of *need* for sex to bridge the abyss created between us from disconnect and lack of intimacy. The completion of that experience for me came together when she finally admitted requiring intimacy in the bedroom to be the expression of our connection together. For me, I required a real connection together *outside* of the bedroom first, then allowing the intimate expression of our connection to unfold in the bedroom, like a flower in the sun.

Our mind's interpretations and definitions of conditional human Love did inevitably create much drama throughout our relationship. These dramas however, were the fuel that stoked the engine of accelerated learning which inevitably came out of our experience together. The catch is, that accelerated learning is only effective when it is coupled with Awareness and Will. It is our Will that provides the power to apply our ability to stay "in feel" with what is really going on in our *internal* world. It is this ability and the Awareness of Spirit, that allowed me to ultimately recognize the difference between my minds human perception of love and the truly virtuous state of Love that comes *through* Spirit. I could feel my Spirits unconditional Love for my sensual cowgirl, and still do, but my human minds definition of love, with its conditions and expectations was in direct contrast. Inevitably, the drama of both our minds expectant love facilitated the event of us breaking up. Something to point out here though is that we were *both* in states of expectation and judgment. Although we were of opposite sex, and brought up on opposite sides of the planet, we both were feeling and playing out the same mind based emotional dramas ... together. Here is another example of my saying that, "We are all the same ... just different."

Contrary to what a lot of people would have you believe ... Being Human is a paradox, because ... it is the same for ALL of us ... and yet unique to each of us.

Being human is a particular parameter of experiencing and as such, the perception and influence of *human* love will be conditional within those *human* parameters of beliefs, ethics, integrity, judgments values and expectations etc. These are all an intrinsic part of the "human domain" of existence. Understanding my design that creates my unique blend of being human for this particular lifetime liberates me from the confines of that domain of existence, but it still can't substitute or replace deliberate experiencing of my life. I began to recognize that the human design is not the true me, but merely a part of the design of my unique *human*-ness. I have been freed to experience my True Self— the unconditional essence that *experiences* BE-ing Human—through intimately experiencing the design of the human vehicle ... I call Peter in this Life.

"Knowing about" Being Human isn't the same as the "knowing" acquired from TRULY experiencing Being Human.

Although the newly developed "Human Design" system is amazingly helpful and accurate, it is still just a partial map of a much more infinite Divinely planned human system. This Divine system is what allows ALL of these interactions to occur; interactions of the physical Body and the Cosmic Soul & Spirit together, which make up the reality we experience as Being Human. It is also worth recognizing that this Divine design, is what we all have equally. It is the vehicle our Spirit drives, to get us to the destination of our higher virtues and spiritually intended experiences.

Being Human is one of the most variable and widest paradigms of experiences available for us to evolve through. Have you ever sat and just watched people be human— without judging them? Have you ever noticed yourself being human—without judging yourself? It is near impossible to not judge when we connect with our human-ness. Judging is yet another intrinsic part of "Being Human". Have you ever dropped into that place of wonderment or maybe bewilderment, just from watching people at events or shopping mall or at simple family gatherings? People watching. I love to do it deliberately, making sure to stay Aware of my judgments and criticisms, but just notice the same-ness of the differences in people and their actions—their thoughts and words. From my observations of the human differences of others, I coined the phrase "We are all the same, just different."

I find it humbling and inspiring to notice how much the same our differences are.

To go to a shopping mall and notice how people outwardly act one way toward another, and then turn the corner and act almost totally different to someone else within seconds, constantly amazes me. The mother screaming at her kids to behave one minute, then nice as pie to the shop assistant the next minute. Have you ever done that yourself? How is it that I can be this way now and in just a few seconds, with a couple of strategic jibes toward my mind's pride ... or theirs ... and it's as if another Being jumped into my skin and took over all my responses ...and defenses. Is it possible this is where the story of Jekyll and Hyde originated? Is there really a Jekyll and Hyde lurking in the dark depths of the resisted consciousness of each of us? I think yes, but maybe it isn't in the depths of consciousness, but simply in the depth of our human-ness. where our contrasting attributes reside. We most definitely don't have the murdering type in our Spirit, but definitely the contrasting types of potential murderer *is* ingrained in the potential of our human-ness. The good news is that they're just our human identities creating an intended human event for us to experience.

Understanding my human identities can be the most liberating experience to free me from the mind's drama of my present human reality.

However, understanding which part of our human-self our identities exist in is the pre-requisite to true liberation. We will explore this much more deeply in the following chapters.

Being human though is such a unique opportunity to constantly experience new situations and emotions. One thing we could say about BEing Human, is that change is a human's constant companion. It is our human reality of opposites, of duality, that provide us with an endless flow of alternate potential experiences. Look at how easy it is for us to change our mind, change our viewpoint in any given moment once circumstances require it to be so. Look also at the emotional rollercoaster we all experience, as we ride from the peaks of sublime joy that comes from simply BE-in our human, to the depths of human suffering that inevitably results from our mind-self's resistance to BEing human. Once again, it is through BEing human that we are able to experience both ends of this paradigm within minutes of each other. To be emotionally involved in any event will inevitably lock you into that event and provide you with so many opportunities to learn new ways of how to BE-in this human world. It can also provide opportunities to change the events you are experiencing by applying yourself and those new traits, those new *virtues* you may have acquired from what you learned from previous experiences.

Every human experience has the potential for me to become a more virtuous human.

Being Human intrinsically stems from a sense of separateness, or rather more accurately, a sense of separateness is what defines the human. Specifically, this separation is what came about through the creation of our Human Soul's self-consciousness and the Spirit's Ego that is our "I AM". Our Soul's consciousness has come about from our Spiritual evolution from formless Spiritual Essence into the dense form of our human "I" consciousness, that is now conscious of its self. To be an "I", I *must* feel separate and individual. Our viewpoints are separate from each other. Some of you may even have the same viewpoints as I do, but does it make us feel connected or was it just a relief to hear that someone else has the same viewpoint as you? Although we may have the same viewpoint we still feel different from each other. If I disagreed with your viewpoint on let's say religion or politics, we will probably become extremely separated again. The belief systems of religion and politics are great arenas for creating vast arid wastelands of separation and disconnection from each other. The extreme results of these arenas of course, as we see all too often in our world ... is death and mayhem. Isn't it ironic, considering that religion for example is supposed to be the common spiritual link for us all to be one with The Divine and ultimately with each other. Even more ironic is that the robes of religion were used to cover up the covert judgments of separation that in days of old, the clergy held against the common people of the land. The desecration of my beloved Hawaiian culture is a great example of this irony through the mind's spiritual identities, self-deceiving judgmental projections. The deception was to bring everyone together with God, but the result was to eliminate anyone that expressed their separateness, their healthy Ego individuality, the very essence of their human nature.

To come here as a Spirit and enter our human vehicle of Body and Soul to have a human experience, the feeling of being separated from the Source, needs to permeate our whole state of BEing. The belief that I am separate is as essential to being human as is the very breath of Life Force that I need to exist and survive as a human on this planet. The power of this basic, human belief amplifies my sense of vulnerability and aloneness. Having this vulnerability and aloneness amplified, ensures that my human experience is mine and mine alone. This process holds the potential for me to be totally present with my individual experiences. From this place, I can learn to master the limitations of this "human" form of existence. This viewpoint, this belief of separateness; which brings with it the dualistic conflict of resistance and attachment, is at the heart of all suffering we experience as a human. Although this later statement may be indirectly true, it is ironically not separateness that creates the suffering, but the resistance to separateness and attachment to oneness that manifest the *conflict* that we experience as suffering.

This underlying feeling of disconnection is the core belief that manifest my human events where I am able to experience being an "I "... alone and vulnerable.

Without the experience of being alone and unloved we wouldn't have the opportunities we get so often, to integrate the self-love needed to experience TRUE oneness or connection with each other. Only the identities inherent within our human being, with their inherent belief structures, can offer us the appropriate human **events** to experience what we need. Only my identities that make up the human-self I call Peter, can house these beliefs and feelings of separation. Even though we are all one; we are all human. Our human identities are the projected vehicles created by our Soul's mind-self to manifest specific human events of emotions and feelings. These are all humanly created for our Spirit True-Self; the TRUE experiencer ... to experience. The Spirit True-Self is the "I" of your Spirit that is eternally connected to each other and Spiritual

Source. It's the aspect that we may feel as this vague sense of the observer sitting in the background of our experiences. You can't integrate self-empowerment without experiencing disempowerment. You can't experience disempowerment without being a victim or rather, BE-in a victim identity that is easily disempowered by others. The creation of these identities is the domain of the Soul's mind-self. More specifically; which we will explore in intimate detail in the later chapters: they exist within a specific component of the Soul, but for now, we will call it the mind-self. This is what it does, and it is brilliant at it. We have many, many identities available to us on call. These identities are created and exist within the domain of our Souls mind-self. As I said, we will go into more depth in this subject through the following chapters.

My intention to explore this core "belief feeling" of vulnerability, aloneness and separation, attracted the opportunity for me to experience a rebirthing process through a spiritual men's group I was involved in. I can feel some of you struggling with the concept of men coming together in a group specifically to explore spirituality. I'm sure a few of my friends from my younger Rugby Union Football days in Australia couldn't even conceive of these three words coming together in the same sentence. Some of them probably couldn't even pronounce spirituality. None the less thankfully, in these days it has become much more common. I believe this is a comforting and reassuring sign confirming the evolution of our collective human consciousness. I have never previously been drawn to any form of rebirthing, as my belief is more aligned with *this*, the life I'm living, and I don't need to bring the past into it. As a side note, ironically the Karma we bring with us is exactly that, our unresolved past from previous human incarnations.

Thank goodness that my Spirit True-Self's intentions to integrate life's lessons have precedence over my Souls mind-self's proclivity for resistance and avoidance.

I was in a group of ten men that met each week to explore our spirituality through open discussions, breath-work, meditations, group alignment and support techniques. On this particular week, we were exploring a rebirthing technique in our friend's back yard pool. As I floated on my back in the swimming pool, my head gently held by the assistant, I dropped my self into a trance-like state of deep relaxation. With Awareness, I could feel my human judgments of "this is silly" and "floating in a pool isn't going to do anything," sabotaging my ability to relax. I decided to connect with my intention to *experience* whatever this is going to be and *experience* to the fullest everything that unfolds.

My awareness gradually began to extend past my rampaging mind and the space I perceived I was in and moved into the actual space I occupy. I relaxed deeper and deeper and began to lose all sense of my body and where I was. As per instructions, I took a large breath and the assistant rolled me over to float face down. Opening my eyes under water and exhaling as slow and little as possible, I eventually began to feel like I was once more in my mother's womb. All noise from outside magically faded and any effort to exhale or even hold my breath eventually dissipated. An amazing sense of being cradled in the womb prevailed. No *need* to breath, no *need* to move. The *need* for breath continued to diminish even more. Time became non-existent.

As I put more Awareness on the sensations of being in the womb, I became aware of feeling free from the constraints of the outside world and even the need to breathe. Actually, I had lost all recognition and attachment to the outside world and I noticed I was experiencing, not my body floating in the pool, but my Soul, suspended in space. It wasn't so much an "I" of my human me that was suspended, but rather the presence of "I Consciousness" that is the True Conscious Self of my Spirit "I AM". That brief, euphoric moment of complete disassociation from BE-in a human, from being in my body as the human identity of my personality, unleashed the experiential memory of moments just prior to my birth. Almost as soon as the peace and tranquility of my Spirit's pre-birth experience was experienced, it was shattered by my Souls mind-self's thump of attention coming back to being in my friend's pool. An explosive charge of terror shook the space between every cell in my body. It was as if life's paramedics had sent a thousand volts through my heart pulling me back from the brink of stepping through the Soul's doorway back to Source. The *need* to have a breath slowly enveloped me again, bringing with it the dread of knowing that once taken, this experience of my Spirit's effortless space would end.

My experiential memory of the warm loving comfort of my connection to Divine Source and re-experiencing my mother's womb permeated with her love, overwhelmed me. The murmur of my friend's voices started to pull me further back to the present moment as tears uncontrollably flowed and mixed with the cold saltwater of my friend's backyard pool. Still face down, I resisted letting go of this experience and becoming human once more. Intimately connected to this resistance was my attachment to my Spirit's ability to experience my Divine Source, which ultimately triggered again ... conflict. It was this conflict of resistance and attachment connected to separation though that acted like an anchor, pulling me back to BE human. I had a flash of an insight into the many previous times, previous lives when I had resisted to BE-in a human once more. I recognized in that moment, that this is where that fearful belief of being human had come from. I could feel the denseness of my body begin to return.

Hearing the soft murmur of my friends debating whether to pull me out or not and which one was going to give me the kiss of life, amplified my human frailties even further. My judgmental macho identity kicked back to life as it strongly resisted going mouth to mouth with one of my male friends. I began to notice my body density increasing as I became more and more present with being in the pool. I became curious to the original sensation of my pre-human experience of resisting letting go of my connection to Source, to cutting my Cosmic umbilical cord to the loving presence and security of my Divine Existence. I realized how similar this was to other experiences I later had as a child. Those times I dug my heels in while being dragged into the house to be punished for something I had apparently done wrong but didn't understand what it was I did. The human event and participants may have been dramatically different to when I was born to this Earth, but the **experience** was definitely the same.

It was an aerie experience however, to still feel the presence of Source around me while having the basic human belief programs of separation being downloaded into me again. It was like those sequences from the Matrix movies. I imagined it felt similar to when

Neo is loaded up with fighting programs to assist his operation in the machine's world and he becomes something different from what he actually is.

I have no doubt that the core consciousness software program for BE-in a human has at its core, a belief or two about being separate.

Insights continued to flow like water bubbling from a spring. This belief of separation is a necessary belief structure which allows us all to operate as individual humans in this Divinely created Earth playground. It is this belief of separation which makes it possible for us all to have our individually unique parameter of experiences throughout this lifetime. If you didn't have this separation belief, then how could you BE the individual you are? If you truly experienced Oneness, if you truly "experience" non-separation, then could you still be the "individual" you are right now? Could you possibly be the one who uniquely grew up the way you did, gaining and holding the beliefs that create the events you experience through, in this present moment? I think not. Without this core belief of separation, it would be inevitable that you would be a completely different human Being than the one you are now. Could you have the experiences you have had, the ones that have shaped and formed who you BE now, if you had started without the belief that you are separate, alone, an individual?

The very basis for any human Soul's individual personality to exist, is to believe that it is separate from not just the rest of the world ... but from Divine Source its Self.

The work of Rudolph Steiner clearly shows us our evolutionary path from before the formation of our "I Consciousness", where we existed in a true state of non-separation, when we were still connected directly and intimately to the Spiritual Realm. Our evolution into "I Consciousness" came with the insertion of the *separation belief,* so we could have a truly individual "I Conscious" experience. Ironically, it is only through our separation that we are able to truly experience the *State of Being* we call *Oneness.* Think about it, how could you distinguish the experience of Oneness, if you haven't first experienced separation?

What could you gauge any experience on, or rather, any state of Being of Oneness; for Oneness is not an experience but a state of Being, without knowing intimately to your core existence ... separation? The real catch is .... you must fully embrace and *experience* completely the existence of separation ... without ANY resistance or attachments filtering your experience.

There is so much Spiritual rhetoric from the many Spiritual Salesmen who would vehemently deny and discredit this viewpoint, as they try to consolidate their belief in you that we are, here and now, all one. Of course, what they say of One-ness is most definitely true with respect to our Spirit-Self, for it is in the Spiritual Realm when we leave this physical material emerald green third rock from the sun, that we do indeed rejoin the Oneness brotherhood of Spirit. However, as a human during this brief lifetime here, we do not exist in One-ness and brotherhood together without separation.

Most of these spiritual salespeople have a hidden agenda to sell you *their* system of obtaining this revered and sort after state of Oneness. Unfortunately, most of these salesmen ... and saleswomen ... have no Awareness of their belief being deeply shrouded in their own resistance to separation and as such, because of this shroud of resistance and associated attachment, are unable to actually BE Oneness. If they cannot BE Oneness, then how can *their* system achieve Oneness? The fact is that being human is so very individualistic, but this doesn't mean that it is a negative thing. There are so many benefits to be a separate being from others, to be a unique form of existence that is capable of creating uniquely individual human events to experience through. If we look at it from a bigger viewpoint than the single self, if we can look at it from a much larger human collective viewpoint, we can begin to see and maybe feel, the important part we each play in the way our human reality operates ... and grows and evolves.

We are each a unique facet, shinning our personal light through the diamond like sphere, that is our Collective Human Consciousness.

Consider that the complete Human Reality is made up of the collective sum of each and every one of the individual realities that we each exist as. This reality that I call Peter, is but a single sparkle of light shining from the glittering diamond that is the Collective Human Consciousness. This collective exists within Gaia, our Earths Sentient Being, which provides us all with the correct *human* environment for this personal AND collective reality to manifest. Each and every one of us shinning our individual light here now, make up the cosmic glow of Humanity. Consider that there are approximately seven billion people on this little third rock from the sun, and each one of us is a completely unique parameter of human experience. One system of self-evolvement operates from the basic principle that the only difference between us is our beliefs. Now although this may be true to some degree, if we look at these minute belief differences and see the profound effect they have on creating our individual reactions and responses, we may see the potential we have for an almost infinite number of human experience parameters to choose from.

Being human; to BE-in a Human, although it may be a collective reality, is first and foremost a personal, individual "experience". We are most definitely simply different aspects of the Cosmic Consciousness from which the Human "I Consciousness" comes from, yet we are the same in respect to our human-ness, our emotions, identities reactions interactions resistances and attachments etc. etc. We all love cry and hate, judge blame and reject. We all have feelings of guilt regret and sadness, of joy happiness and elation. We are all victim's victimizer's and controllers ... and many more identities ... yet ALL the same ... just different. All of these human traits etc. exist within each and every human BE-ing existing here now on this planet. All of these traits and identities when looked at objectively and openly, seem to originate from a common human blueprint structure, yet they all have their own unique flavor and applications unique to each of us. It is as if we all have a core generic "Human Blueprint" of identities, emotions etc. that we get to wear as human suits throughout this Life walk together. We then get to dress our suits up, make them uniquely individual and tailored to our specific parameter of experiencing for this lifetime, that will benefit our unique True-Self's evolution through our lifetime here now.

When we start to see the same-ness that lies within Being Human, we can then drop the special-ness our mind likes to place between our self and the rest of the world. A simple fact is that we are each unique, not special. Special is only a viewpoint of our mind's creation, designed to prop up our fragile mind-based identities resistance to being vulnerable. *Special* is our minds viewpoint and its expression of separation. Special disconnects me from the rest of humanity. Special starts to demand "special privileges", which ultimately the mind will justify taking from others. Special puts one person above or below another, breaking the true spiritual connectivity between each of us Human's ... here Be-ing. Special has me resist what I see in others and ultimately serves to be yet another form of avoidance of what the world is reflecting to me of my self, those elements I don't want to see about me.

The bottom line of Being Human is that we are all the same, we are all human, we are all BEings of Spirit Consciousness here now having a human experience. We are also all here supporting each other in sometimes dramatic and even aggressive ways to become more, to be better than we are at this present time, to become a more virtuous human.

If any of this resonates in any way within your core, then does it naturally stimulate you to ask more questions about Being Human?

Could some of those questions be ....

- Is my human-self ... my True Self?
- Is my human-self merely a personalized vehicle I get to use in this present dimensional reality to expand and evolve my True-Experiencing-Self?
- Is the purpose of Being Human simply to create a more virtuous human vehicle capable of housing and supporting a more evolved experiencing True-Spirit-Self?
- Is the End-Game of all of this to evolve us back as a once more unified Human Soul & Spirit, fully conscious in the Oneness again that is ... our Divine Source?"

Chapter 4

The Self's of Being Human

So what kind of statement is, "The Self's of Being Human? When I first posed this title as a question to my partner and asked her what she thought, her immediate response was ... as expected ... "that's not a true statement and doesn't make sense." I replied that I knew that and that it's a deliberate use of words to challenge the mind's reference points and hopefully stimulate some right questions that would connect us with what it is to "BE a self". Hopefully, we may be able to expose and experience the differences between what I call the Human and Spirit Self's that make up our Human BE-in-ness as a Cosmic creation. So, let's explore a bit about what a "self" is, and then move on to see if we can find the "self" or "self's" that may be in each of us and as such, make up the whole Human Being that we are.

The conquering of self is truly greater than were one to conquer many worlds.

Edgar Cayce

Here are some "self" definition's out of our Wikipedia for examples to help start our exploration.

- *The philosophy of self seeks to describe essential qualities that constitute a person's uniqueness or essential being. There have been various approaches to defining these qualities. The self can be considered that being which is the source of consciousness, the agent responsible for an individual's thoughts and actions, or... the substantial nature of a person which endures and unifies consciousness over time.*

- *The psychology of self is the study of either the cognitive and affective representation of one's identity or the subject of experience. The earliest formulation of the self in modern psychology forms the distinction between the self as I, the subjective knower, and the self as **Me**, the object that is known. Current views of the self in psychology position the self* as playing an integral part in human motivation, cognition, affect, and social identity.

- **Religious views** on the self vary widely. The self is a complex and core subject in many forms of spirituality. Two types of self are commonly considered - the self that is the ego, also called the learned, superficial self of mind and body, an egoic creation, and the Self which is sometimes called the "True Self", the "Observing Self", or the "Witness". Human beings have a self—that is, they are able to look back on themselves as both subjects and objects in the universe. Ultimately, this brings questions about who we are and the nature of our own importance. Traditions such as Buddhism see the attachment to self is an illusion that serves as the main cause of suffering and unhappiness. Christianity makes a distinction between the true self and the false self and sees the false self negatively.

From these definitions we can see there are varied views of what a self is, but still there is a common thread throughout all of these systems of understanding. That common thread is one of being an individual, of an experience of the difference of ones Being to other forms. It is an *ability* to acknowledge one's separateness from an external world reality and able to make a distinction between one's inner and outer realities. From the philosophical viewpoint, the self can be considered that being which is the source of consciousness, whereas through the teachings in Rudolph Steiner's Anthroposophical viewpoint, the self is a **product of consciousness.** Still with Anthroposophy, it is understood that the "self" consciousness emerged through our evolution into our pre-separation existence. Prior to this time, we were not in such a solid and dense form as we are today, but still in direct and intimate connection to the Spiritual Realm. Our Human's Spiritual evolution into our present "I Consciousness" produced the "self" that we are today, and with it, our current state of separation from the Spiritual Realm.

Consciousness is simply the ability to be conscious of my existence as an individual, different and separate, thus creating a Self ... to be conscious in.

Before our collective evolutionary jump into "I Consciousness" thousands of years ago, we didn't have the ability to recognize, experience, perceive or to even think about our existence from the individual viewpoint of a self; as an experiencing "I". Eventually with this "I", and the "self" unifying quality of its inherent Spirit Ego Body, came our capability to recognize one's self as the experiencer, as well as what is being experienced. All of this came about through our emergence into "I Consciousness". Unfortunately, through this emergence into the consciousness of "self", we lost connection with the true spiritual *origination* of our Self. Through the intellectualization that has become inherent within the "conscious thinking I", we have become blind to the experience of the *spiritual* element that is our "True-Self". The self has been humanized, and as such, its significance has been devalued to its most physical and assertive ... intellectual self.

A self has functions and abilities that are different, separate and unique to its self, as opposed to other self's or the environment it exists in. Although I have said, and will say often throughout this book, that we are all the same just different; in no way am I suggesting that the self that we are, is identical as any other self living on this planet. Although our Collective Quantum Leap into "I Consciousness" is one of a collective and not a *purely* singular individual event, the resultant "self-consciousness" or Awareness of and existence as—our self, IS a completely individual one.

I have chosen the concept of the self for its simplicity in describing the aspects of consciousness that makeup being human. These concepts we are about to journey through here and in later chapters as we go deeper into their intricacies, may challenge your minds framework of comfort zones. I invite you to step out of your mind's need for complex definitions for a while, and explore these concepts with your experiential Self, *feeling* for their simplistic wisdom; of which is waiting to reveal itself to you. My goal is that within this simplicity, we may see the greater role of the Human BE-in, in the bigger picture of the evolution of our Spirit of Man and Humanity as a collective. These concepts have been applied throughout the ages in many forms, from western psychology to shamanism and Hawaiian Huna spirituality, along with countless others throughout this world, with varying descriptions. In ancient Hawaiian Spirituality which spans the past thirteen odd thousand years, their intimately experiential connection to our Cosmic origination gave them the understanding of the human makeup, to be a combination of three specific components to our human existence and evolution.

To note here, is that thirteen odd thousand years ago, our human evolutionary stage was still in the time of no Ego "I" consciousness. What that means is, that the original Hawaiian culture still intimately held onto their connection to the Spiritual Realm, right up to the point of the European invasion and the more intellectual influence of the western Intellectual Soul came along. Because of this, the Hawaiian understanding intimately experienced these elements as self's, as deeply spiritual elements of the Human Being, which have their own functions and purpose for our human journey here. They also experientially knew the real purpose for our "I" consciousness ability; which is to unify these "self" elements, as the keys to maintaining our connection to the Spiritual Realm. Because of their isolation for such a long time, their wisdom of the self's and their Spiritual connection to The Divine Source, was maintained untainted for a much longer period than almost all other ancient culture. The Hawaiian names for these elements is unihipili, uhane and Aumakua.

In western psychology it is the concept of the sub-conscious, conscious and super-conscious. The western concept comes from our later period of development and consequently, is one of a more mental or human understanding if you like. By the time the western Soul-mind had conceptualized these components, the concepts were intellectualized from a mind-based viewpoint pretty much void of Spiritual connection. Some spiritual practices of today describe them as the low-self, mid-self and High-Self. Our own intellectualized western spirituality of "New Age" thought, often use the terminology of Body, Soul and Spirit, or Body Mind and Soul. There are many other descriptions and labels or names from many other cultures and practices around the globe for these self-aspects of human consciousness. I don't want to get into a long list to try to define or describe them all to you. These are simply the different aspects of consciousness that make up the you, which you are here and now. Hopefully we will see throughout these pages, that the intellectual minds use of mental descriptions to try and understand experiential concepts of what we're talking about, can quite often be a poor attempt to convey the true characteristics, attributes or abilities etc.

Understanding comes from the ability of the rational mind to mentally <u>know</u> <u>about</u> something, by creating concepts of that thing through thinking.

Wisdom comes about through the full experience and integration of something by my experiential True Self, to the level of simple intimate <u>knowing</u>.

My intention here is, wherever possible; to always create the opportunities for you to experience or at least see these aspects that make up you and every other human being here on this planet. This is also another instance of how we are all the same, just different. Every single Human BEing on this beautiful emerald green third rock from the sun, is made up of these very same aspects of consciousness. For arguments sake, throughout this book, I will call them self's, and refer to them as the Body-self, Soul-self and Spirit-Being-Self. As you will see, in the greater sense, although they are all intimately connected and related to each other, they are all their own self with regard to them all having their own unique realm and functions, purpose, attributes and abilities.

Although they are to a certain extent in-dependent from each other, they are very much connected and dependent on each other, through the very intention of having this human experience. They are so interwoven that it takes a deeper sense of *Aware-feel* and discernment than we normally use, to recognize the differences from one self to the next. Although Awareness is potentially intrinsic in each and every human BE-ing walking this planet now, a *trained* and *grounded* Awareness in our human-self is essential to accurately discern and recognize the differences. They are so interwoven that I can quite often feel confused and discouraged when trying to understand when asking the questions, "who I am?" and "what I am feeling?" or, "where does that react or stimulation coming from?". Just when I think I have a grip on how I operate in the world, a different aspect of "me" shows up and turn's my world upside down—again. Sometimes, I'm reacting and responding to things without any wish to do so or idea why. Respond and react, from one self to another, from one identity of the Soul-self to another, from one survival instinct of the Physical Body-self to another, from one experience of the Spirit-BEing-Self to another. Without Awareness, there is nothing deliberate, just react and blindly respond.

To know thy "Self" … is to know God.

Hopefully, by the end of this book you will have experienced the differences, or at least get a sense of the difference and be inspired sufficiently to experience more of the amazing power and dynamic union of YOUR three Self's together—as the Human YOU BE-in. To leave out or separate any one of these self-aspects, makes this human experience not simply difficult to comprehend, it makes it impossible. They are so intrinsically connected that it can be very difficult sometimes to distinguish between them and know which one I am operating AS or through in any moment. The amazing healings of old from the ancient Kahuna were only possible, because they intimately experienced the difference between each of the self's and their unique attributes, functions and faculties etc. For example, the unihipilli or physical Body-self, couldn't heal an ailment or dis-ease that originates in the uhane or Soul-self. My Kahuna once shared the difference between an illness; which is a dis-harmony or dis-ease within the unihipilli physical Body-self, and a sickness; which is a dis-harmony or dis-ease within the uhane, the Soul-self. We can't heal a sickness solely with a treatment for an illness, however … we can heal an illness with a treatment for a sickness. In other words, you can't heal the Soul-self through the Body-self alone, but you can heal the Body-self through the Soul-self. To go one step further, you can heal the Body and the Soul through the Spirit, what the Hawaiian's call the Aumakua, but you can't heal the Spirit through the Body and Soul alone. Yet even another step further, it is the Body and Soul together that make the evolution and wellness of the Spirit possible. This is made possible through this "Human Experience" here on Gaia Mother Earth.

Are you out of your mind … yet?

Stop and breath for a moment into this last paragraph and feel for the simplicity in these statements.

Every single human being here now, living and breathing on this glorious emerald cosmic rock, is made up of these very same three "self" aspects of consciousness.

This is another instance of how we are all the same, just different.

There is a hierarchy of influence of one self upon another and knowing this sequence of influence can sometimes provide instant healing through one, or sometimes even all of the self's. This understanding became wisdom for me when I experienced these differences many times over throughout my Conscious Bodyworks practice.

Taking the knowledge that my Kahuna shared, and then applying it in my practice to the point of "experiencing" the differences within my clients … and my Self, revealed the wisdom that began to guide me deeper into all the realms of the self's that make up our Human BE-in. The profound resultant healings that came from gradually *knowing* which *self* is, the originator of my client's condition is … or mine, stimulated this material I am sharing about now. So, let's see if we can get a feel for the differences between the "self's" within us, so you can become wise to their use and application in *your* world. In the later chapters we will explore more deeply into the elements of these "self's" and how we can heal and maintain a very high level of wellness of Being, simply by deliberate experience and alignment of our three self's.

According to an ancient Hawaiian Philosophy, our purpose for this life time here, is to unify and align ALL of our Self's in one harmonic space together.

The most in-depth, extensively detailed and accurate descriptions of the make-up of our human existence that I have found, can be studied through the extensive works of Rudolph Steiner's Anthroposophy teachings. His work is so extensive that although he doesn't call them self's; through his spiritual-science research, he has been able to brake the Self's down further again into the spiritual components within each. He was/is an enlightened Initiate of an extremely high order and as such, his detail which comes directly from the spiritual realm, is immense, intricate and deeply revealing. I will try to simplify these down further to make it easier for us all to comprehend and experience these wisdoms within our own … present day Self reality. If we can see and agree that although we are ALL Human, we are; each and every one of us, an individual self, with our own characteristics, abilities, capabilities, functions, skills etc. etc., then we may notice the differences that make us unique … yet the same. I won't go into too much detail right now, as this detail will reveal itself in the later chapters here, but I will try and give you an outline, a beginning perspective that we can build on later. Using this Awareness and skill to notice differences, let's explore now the realms of the Three Self's, and see if you can distinguish the differences in the Self's that make up the Human that *YOU* … Be-in.

Body-self

The first self I will call our Physical Body-self. This self is made up of our physical body along with the etheric or Life-Body. Although our physical body seems self-explanatory, and there is already so much documented *physical* research on its physical makeup and perceived requirements, there is a perspective of it that is rarely looked at. Our body is not just an organism that we are randomly given for this Lifetime to get around this planet in. It's not just a vehicle, but rather a Cosmic Being, a *living instrument* that is capable of transmuting creative spiritual energy from a formless Spiritual intention into a physical form. This gives it the ability to manifest all kinds of human events for us to experience. Your Body-self is your sensory organ for creating in this material physical world reality ... and bringing this world into your BE-ing. It is also at the same time, a Super-sensory organ capable of communication and manifestation between your physical AND Spiritual worlds. If you will, it is an instrument that acts as a transmitter and receiver. Contrary to a lot of intellectual mind-based self-development technologies and indoctrinations, it is actually our physical Body-self which creates and manifests in our human world, not our Soul-self. Your Body-self is the final filter that determines the 'form' that your human events and experiences will manifest as and how they are received.

My Body-self is what makes it possible for my human reality to manifest in this materialized world.

My Body-self is the sensory organ that also makes it possible for my Spirit True-Self to "experience" its Self in this physical reality.

The etheric-body is the Life-body of this Body-self. Life Body means what it says, in that it is the source of "Life" for your physical body to grow, exist and connect with the Spiritual Being that is our planet, what we call Mother Earth. It is this Earth Being that creates the physical environment for your Body-self to exist in. Your physical body cannot exist without this Life-Body ... or this Earth Being that it lives in. At death, it is the departure of this Etheric Life-Body that allows the physical forces of destruction and decay to carry out the breaking down of the physical body and return its elements back to the Earth. This etheric Life-Body, not just sustains and feeds the physical Body-self while you are alive, empowering its growth and effectiveness through this human Life walk, it also rejuvenates the life in the body by managing the physical forces of destruction being constantly placed upon it. Along with this, it also stores all the life-experience memories you have during your current physical Life here. It is through the Life-body that your physical body is connected to and draws from, our Earth's Etheric Life field. Have you ever felt the Earth's subtle energies through your body when you walk in Nature or swim in her natural waters of ocean lakes and streams etc.? Have you ever notice how revitalized you feel after such a walk or swim etc.? Go ahead, take a moment now and recall times when you have experienced this. It is your immersion in our Earths Etheric Life-Body through these kinds of activities, that reconnects these two etheric Life Bodies and consequently regenerates your physical body. This regeneration after being in Nature's environment, manifest as a sense of "Health and Vigor" within your Body-self.

You are experiencing these rejuvenating effects of the Life energies from the Earth on your etheric Life-body; which is continuously and intimately connected to our Earth's Etheric Life-Body. The instrument that is your physical Body-self, manifest these energy effects as sensations which are able to be experienced as a Body-self reality. Our intended experiences, whether originating from our Soul-self or Spirit-Self, ALL manifest by way of our physical Body-self. A physical illness can be a disruption or interference with your Body-self's ability to transmute and manifest this "intentional" energy from your Soul or Spirit Self's, into an experiential form. This disruption or blockage, results in what we call illness or disease. As this energy gets blocked, builds up and is trapped in the physical body system, ultimately it will manifest as the physical conditions we call disease. The system of Acupuncture is one system that works on releasing or unblocking these points of disruption. I have had many instances throughout my Conscious Bodyworks practice where simply discharging these blocks etc. and opening up the flow of Life Force once more, instantly created physical shifts and changes. The discharging through the Conscious Bodywork however, is done by the client simply, but deliberately, experiencing the originations of the blocks which they themselves had placed there. These changes and shifts we would often call a "miracle healing", were in fact very natural and unordinary results of a cosmic system of physical creation ... of Life its Self.

My Body-self is my human sensory instrument for manifesting everything intended by your Soul AND Spirit for this human existence.
My Body-self doesn't judge right or wrong ... it just manifests and receives.

I have a practice of 30-day fasting, of not having any solid food and only fluid for a whole month. I originally intended this practice to remove old habits and clean and tune my Body-self to be a more effective instrument for experiencing my Life through. With Awareness, I began to have acute experiences of the differences between the self's of my human existence, specifically at first, between my physical and Life bodies. Through meditation and insight from the deliberate experiencing of my Life-Body, its process and function of enlivening the physical body were revealed. At the same time, I was doing intense physical landscape work as well as my Conscious Bodyworks practice. Now, one would think; and many of my friends etc. did at the time think just this, that I should run out of steam, be depleted of energy and even get physically sick from the combination of this intense fasting and long extended hours of extreme physical activity. One of the hardest parts of that whole journey was to NOT allow my Soul-self to take on everyone's concerns for my health. At the same time, I was intensely amazed and interested in the fact that my Body-self was not breaking down as well.

A revelatory experience which integrated a new ability into me, was to deliberately connect my etheric Life-Body to the Earth's Life-Body, and just allow my physical-body to absorb and *drink* if you will, from our Earth's *Life-Giving* source of etheric sustenance.

This became my practice every time I would recognize any sensations of hunger. In those moments, I would simply stop and allow my Body-self to *feed* its self from our Earths Etheric Life-Body. Amazingly, the physical sensations of hunger would discharge within minutes, even seconds quite often, and my physical and etheric bodies would feel regenerated and empowered again. It became quite humbling really to see younger and fitter bodies half my age, quite often fall by the way with fatigue, in need of lunch breaks etc. For me, the longer the fast went, the more my need for food and my hunger pains diminished to near nothing. The more I allowed my Body-self to absorb what "IT" needed and felt and experienced my Life-body enliven, the less physical matter I needed to put in my physical-body to *get* nutrient from. What I began to notice also, was that my sensitivity through all my subtle bodies became extremely heightened and acute also. This was not just a physical body sensitivity that heightened, but my Soul's Astral and Spirit's Ego bodies heightened in sensitivity also, along with my Spirits experiential connection to all of my subtle bodies.

My Body-self will create a physical event for everything it is directed to manifest.

Obviously, I did lose some weight through this *fasting journey*. I pretty much had no need for food by the end of the 30 days and did wonder why I was going back onto food again. By this stage, my acute sensitivity revealed it was not just time, but necessary to start eating again. The new ability I had gained from this journey however, was to no longer need the mandatory indoctrinated three-meals-per-day eating routine. I have found since, that my Body-self doesn't need to be loaded down with food, but does need some specific elements of food, to maintain the physical structure of the organism and compensate for the naturally occurring physical *forces of destruction* acting on it from the physical reality of our Earth's environment. Food is also another way to bring into its self, Life Force, to strengthen its Etheric Life-Body as well. This is why the quality of "live food" that we put in our physical body is so important. This is also why dead food, or *fast* and over processed food that has had most of the Life Force released from it through modern day productions, is so detrimental to our Body-self. High potency *live food* is necessary to assist the body, in not just the breaking down and reconstitution of the elements in the food; which are necessary for the body to use in the regeneration processes of its physical structure and form, but they bring in "Forces" essential to the enlivening of the Astral Body as well. It is the *Life Force* in the food that the body requires to break down the physical components in the food. Without sufficient Life Force, the food can't be broken down sufficiently and consequently, it can't be utilized by the body.

I would suggest that ninety percent of the chronic health issues around our world now could be contributed to the lack of Life Force remaining in our food supply after modernized food production. My Kahuna once explained that every step in the process of food production; from the pulling of the plant, to the rolling and touching of it on metal surfaces, to the cut and removal of old dirty or damaged leaves, to simply make it look better; ALL release Life Force from the produce. Consider that these processes start the release of this Life Force, and it continues to be released right up until you eat it. Consider how much Life Force is left, if that produce was picked and packed two weeks, or even in some cases of our modern techniques, two months prior to you eating it. How much Life Force, if any, is actually left in a packet of chips or any packed, processed or synthesized food.

When I interrupt my Body-self's ability to be the receiver and transmitter of Life-Force, of Life's creative intentional energy, it will create for its self, a hunger for more physical food. This addiction for food, stems directly from an inability of my Body-self's ability to satisfy its need for Life "forces". From this premise, we can begin to see that, the obesity issues that plague our material world at this time, may well spring from a dis-connect of our Body-self from its TRUE source of sustenance … from "Life" its self. The true origination of obesity may well be a disconnect between our physical-body and our etheric Life-Body, along with an overcompensating intellectual perspective of our Soul-self, all of which is compounded by the final *nail-in-the-coffin* of … *dead food.*

> *My physical Body-self, through its sensory system and ability to transmute energy into a physical manifestation, is the end of the line for ALL intentions to be manifest in this world, whether of Soul or Spirit nature.*

A great example of the body manifesting unconditionally is an experience I had during my second 30 days of fasting. I was about 20 days into my fast when this one particular night, I had opened the fridge to clean it and my eyes fell on a jar of peanut butter. At the time, peanut butter was a seductive addiction for me to the point of having more spoon scoops directly from the jar, than slices of bread slathered in this pasty delicacy. Now by day 20, I had a good handle on the hunger element of my fast and as I said earlier, allowing my body to "*force*-feed itself", meant the body was being satisfied through the Planets Life-Body. So, when I opened the fridge door and my eyes fell onto the jar of peanut butter, it was my Soul-self's mind that attached to the peanut butter and almost immediately; as the mind is so skilled at doing, sent its message which stimulated the Body-self to create sensations of hunger. In a flash, my mind backed up this command to create, with a steady flow of distracting and justifying thoughts like "it would be OK to just have a scoop or two", and "it's not really food after all", and "oohhh, yum, you know how much you LOVE peanut butter". At first, I thought that was quite funny really, because my mind was trying to convince its self that it was OK to eat. With a little more Awareness, I realized that my Soul-self's mind was actually trying to convince my Spirit-Self to give up its hold by intention, of the whole fasting journey. For my Soul-self, peanut butter had quite often become a *comfort food item* used to sabotage Spirit-Self's action commitments. It was too easy to sit down with a jar of peanut butter and flick the dreaded Soul killing, Spirit strangling TV on, and pig-out until my Body-self became too uncomfortable to get up and do anything. We all have at least one of these sabotage addictions we allow our mind to run … right?

Supported by my Awareness work; which we will discuss more deeply later, and my consequent heightened Awareness from the fast cleansing; I was able to notice that these thoughts were of my Soul-minds creation and not actually how I was *feeling* within my experiencing Spirit-Self in that moment. When I caught this moment, I brought my Awareness to my Body-self to notice if it was actually hungry or not. Through the light of my Awareness, I asked was it actually in need of food and craving for sustenance, or not. Ironically, when I *felt into* my body's condition, there was no hunger or fatigue at all to be found. This moment of revelation shocked me throughout the core of ALL my Self's. I realized and actually fully experienced in that moment, the effects of my Soul-self's mind on my Body-self. The speed of thought that everything happened was also shocking to me. The deepest and most revealing of all though, was the direct and complete response of my Body-self to the influencing thoughts of my Soul-self. My Body-self immediately, without any questioning, without any scrutiny, without any moment of contemplation spun straight into action and created the sensations of desire throughout its whole organism for that most tempting and tasteful goo.

The Body never questions or disobeys any command for creation ... from either the Soul or the Spirit.

When my Soul commanded the sensations of desire, my Body-self responded with corresponding physical desire sensations throughout its whole self. When my Spirit, through its Awareness asked my Body how it actually felt, it responded immediately to my Spirits request with the truth of no hungry and without desire. It wasn't my Body that was hungry, it was my Soul-self's mind manufactured desire. The transformational insight from this whole event, was the experience of the undeniable difference between the Body-self and mind of the Soul-self. The most empowering and transformative insight of all was experiencing the intimate and intricate functions, capabilities and greater purpose of our Body-self. From these first beginnings, each meditation on this topic, each fasting experience since, has revealed deeper and more extensive elements of the Body-self's role in the bigger picture of our Earth Walk here as a Human BEing.

Soul-self

The second self is called our Soul-self. Its elements are unlike the human physical elements of the Body-self and exist within the non-physical *human* element of its Astral realm. In psychology, the terms sub-conscious, conscious and super-conscious are used within this realm, but I have found this to be out dated information and misleading to what the actual *experience* of these aspect really are. It is almost like the psychology depictions of these aspect come from a more intellectual understanding, from a mind-based understanding of these aspect of Soul. Steiner's Anthroposophy ironically has named and broken these aspects down further as the Sentient Soul, Intellectual or Perceptive Soul and the Consciousness Soul. These Soul aspects or components that make up your Soul-self are housed, so to speak, by the Astral body of our Soul. I find these depictions much more appropriate and aligned with the actual "experience" of these bodies of the Soul-self. I would suggest that it is the Intellectual Soul aspect that has created the psychological labels of sub-conscious, conscious and super-conscious etc.

The sentient component of my Soul-self is how I am able to "sense" all the elements of my human form of existence.

The Sentient component is the specific aspect that makes it possible for your Soul-self to "feel" things, or more appropriately, "sense" them, to be responsive and recognize outside and inside influences. This sense-ability is what gives your Soul-self the ability to receive the Body-self's physical world inputs etc. of the senses, of smells, touch, seeing and hearing etc. This is your Soul-self's ability to feel Life, to connect with and communicate in a *sense* with the Body-self's etheric Life-body. This is where and how your Soul-self accesses the Body-self's etheric Life-body's storage of your memories, your Life events and experiences. Feel for this specific element within your-self, that "picks up" the external things coming from our external physical world through your body. Feel for the subtlety of this ability and particularly, see if you can get a *sense* of the specific unique-ness of this ability, the difference of the senses and the range or scope that it exists ... within *you*. In the later chapters, we will be able to increase your ability to truly *feel / experience* these differences. For now, just allow yourself to get a sense of this component, without having to make anything definitive right now. In a real sense, this sentient component of your Soul-self is the link between your Body-self and your Soul-self ... between your Body and Soul.

The Sentient Soul is also the component that houses your feelings and emotions, your desires and passions etc. If you can imagine your physical Body having the 5 normal lower senses of sight, sound, smell, taste and touch, and your Soul having another 7 higher senses of Life, language, balance, movement, thought or concept, warmth and Ego. Although all these seven senses are not all located within the Sentient Soul component, they are however existing within the whole of the Soul sphere of your existence. Rudolph Steiner's Anthroposophical research has much more detail of the relationships of all these senses than I am willing to go into for this exploration. I encourage you to explore his works for much more understanding of these. For this journey, I wish to stay a little lighter for you at this point. The later works here can help your understanding of his deeper works. This Sentient component of Soul is the Souls feeling capacity.

The Intellectual or Perspective Soul gives me the ability to create my perspective of things.

The Intellectual / Perspective Soul is that component of your Soul-self that gives you the ability to *BE* the individual you are. It's through this component that you can make or have a particular perspective, to form unique viewpoints that allow you to see or experience something from. This is the Soul-self component that particularly forms a major part of your human personality for your unique and specific Life-walk through this human lifetime. This is the component within your Soul-self that enables you to create perspectives of things. A perspective is how something is viewed or the result of something being viewed felt or sensed. A lot of confusion in our human reality can come from an imbalance in this component of Soul-self. Confusion is created through this faculty that manifest intellectual filters and concepts; which ultimately cloud the purity of the sensations coming from your Sentient Soul. Your Intellectual Soul perceives what your Sentient Soul's true *sense* of what something actually is in your human reality. The Intellectual component of your Soul-self is the component that houses all of your identities and beliefs etc. This is where your *personality* for this lifetime is created and formed. It is through this element of your Soul-self that all of your resistances and attachments originate from. It is so easy to be misidentified AS these unique personality identities housed within this component, because they are so subtly pervasive in all spheres of our human reality. This element is how you perceive the world through your human-self. This pervasive identity warehouse of your Soul-self is so interwoven into and as your individual personality for your present human existence, that you can mistakenly believe it to be your experiencing *True* Spirit-Self. We will talk in more detail of the makeup of this particular component a little further on. This is where the thinking capacity of your human Soul-self resides.

The Consciousness Soul component of my Soul-self is how I am able to BE conscious of your Self.

Your Consciousness Soul element of your Soul-self is what gives you the consciousness, or as I said earlier, it is the conscious component that creates the "self". This is not to be mistaken for an identity or personality or individual that lies within the previously explained Intellectual Soul component. Your Consciousness Soul element IS consciousness; it is your "cosmic intelligence" which is able to recognize differences between the physical and Soul elements of your human self. The Consciousness Soul is the component that makes it possible for your Spirit BEing-Self's attribute of Awareness to enter your Soul-self. This is a tricky one to detect really, because it is much subtler as a self goes and is the link between your Soul-self and Spirit BEing-Self. Being this conscious linking component means, that there is a kind of blending between these components of your Soul-self that, from the intellectual perspective of the Intellectual Soul-self, the human Soul-self and the Spirit BEing-Self can *appear*, to be one and the same. The upside of this blending is that it is what makes it easy for you to ground your BEing-Self's attributes and higher virtues of Awareness, compassion, forgiveness etc. etc. into your human Soul-self. The down side is that it is also easy for the Intellectual Soul to deceive; through its constructed spiritual identity, to mentalize, imitate and falsify these higher attributes of Spirit, effectively blocking the true grounding of your Spirit in your human. The result of this, is the mental projections of a "spiritual human", with seemingly amazing mental concepts of the Spiritual Realms, but void of true *spiritual* experience. The give-away of this spiritual salesman, is that their concepts are generally describing a blissful and awe-inspiring spiritual state, separate from an illusory human state. Another giveaway is their deceiving promise of obtaining this spiritual bliss state through *their* system of consciousness practices.

The only system of consciousness that can access the Spiritual realm of Being human ... is within you, and you are the only one that is capable of accessing and using it.

Although this blending between Intellectual and Consciousness Souls can make it difficult to distinguish the difference between being conscious of something and having an intellectual perspective of that same thing; there is most definitely a distinctive and important difference to become experientially Aware of. It is the lack of an "experiential" difference that allows the Intellectual Soul's spiritual identity to continue to block the Spirit's *TRUE* virtues and attributes from being grounded into your human-self. Many Self-Realized Masters have shared that it is the final experiential Awareness and surrender of our mind's *spiritual identity*, or spiritual ego as some refer to it by, as the moment of true freedom from the human-self's deception. This provides establishment of one's existence in the Divine gift of True-Self Realization. It is the Consciousness-Soul component that brings with it the Will capacity and it is this same Will that is needed to maintain the Spirit-Self's grounding in the Soul-self.

It is the grounding and integration of my Spirit BEing-Self into my Human-self, that will ultimately evolve me into a TRULY Spiritual-Human-BEing.

I hope from this more simplified depiction of the three components that make up your human Soul-self, it might make it a little easier for you, to maybe detect the subtle differences of these components within you. Don't be concerned if you don't *seem* to get it clearly right now. Just get a "sense of them" without looking for a solid definition just yet. Use the *Sentient Soul* element of your Soul-self to get this "sense" of what you have just explored. There is no need or benefit for rigid definitions at this stage. As we go further, you may get a better feel for them and how they operate ... and deceive ... within your own Life-walk here. Remember that these three components exist through a blending of each, with the Intellectual component sitting in the middle of them all as the "*seat of the human Soul*" in its current evolutionary stage. Having just entered the Consciousness Soul stage of our evolution, we are now able to develop our consciousness capacities much more than ever before. With real Awareness of these components, you will understand so much more of your mind's identities and their deceptions of self, all of which are manifesting from the Intellectual Soul. This is done simply to create your human personality for this particular Life's walk. To experience your identities as your constructed personality for this particular Life and not your true experiencing Self, can be incredibly freeing.

The unifying environment that makes it possible for all three soul components to come together ... is the Astral-body.

As I said earlier, your Soul-self is comprised within your astral-body. It is the astral body which is the environment that your three soul components of Sentient, Intellectual and Consciousness Soul co-exists and operate and develop in; of which you have just explored. Your astral body is in a sense, a uniquely spiritual energetic environment that makes it possible for the three components of your Soul-self to exist, operate and co-create your human Soul-life together. Your astral body is a kind of congealing environment that bridges your Spiritual and physical world realities together within the Soul.

I must mention here that the present understanding of the ego is not as such, a component of Soul; however, it is necessary to mention it at this point to bring some clarity to some debilitating perspectives about the ego before we go on. From some perspectives, there can be said that there are two ego's within our human-Being-ness. According to our present understanding, or could I say indoctrination, we have within us a small ego, and a large Ego. The small ego is associated with the Soul-self, and the greater Ego is associated with the Spirit True-Self. For most of my life, I have been conflicted with the commonly prescribed association to the small ego and its perceived inhibiting intent on the Soul. Finally, after studying and spiritually researching the Anthroposophical teachings of Rudolph Steiner, with his initiated wisdom that the Ego is the body or housing of the components of our Human Spirit, my conflict was extinguished, and he affirmed what I had always felt, yet unable to distinguish.

According to most commonly accepted belief, but put in my terminology, your small ego is that "self" consciousness that controls and orchestrates your three soul components within this astral environment. Now, this ego has gotten a pretty bad rap as far as I am concerned. So many present day intellectual spiritual salesmen with their systems and programs of so called self-evolvement etc., profess the shame and deceptions of this ego. It is so easy for them to blame all that they cannot accurately explain or let alone experience, on this poor ole ego. Our perspective of the ego has become a tremendous scape-goat for all kinds of denial, hidden-agendas, lies and manipulations of the mind.

A part of Freudian definition is;

- *The ego is the organized part of the personality structure that includes defensive, perceptual, intellectual-cognitive, and executive functions. Conscious awareness resides in the ego, although not all of the operations of the ego are conscious. Originally, Freud used the word ego to mean a sense of self, but later revised it to mean a set of psychic functions such as judgment, tolerance, reality testing, control, planning, defense, synthesis of information, intellectual functioning, and memory. The ego separates out what is real. It helps us to organize our thoughts and make sense of them and the world around us.*

Looking at these aspects that Freud talks of, we can see a slight common strain through it that the ego is the aspect that organizes, that controls, orchestrates and even commands these attributes of perception, thought, planning, intellectual functioning etc. Now let's see if any of these attributes correlate with the three components of your Soul-self we have just explored. Can you see that there are specific attributes or functions that Freud refers to with the ego, of controlling or orchestrating etc., which are also specific functions of your specific soul components of Sentient, Intellectual and Consciousness souls?

To explore even deeper, we can see that through this orchestrating etc. of this *perceived* ego, there is a *"quality of thinking"* necessary, which this ego supposedly uses to manifest its orchestration of these soul force attributes and functions etc. With Awareness, it is possible to experience a difference between this *quality of thinking of the ego* and, *the true quality of higher thought that can be Willed through our Consciousness Soul.* Your ego's quality of thinking is what it uses to orchestrate the "Soul Forces" emanating from your Sentient, Intellectual and Consciousness components of your Soul-self. Your mind has also been associated with this ego as it uses it to reason and rationalize its way through our physical human reality. It is this ego concept that is meant to explain your existence as one of a very human materialistic thought world; one without direction, randomly flipping from one "sense" from the Sentient soul to an overanalyzed mental perspective from your Intellectual Perspective soul and then into an overinflated conceptualization of self from your Consciousness soul. It is suggested that without the ego, we would not be able to bring these sensory and super-sensory elements of perceptions and experience etc. into any purpose or constructive use for the evolution of our human or Spirit. It is believed that it is your ego that is responsible for the successful correlation and use of these elements, to make your human life-walk here one of harmonized self-realization and revelation through higher thinking and guidance. My question is, if this lower ego is doing all of these things, then what is the "you self" that you are, doing through this Life walk? The fact is that it is your Being that is your Spirit-Self that facilitates this, not the perceived small ego. It is your Spirit that gives your human the potential to be a fully conscious, super-sensor-ably pure human. With Spirit grounded deep at its core, we are driving on to become an enlightened species in the Divine Cosmos.

This concept of the small ego is not what orchestrates the symphony of these three components of my Soul; from which produces my human for this current walk.

It is the Consciousness Soul which brings to this human Soul-self, the ability to think in the higher realms of the Spirit.

Through the spiritual development into your current densest yet intellectual human form, you have gained the Consciousness Soul component, which gives your Soul-self the ability to think in the higher realms of Spirit ... as a conscious self. Contrary to most western intellectual spiritualist, it is actually through our Consciousness Soul component and not our ego, that we are capable of higher thought, which consequently reconnects us back to the spiritual realm. Your true Ego is the Body, the spiritual environment of your Spirit-Being-Self and is NOT an unruly consciousness child of deception and illusion. Your true Ego is NOT hell bent on sabotaging all your efforts to ascend to higher spiritual states of Being. On the contrary, it is the very *means* by which you are able to ascend. Your greater, higher Ego is actually the very vehicle you need to bring your human into the realm of a truly Human Spirit Being. Your true goal for your small ego, should be to see through the deceptions of this *concept* and experience the true higher Ego body of your Spirit. From there you may strengthen *IT*, to develop its functions, attributes and abilities to stand fast, to stay on task, to be able to make definitive decisions based on clear *higher* thinking permeated by spiritual concept and insight. The quite common concept now days, that the ego is a detriment and hindrance to the development of our Human Spirit, are deceptions perpetuated by deflecting forces with intent to prevent the grounding of the Spiritual realm into our human consciousness.

These dark deflecting forces have influence on your human through your lower nature. A weak Soul is open to these darker forces, which is the reason many of us predominantly live in our human's lower nature. A weak Soul is responsible for your Intellectual components identities and materialistic viewpoints being asserted on your world. A weak Soul without a well-grounded Spirit Ego body, is powerless to identify any and all outside influences that will have your human flopping along without direction, purpose or conviction. A weak Soul is incapable of utilizing the Will sufficiently, which is essential for aligning and orchestrating the three components of your Soul-self. Weak Soul forces results in an inner Soul environment of wavering confusion, conflict, doubt etc., etc.

A strong Spirit Ego embodied by your Soul, gives your human a strong and coordinated harmonic use of your three soul components, producing a strong flow of soul forces that manifest in this human reality. A strong Ego is the "I AM" individual that we see consistently stand up and do "the right thing", in spite of the consequences. A strong Ego is what is necessary to be able to wield a strong Will to direct and create with.

My Ego is actually the vehicle of my Spirit ...for my salvation out of the traps of the lower nature of man.

In truth, the label of strong or weak are also misleading conceptions of the state of the Ego. Strong or weak generally have construed judgments of right or wrong actions of the Ego attached to it, rather than declarations of the actual state of the Ego. A truer depiction I feel would be one of healthy or unhealthy. Just as with the physical body, health determines the body's ability to perform certain tasks or functions. So too does it apply to the Ego. When an Ego becomes unhealthy, it is closed in and disconnected from the Soul. Thinking becomes clouded and manipulated by the influences of lower BEings, trapping one in the lower materialistic nature of man. Trying to release or renounce the Ego is a common self-deception and self-sabotage of the darker deflecting forces of influence on the spiritual identity of our Intellectual Soul, with its intent for us to not own or take responsibility for the completeness of one's human-self. The misuse of our mind concept this way also stems from the subversive direction and lower thinking of our Soul, as it drowns in the lower nature of man without higher guidance.

When an Ego is healthy, it is connected to the Soul via the Consciousness Soul component, which is now open and receptive. Its thinking is permeated with streams of higher thoughts from the Spiritual Realm and it is cognizant to the directions and influences from our Higher Spirit-Self, as well as from higher, more benevolent creator BEings. A healthy Ego is one, sound in its own Spirit based space, confident in its open communication with the Spiritual realm. A truly healthy Ego has been transformed from a servant to the lower nature and forces of our materialistic human reality, into a Divine instrument and conduit of our Spirit-Self's highest intention to spiritualize our human BE-in. Through this last statement, I hope you may sense the difference between our small ego and our greater true Ego body of Spirit. This concept has been shared by so many teachers previously, but you may have felt confused by it, as I often did. I hope this simplifies it for you, as it did for me also.

So how do we improve the health of our Ego? We will go into further detail with some helpful tips in the later chapters, but for now know, that it is simple. In its simplest form; to improve the health of your Ego is to simply spiritualize your Soul by *grounding* your Spirit BEing-Self into your Human-self. Now I am going to introduce yet another self here into what may already be starting to look like a complicated *self-picture*. My term of Human-self, from this moment forward, will always be referring to the combination of your Body-self; which includes the etheric life body and Soul-self. In truth, the human element of your Human Being for this Earth-walk, is the co-creating combination of physical Body-self, Etheric Life-Body and Soul-self. Hopefully, we now have from what we have been talking about so far, some clarity on the components and bodies that make up your Human. To break it down further for clarity, your Human-self is made up of your physical body, your etheric-body, your astral-body as a collective of your Sentient, Intellectual and Consciousness Soul components. Now that we have some clarity of the "Human-self" relevant to our label of a "Human-Being", let's see if we can get some clarity on the "BEing-Self" aspect of the label.

My Human-self is what I get to use and <u>experience</u> through, for this present human Life-walk.

The last "Self" of Being Human, is our experiencing Spirit-BEing-Self. The greater Ego is the body that houses this Spirit-Being-Self and its relationship to the Spirit, is the same as the Astral body has to the Soul. Now if you are starting to real from all the *self-talk*, and you're starting to go "*out of your mind*" as it starts producing thoughts like, "oh boy, here we go into wackoville" or "man … this guy has really lost it" or even, "what the hell is this guy on?", then try to relax and let go of definitions etc. for a moment longer and bear with me. Try to just *feel* for the components we are going to talk about here and see if you can see where they work or seem to act in your life. If you were able to get a sense of how the human elements we have discussed already come together within the Body and Soul; and it makes *some* sense to you that they all exists as the human aspect of yourself, then this BEing-Self component should make some simple sense to you also.   Feel for this element as the *Be*-ing element of you. This *IS* your True-Self, that part of you that just is, that simply BE's with things, Be's with nature when you walk in it, with silence or even BEing *of* silence when you are on your own or meditating etc. This BEing-Self is that aspect of you that is simply Aware of things, without defining them, or the experience you are having of them. It is the Self that is capable of BEing Aware of the "differences" of the energy in a room when you walk in to it. This Awareness is "supra-sensitive" … right?   Supra-sensitive to the point that it detects the subtle differences in things, in ALL things. It is not a "sense" of something, it is an acute *Awareness* that there is simply a difference between one thing and another, without *needing* to define what that difference is. This Awareness is not a *sense* you feel in the body; it is a super-sense you feel in the space you occupy … in the core of your BEing … not your physical body. In truth, when you feel it in the space you occupy, it is actually, your Ego Body you are sensing in. This Being-Self is the Self that is intimately connected to the spiritual realm through among other things, this attribute of Awareness and its ability to "feel", or more accurately … *experience* with this Awareness. This *ability to feel* is not the same as our human sensory feeling ability we spoke of through the Sentient Soul component, nor is it the "feelings" that so many consciousness systems have us chase, like a rabbit down the burrow. Feelings are what your concept of mind, within its Intellectual Soul construct, creates and transmits through your Body-self to help bring about and manifest the *human events;* of which your BEing-Self *experiences.* Can you get a sense of this difference between *feelings* and your *ability to feel* or rather, *experience* your life?

My Being-Self is the "experiencing" aspect of me, as a Human … BEing.

We will go into much more detail about this *feel/experience* ability in the later chapters as well. So, if you can understand Awareness being an attribute of your BEing-Self, then let's go a little deeper and see if we can identify some more subtle aspects to our BEing-Self.

As with our Soul-self, our BEing-Self is also broken down further into three elements of this even higher form of consciousness. Once again, I do like the definitions of Rudolph Steiner with respect to this BEing-Self. Through his initiated experience of these components, he has labelled them as, the Spirit-Self, Life-Spirit, and Spirit-Man. I understand that I am treading on thin ice to try and successfully explain these aspects that have, since way back in our conception into this Ego "I" Consciousness, been so amorphous, so un-definable, so un-translatable that any intellectual idiot would just simply not go there. Well, I don't feel like an intellectual idiot so, I'm going there. The problem, I believe, where most have failed in trying to describe this realm, is that they have attempted it from an intellectual perspective of a spiritual realm outside of one's self, rather than an experiential one of the spiritual realm that already exists within one's Self.

When I was writing my first draft of this book; which at that time was actually quite a different book to what this one has now become, there was a time when I was shown the difference between writing from "feel" and writing from the mind. The particular chapter I was writing was called "Being Human", and the section I was writing about was on the mind and its inability to experience and feel with Awareness. At one point I noticed, that what was going down on paper seemed very complicated with lots of words attempting to describe what I was feeling of my "experience" of this topic. When I noticed this complicated and wordy passage, I stopped and sat back a little frustrated and annoyed at myself. As I sat there *feeling into* the whole section; with my Awareness of course and not my mind, I said to my BEing-Self, "why is it coming out so complicated, when the reality is that it is so simple?". I got up from my chair, walked into the kitchen and started to make myself a cup of coffee to try to chill out and get another perspective on it from my Intellectual soul. All of a sudden, I just started laughing my head off and couldn't stop. My partner at the time; which happened to be my ghost-writing sexual cowgirl from my previous story; but at a MUCH better time in our relationship, came running out laughing also as she felt the humor in my "Ahh Haa" moment. Of course, she asked what was so funny. I explained my dilemma of complications and answered, from the blinding revelation of my BEing-Self's most distinguishable inner voice that, "this work is sooo stupidly simple, that you have to make it complicated enough for the readers mind to be interested in understanding it."

Since then I have come to realize that I am not needing to speak to the mind of the reader with these stories and concepts but attempting to communicate with the Spirit-BEing-Self that *IS* you, the individual on the other side of this page which already experiences the concepts I am presenting through the stories. Ironically, your Spirit-BEing-Self understands intricate simplicity, and is neutral to complicated mental concepts.

When simplicity speaks to me, my Spirit is speaking ... I need to listen to it.

Another help here from our world-wide wiki for the meaning of Spirit is;

- *The English word **spirit** comes from the Latin spiritus, meaning "breath". It is distinguished from Latin anima, "soul", which nonetheless also derives from an*

*Indo-European root meaning "to breathe". The English word **spirit**, from Latin spiritus "breath", has many different meanings and connotations, most of them relating to a non-corporeal substance contrasted with the material body. It can also refer to a "subtle" as opposed to "gross" material substance, as in the famous last paragraph of Sir Isaac Newton's Principia Mathematica. The word spirit is often used metaphysically to refer to the consciousness or personality. The notions of a person's spirit and soul often also overlap, as both contrast with body and both are believed to survive bodily death.*

There are two descriptions from this I would like to look at. One is that of Spirit being a subtler substance as opposed to the gross material substance of the body for example. I would suggest that the Spirit is also subtler than that of the Soul, even though the Soul is still a much subtler amorphous state than the Body. So, in respect to the difference between the subtle states of existence of our Body Soul and Spirit, we could say that they are each subtler than the last, going from physical Body through the Soul and onto the Spirit essence. The other point of reference is the one that the Spirit is derived from the word meaning "breath", and the Soul is "to breathe". This is also a great indication of the dynamic truth between Spirit and Soul, in that the Spirit-Being, the breath of the Divine Essence and the Soul, is what makes it possible for the Divine Essence that is us, *to breathe* the Divine breath into our Human.

It is my Spirit that breaths the Divine Presence into my Human.

So, the first aspect of your Spirit, or if you like, the attribute or "state" of Spirit existence is the Spirit-Self.

Imagine if you will, what we have already covered with respect to a self being that individual consciousness, that *self*-consciousness. Now understand it as an individual Spirit, an essential essence of the Infinite Divine Unity which is capable of individual existence and Awareness. This Spirit-Self element is, in a greater sense, the link between our Consciousness Soul and Spirit ... its Self. This is the aspect of your BEing-Self, which has a vague *super-sense* of a connection to all, a connection to the Divine, yet there is no direct experience for your Consciousness Soul element to directly associate with it. As we discovered before that the linking agent between our Body-self and Soul-self is the Sentient soul element, then so too is this Spirit-Self and Consciousness Soul, the linking agents between your Soul-self and BEing-Self. Remember we said that your Spirit-BEing-Self was the experiencing Self, well this component or function that is your Spirit-Self, is that aspect where *true experiencing* takes place. This is the *experiencing element of you*, the component that has and utilizes, your ability to BE Aware, to *feel and experience* with and through its attribute of Awareness.

It is, through this linking between my Consciousness Soul and Spirit-Self component of my BEing-Self; that makes it possible for my Human Soul-self to ultimately become "Consciously Aware" of my Spirit BEing-Self.

In a sense, or should I say super-sense, the Spirit-Self is the component that experientially connects your human self-consciousness, to the Spiritual realm. At its full development, the Spirit-Self transforms the Soul-self into a Consciously Aware Spiritual Human BEing.

The next element of your BEing-Self is your Life-Spirit.

This element is similar to your etheric body, in respect to the way the etheric body enlivens and sustains the life in your body and rejuvenates and regenerates it. However, the Life-Spirit brings from a different sphere of Life and services the finer realm of Spirit. This is how *Spiritual Life* is brought into your Human-self. In a sense, it is the level of development of this component of Spirit, that determines the degree and parameter of Spiritual Life we can bring into our Human BEing. The function of this component of Spirit, is to not just bring Spiritual Life into our Human, but to regulate the amount or degree of Spiritual Life entering our Human-self. The amount of Spiritual Life entering your Human BEing is relevant to the level of consciousness your Human BEing is at. Your Life-Spirit component regulates these amounts to ONLY what your Human Consciousness is capable of handling, or more correctly, what your Soul can embody. It is through this *force* of the Life-Spirit, that the wisdom of the Spiritual Realm can be transferred into your Human Consciousness via the Etheric Life Body. Through the final embodiment and development of your Life-Spirit, your etheric Life Body is transformed and integrated into an organ for not just experiencing Life, but intimately experiencing the Life of the Spiritual Realm.

My Life Spirit component brings Spiritual wisdom to my Human-self.

The last component of BEing-Self is the state of Spirit Man. Most of us have no doubt heard at some point in time of the word Human Spirit etc. Spirit Man is this state of BE-in that is nearly impossible to describe in the words and meanings of our todays consciousness, but let's give it a go anyway. Firstly, let's not get too rigid with our need to understand and allow our-selves … all aspects of you … to be fluid and flexible, to be open and receiving, letting the information filter through ALL of the aspects of you that is your Human BEing … without trapping it in your Intellectual Soul's mind.

Spirit Man is that highly evolved component or actually, attribute of your BEing-Self that is capable of transmuting your Human-self. Specifically, Spirit Man will transform your Body self into a Spiritual function of your BEing-Self. At this stage of evolution, where our Spirit Man is fully developed and becomes an active and fully operational "state of BEing" within our Spirit-BEing-Self, its function if you will, will be to transform our whole Human BEing into a Creator Being. This transformed Human Being will no longer be bound by physical laws, no longer bound within a physical body, and operating in intimate integral alignment with Divine Purpose. It is in the development of this component of your Spirit-BEing-Self, that your current body will transform into a new form, one more suitable for existence in a new dimension of existence. This transformation will be one determined and orchestrated by YOU, as a higher BEing Self.

Obviously, at this point in our evolutionary path, we do not have this capability or that of Life-Spirit, and even our Spiritual Teachers and Master's haven't achieved this level. Our world reality, our Earth Station Gaia is evolving with us, yet is not capable of sustaining this level of Spirit development yet. Therefore, our great Master's have not been able to stay with us here on Earth. We will talk more about this in the later chapters also.

So, let's look at the components of Spirit and their functions that make up your BEing-Self.

- Your BEing-Self is made up of the Spirit-Self, Life-Spirit and Spirit-Man. Your Spirit-Self's function is one of a super-sensory Self that is not just "conscious of self", but Aware spiritually of all forces and aspects within and without of your whole Human BEing.

- Your Life-Spirit's function is to enliven your Body Soul and Spirit with creative Spiritual Life, which brings with it the wisdom of the Spiritual realm.

- Your Spirit-Man is the fully evolved BEing function of you, that transforms not just *you*, out of the physical Human Realm, but transforms the Human Realm of existence its Self, into a new form of Higher Spiritual Consciousness. When I talk about "spiritualize our Human", I am talking about developing, aligning and harmonizing ALL of these components within our Body, Soul and Spirit BEing-Self.

From there, I then ground my BEing-Self into my Human-self, thus permeating my Human with Spiritual attributes and virtues.

So, let's do a final recap now on all of the Body Soul and Spirit Self's of BEing Human.

- The Human ... BEing that I am, is made up of my Body-self, Soul-self and Spirit BEing-Self.

- My Body-self is made up of my physical-body and etheric Life-body. Its function is of a physical world sensory instrument for transmuting spiritual intention into physical reality through manifesting events in our collective human theater. It is also the instrument that makes it possible for Spirit to enter, move around so to speak and experience this physical reality of matter.

- My Soul-self is made up of my Sentient Soul, Intellectual Perspective Soul and Consciousness Soul. Its function is that of a sensory and super-sensory *conscious self*, within this human reality existence. This self is the complete conscious personality structure of the *human* that you BE. This self creates the potentiality of "human experiences", through the human events created by its identities, beliefs, passions desires and emotions etc. These events manifest in this human reality within our Earth existence, for our Spirit-BEing-Self to *experience* human reality.

- IT is my Body-self and Soul-self together, that make up the Human-self that I exist as in this gross physical reality. This Human-self as a totality of these self's just mentioned; by which ALL human events are made possible, but only exists within this Human Domain of existence. The Human-self is transient and is not an eternal self, even though the Soul is.

- My Spirit BEing-Self is made up of my Spirit-Self, Life-Spirit and Spirit-Man.

- My Spirit-Self's function is that of Awareness of Spiritual existence as an individual Spirit Essence, but still fully connected to the spiritual realm. This Self brings the potential of Spirit Awareness into my Human Consciousness.

- My Life-Spirit's function is to bring "Spiritual Life and Wisdom" into the Soul and BEing-Self, making it capable of enlivening the Soul-Self with Self-Awareness and spiritual wisdom and ultimately transform the etheric Life Body of my physical vehicle for this life walk. It also makes this BEing-Self capable of creating in both the Human and Spiritual realms.

- My Spirit-Man's function is one of a fully evolved Creator BEing with full autonomy over one's own evolutionary destiny and the manifestation of the environment this complete Human BEing exists in.

Although we are not at this end evolutionary result of our fully developed Spirit-Man, we—each one of us, do already have the potential of all of these Self aspects available within us here and now. Obviously, just by observing our world and the destructive actions of many and the extremely intellectual and materialistic developments and operations of so many more, we can comfortably say that our Human Realities evolutionary stage is somewhere around the intellectual / consciousness soul stages, yet with the potential for the embodiment of our Spirit-Self Awareness. Dr. David Hawkins, one of the master Initiated Teachers for our time, who pioneered the use of Kinesiology as a spiritual practice and tool; created a "Map of Consciousness" depicting a Scale for our humanity as a collective. According to his calculations, the percentage of population that live and exists *below* the level of "Truth" is 78%. Shockingly, only 4% of our human population live at the level of Love, and .04% live at the level of Unconditional Love. On studying these findings and the others he calculated, then looking into our human world reality through the neutral unbiased Awareness of our Spirit-Self, we can see and *BE* with the problems of our world from a whole new perspective and understanding.

The Self's of BEing Human, is a fascinating and incredibly interesting study to meditate on; of which this chapter is just a scratch on the surface. This scratch however, has the potential to free you from the small and narrow perspective of your *concept of mind's* tiny domain of existence. To get out of our mind, and not just see, but fully experience the vast vista of the spiritual world we actually exist in, is liberating to say the least. It is not only liberating, but incredibly empowering in its simplicity. We have been misled for so long by so many spiritual salesmen and women of our present time. They flood our Intellectual Soul right now with seductive mental concepts, systems, processes and exercises, all professing to be spiritual in nature, but never getting us past our Intellectual Souls' realm of the mind's false spiritual identity.

It is through the development of my spiritual senses, the super-senses of my Spirit-BEing-Self and grounding them solidly in my Human-self, that I will free, align and harmonize ALL of my selfs ... as I get ... out of my mind.

So, although these new concepts all may seem a little complicated for some of you, let's take them forward now and see if you can see how they are already operating and producing your life. From this, you may be able to grasp the later chapters where we can see how to deliberately develop the forces and capacities within these components; from which your "I" will harmonize the complete BEing that you are as a human.

Chapter 5

Experiencing

From our previous chapter, I hope you may now have a somewhat clearer idea of the subtler components that make up the Human that you are. I appreciate that it may seem more complicated or confusing for some of you, but remember the definition earlier about confusion only coming about when there are pieces of information missing? Take a breath and carry on so you can hopefully bring in the missing pieces of information and complete the picture we are forming here of the Who you truly BE.

Understanding that we have a Human-self and a Spirit-BEing-Self is all well and good but; then what? Do all those aspects just get muddled up together, just so we can wing our way through Life confused and bewildered, and hopefully, we survive at the end of this drama filled human life with a bit of what, Divine insight, from which we might learn what … something? What if we don't ground any of our Spirit-BEing-Self's higher attributes and virtues in our human and we don't become anymore virtuous than the day we came here? Does that mean we won't learn anything? Does it mean we don't evolve or grow as a BEing? In the next chapter we will dive more deeply into the "Purpose of BEing Human", but for now, let's see if we can find what the dynamic *force and relationship* is between our Human and BEing Self's. Let's see if we can find what might give our Life-walk here a little more purpose and joy than just … learn something. It is *this* force that makes it possible for us to not just learn something on our journey through this Life-walk, but to develop aspects, forces and capacities of *all* of our Self's. This force is what not only integrates and aligns ALL of the aspects of our Human-self, but it also grounds our Spirit-BEing-Self deep and solidly in our Human-self. This force is also what makes it possible for us to infuse new elements or attributes into all of our Self's. Ultimately this may create the Higher Human Spirit we all may wish to BE … along with some filament of purpose, peace and harmony that might turn Life into inspired living. Through my Conscious Bodywork practice, this *force* that plays a massive role in the wellness and health of our Body, Soul and Spirit Self's, has been revealed to me many times. When this force is used deliberately and most importantly … consciously with Awareness; our evolution into higher states of BEing Human can be accelerated. In actual fact, when we consciously use this force, Life itself flows effortlessly through us unabated. Another interesting side product of using this force consciously, is that a profound peace can permeate all of your Human existence in the present moment.

This force is my ability to "experience" Life ... and this "force/ability" is a capacity of my Spirit-Self element within my BEing-Self.

The first thing to clarify however, is what exactly is experiencing? When I started to feel into and study the intricacies of experiencing, I found it interesting that no one has ever really shown us or explained exactly what *experiencing* is; the actual *ability* that is experiencing, or how to do it. Through research to find some form of an existing definition for experiencing, I was shocked to not find one single true definition of the *ability* that is ... experiencing. There are plenty of definitions of what an experience is, but not one of what the actual force or dynamic that IS experiencing. It seems to be something that's just taken for granted that we know how to do it etc. Although it is true that we all, without exception are here *experiencing* life as a human being, it isn't true that we are all *fully* experiencing it ... let alone deliberately or consciously experiencing it. It is only with deeper Awareness that we're able to explore, find and hopefully, come to *know* the differences between whether or not we are experiencing our life or not; whether we are experiencing Life or resisting Life: whether we are experiencing Life or simply analyzing, rationalizing and intellectualizing our Life.

Am I in my mind intellectualizing Life ... or am I out of my mind ... experiencing Life?

Experiencing, what is it exactly and how ... do we *experience* anything? If you look up the internet Wikipedia, we get differing definitions. These definitions range from skill and knowledge acquired of things, as in being very experienced in how to do etc., all the way to the other end of subjective experience.

Wikipedia's subjective definition states,

- *"Subjective experience can involve a state of individual subjectivity, perception on which one builds one's own state of reality; a reality based on one's interaction with one's environment. The subjective experience depends on one's individual ability to process data, to store and internalize it. For example: our senses collect data, which we then process according to biological programming (genetics), neurological network-relationships and other variables, all of which affect our individual experience of any given situation in such a way as to render it subjective."*

This of course, is more a definition or description of what a *subjective experience* is, but it still doesn't give us any clarity of what the experience *ability* is. I have struggled with these kinds of definitions for quite some time, as they felt incomplete for me. I feel these definitions have come from our Intellectual Soul, as its *interpretation* of what is happening from the Human-self perspective. This though, doesn't take into account, any higher viewpoint of *experiential* understanding.

Another definition is:

- *direct personal participation or observation; actual knowledge or contact: an experience of prison*

- *a particular incident, feeling, etc, that a person has undergone: an experience to remember*

- *accumulated knowledge, esp of practical matters: a man of experience*

Here again, there is no clarity of what the *ability* that experiencing is, but merely tells us what the end result of experiencing is, the actual experience event. The closest I could find to what I am exploring with you here, was in the Merriam-Webster Dictionary which stated, "the act or process of directly perceiving events or reality". This is the only one I could find that has any reference to an ability, as it refers to "an act or process". Even this however, still hasn't got it all for me, because there is no detail or picture of what the act or process is, or where it comes from, or what part of Body Soul or Spirit is it an activity of.

Experiencing, takes in much more than just processing the human sensory data of the events we are involved in. There are so many unseen influences that are beyond the data stream of our purely human reality. Although my experience may well be subjective from the perspective of my human personality self, however *experiencing,* or my *ability to experience,* is not just an objective response. It not only takes in and is, a response to the influences presented to me by the events of my human life, but also takes in the full spectrum of subtle Divine influences such as Karma, higher intention, Cosmic influences and this specific Life's purpose for MY Earth-walk etc. All of these influences and forces etc., all bring about the events that I may experience. All of these influences etc., have a direct effect on the event that I am experiencing, along with an indirect effect on how I experience it also. These however, still don't have any effect on my *ability to experience.* These latter influences are beyond the sensory ability of my human form; beyond my human personality's ability to collect data. However, all of these influences are so intimately interwoven that it is easy for us to believe that they are all one and the same *experience.*

When my first marriage broke down, there was incredible uncertainty and emotional upheaval between my wife and I and consequently, each of our three daughters. From my human personality perspective of these *events,* coming from the Intellectual Soul element within my Soul-self, my subjective experience may well be one of uncertainty and emotional upheaval, but my objective experience was a more conscious experience. This simply means that I was conscious of the event taking place and the emotional reacts and responses I was under the influence of. This objective conscious experience happens from within the Consciousness Soul component of your Soul-self. Notice here that it is still within the Soul that both of these "experiences" originate in. Ironically, there is no definition of "objective experience" within any dictionary that I could find. Let's see however if we can get a picture of what that might look like anyhow. This objective experience however, although *is* one of consciously looking at the event etc.; of being conscious of my-self (the subjective self) in the event, this is still however not where my *ability to experience* all of these influences; to experience the state of my BEing in the event, is coming from. The truth is that there is a third and primary experience that is always going on within the events we are experiencing. This third experience is the one of the *observer-experience*. This *observer experience* ... is where the true experience is happening ... within your BEing. This experience is the one of how you are truly BEing in the event, how it is affecting your state of BEing. This *experiencer* is the one who is actually having the experience, the true or Higher "I", that is the true "you" actually being in the human event ... *experiencing* it.

We are all Spirits who come here to have a Human experience.

Through the *observer experience*, from outside of my subjective personal judgments, emotional reacts, resistances, attachments and descriptions etc. of the *human event*; from outside of my objective *conscious looking* into the event and all its personality dramas and emotions etc., there is my Aware Observer bringing ALL of these influences, emotions, responses and reacts etc. etc., into my BEing. This *observer experiencer* is the aspect of my Spirit-Self that experiences the *spiritual* truth and purity of the true *event experience* created. This happens without attachment or resistance to the event, without personalizing and emotionalizing its experience. In my marriage breakup through my observer, through my Spirit-BEing-Self, there was a *spiritual* Awareness of a complete dismantling of the family structure we had all been living by for so long. My Life, along with the life of my wife and three daughters, was at a massive turning point. Nothing would ever be the same as it had been, from that moment forward and what would happen from that moment forward was completely unknown. This was not just a physical shift of all of our material existences; this was a massive shift in all of our spiritual paths from that moment forward.

So, we could say that, my *observer experience* is a spiritual one of no drama or resistance to the presently intimate and personalized subjective *events* unfolding, nor the conscious objective experience being seen of the event. My *observer* experience was more of an acceptance of what is happening and what is changing etc., but the experience taken in has far more detail and texture in it than what the subjective or objective are capable of. This *observer experience* was also very different and calmer, more non-attached than the highly dramatic and emotionally charged subjective and consciously objective experiences of my human personality ... of my Human-self. What's revealed through this event of the marriage breakdown, was that I noticed my *observer experience* was coming from a place that seemed to be *observing* the subjective experiences I perceived I was having within the event ... yet totally involved in it, but not identified as it. With Awareness, I could *feel* a difference between these two subtly opposite experience aspects within this same human event. What eventually was revealed was, that although they both could most definitely be called experiences from certain perspectives; for an experience is that which comes from within an event ... I was not however ...*experiencing* both equally.

The fact was, that I wasn't actually experiencing both at all. What was revealed was, that I was only truly *experiencing* in the real sense of the word, one thing ... and the thing I was experiencing, was my Spiritual experience of the <u>event.</u> This experience however, is NOT_what is normally perceived as the *subjective experience.* The real experience was happening in my Spirits *observer experience* of the subjective and objective event. Even though the objective experience was in a sense observing, because it was an experience of being conscious of my human-self in the event, it wasn't capable however, of taking in all of the influences and effects being played out by all of the parts and influences involved in the drama. The objective experience was conscious of the parts, was able in a sense, to see the parts, but wasn't really able to fully feel and experience everything that was taking effect ... on all levels and especially not the spiritual level. This *observer experience* however, <u>IS</u> capable of taking in ALL the aspects and influences being triggered and manifesting by and through ALL of the event, along with all of the identities and emotions etc., yet it has an Awareness of the spiritual effects on my BEing from all of these influences etc. as well.

> *<u>Experiencing</u> as an activity or capacity, is a spiritual activity ... not a physical or even a Soul activity.*

I feel we have been misled for a long time now, in that our Human-self, the every-day *creator* of our human events of emotional interactions etc., is the actual YOU, having the real experience. Truth be known however; is that the human experience has ALWAYS been Divinely designed and intended for your Spirit-Self ... not your Human-self. Only when Humanity has evolved further, and the Spirit-Self has transformed the Astral Body of your Soul-self, that your human will begin to truly have experiences of its own within its *then* spiritualized Human-self. As I said earlier, we are all Spirits who have come here to have a human experience, but this particular reality can only come about from ... within matter. The only way for Spirit to experience a reality of space, time and matter, is through our human existence ... within ... space time and matter. These elements of space, time and matter, do not exists in the Spiritual Realm as a direct spiritual reality. The vehicle that is YOUR Human-self, is the only way through which the Spirit Realm; specifically, through your Spirit-Self, can experience the reality of these elements of physical existence. There are much more higher consequences in the Spiritual Realm that come from our collective human experience; of which we will look at in later chapters.

> *My experience is not the human event my Human-self is creating; my TRUE experience is how I BE-in and with ... that event ... spiritually.*

What revealed itself to me, was the subtle difference between the *observer* and *subjective/objective experiences*. Much more interesting however, was the actual dynamic force that is our *ability to experience* something. This force exists within the Spirit-Self. It was this force that is <u>experiencing</u>, the ability itself and its relationship within the Spirit, that flooded my Awareness with a flash of insight into the true nature of our *experiencing* purpose for this human Life.

My subjectively conscious experience was indeed heavily involved in the human event of the marriage breakdown, with all of its reactive emotions, passions, desires and of course, dramatic identities of victim poor me, controller, arrogant etc. etc. All of these dynamic interactions between the chemical, neural, emotional and physical sensory effects coming from ALL the human components of my Human-self—which includes the Soul-self of course—were only experienceable in their totality, via the true *ability to experience* that lies within the Higher "I" of Spirit-Self. The *perceptions* of a subjective experience that was, in actuality, the *whole* <u>event</u> of the marriage breakdown, are all created within the Soul-self. Because these perceptions are so personalized; because we have become so identified as our Human-self, and so disconnected from our True-Self, our Higher "I" Spirit-BEing-Self, we have come to believe that our subjective human event is what our actual experience is.

Can you see any correlation here with the Soul-self element mentioned in the previous chapter? Can you get a sense of the Intellectual Soul being the creator of our identities, emotions, desires etc. etc., and the Consciousness Soul being conscious within it? Don't worry if it's not clear yet, we will dig deeper into these connections later and bring more information in on that. It is through my Soul-self that my subjective experience is ... created. It is my Soul-self that brings about the *events* of my human reality from interactions, actions and responses, along with all the emotions and drama necessary to humanly enliven such events. When I felt further into this subjective experience, I also noticed all the physical elements to this experience as well, like the emotions that manifested in my body sensations of heat and anger for example, and how this sensation then triggered certain physical reactions in my face and body, making it tense up and squash into a violent and very rigid expression. This expression then of course, was projected out into my wife's space also, triggering a react from *her* victim identity to then protect herself which in turn, stimulated her victimizer identity to attack me back through guilt and innuendo, with intentions to disempower me.

The drama and trauma of my human events are created by the components of my Body and Soul self's, which are of course the Human-self ... that I am.

From this, we may begin to see the *drama dynamic*, by which our human identities create events through. I'm sure that most, if not all of us, at some stage throughout our life, have participated intimately in these drama dynamics also. If you are human, whether you have a well-grounded Spirit or not, then I am sure you have experienced this many a time throughout your life so far. So, from our new and deeper understanding of the makeup of our Human-self, through our Body and Soul Self's, we may see that our *subjective and objective experiences,* are what is created in and by our Human-self. Take a moment and reread the subjective definition below.

- *The subjective experience depends on one's individual ability to process data, to store and internalize it. For example: our senses collect data, which we then process according to biological programming (genetics),neurological network-relationships and other variables.*

We can see that all of the subjective elements defined in this definition are all *human* in nature and actually all correlate with the attributes of the Soul-self we explored in the previous chapter. The processing of the data from our senses comes through the *sense*-ability of our Sentient Soul, sensing from what our etheric body is embodying through the senses of our physical Body, and all being processed and rationalized by our Intellectual Soul. The chemical, biological and neurological etc. aspects of course, come through our physical body and are transmuted through our etheric. They all come from our human reality through the physical senses. They also, all have to do with the human event we are in, as it is created by and through the work of our Body and Soul self's that make up, once again, the Human-self we all are.

You see, this is indeed a *subjective experience*, because the subject participating in the experience, or more accurately, creating the *event* being manifested ... is your Human "self". Your Human-self is certainly the subjective participant, and it is the Consciousness Soul element of your Human-self, the part of you that is *conscious* of its self and being separate from everything, that holds the perception formed from the Intellectual Soul component, of BEing the *experiencer,* of the event. It is precisely because of your consciousness of being separate; from which the false impression that it is the Human-self *doing the experiencing* comes from. There is no doubt that my subjective experience is most definitely, the "human event", but let's explore some deeper questions about this.

Can you actually feel, any *force* that is the Human-self's *ability* to actually feel, integrate and *experience* any of this? Even from the point of view of the small ego, your "I self-Consciousness", which is the complete thinking Human-self itself; is IT, actually *experiencing* any of this, or is it simply conscious of it all as a self that deceptively *appears* to be experiencing the event? Is it simply because it is conscious of the elements in the experience in which emotions and "feelings" are involved? Is your *ability to experience*, the same as BEing Conscious of the experience? Is it simply the separateness of the every-day "you", that gives the appearance of experiencing ... simply by BEing Conscious?

My subjective experience is what I am doing, what I was creating in the human event of my marriage breakup, which is made up of all of the feelings emotions desires passions etc.

*My observer experience is how I am Being ... within the human event. It is how the event **affects** me as the Being ... not as the personality doing.*

There is no wonder that my *subjective* experience of the event is dramatic and emotionally charged, when we look at it from the understanding of the co-creation of my human event by the components of my Human-self. It is particularly clear that the individual traits and intentions of the identities involved, have a massive contribution to the resultant *event*. The subjectivity of my human-ness is inherently grounded in *attachment to the event* through the emotions etc. generated by my identities within my Intellectual Soul. Now, having intimately experienced the makeup of my human-ness, I can see how my human-ness isn't actually experiencing the event, but much rather just emotionally creating it. As I mentioned before, the Soul-self's identities of the Intellectual Soul component and particularly its Spiritual identity; which we will cover more thoroughly in the next chapter; all of these mind-created emotions etc., create the deception; the self-deception, that I am *experiencing* this event. By exploring this perception deeply with non-attached Awareness, it will reveal that it is merely a *perception of your Intellectual-Soul* that this human event of emotional attachments etc. ... is the actual experience. The truth is, that my real <u>experience</u> was not the emotionally charged data details of the event being played out, but rather the all-encompassing effect of the event on my Higher "I", Spirit-BEing-Self; that which is the true observer and true experiencer. It is this Higher Self that is *experiencing* BE-ing Human ... and the events influence this BEing. More accurately, it is the Spirit-Self element of your BEing-Self that is the *observer experiencer*. This is made possible, because of the Spirits capacity through its organ of Awareness; of which true experiencing is made possible.

My Consciousness Soul gives my human the ability to be conscious of its self, individual and separate from its environment.

My Spirit-Self organ of Awareness gives my human the potential to BE an experiential Consciously Aware Human.

Some circles believe, Awareness is associated to consciousness, but although this may be true from a certain perspective, that everything is consciousness and namely from the rationalized perspective derived at by our Intellectual/Perspective Soul component, I feel that comes from a more *cognitive perspective* from an intellectual consciousness, and not an experiential one from Awareness of Spirit. Because our Soul is only able to be conscious at this present point in our evolutionary progression, it is unable to be truly fully Aware. When the state of your Soul and its forces are sufficiently advanced to be able to ground all aspects of your Spirit-Self in your completed Human-self, your Consciousness Soul will not just be able to be conscious, it will then make it possible for your Human-self, the human you, to house your Spirit-Self within it, and fully embody its spiritual capacity of Awareness.

To put it simply, when my Soul forces have developed enough, and my Human has become fully conscious of ALL the elements of both its Soul and

Spirit self, it will then be possible for me to be fully enlightened with full Awareness.

This used to be a long way off for us as a conscious species. According to the Spiritual Science of Rudolph Steiner's Anthroposophy, we are now at the peak of our "I Consciousness" evolution, which means we already have the ability to bring Awareness into our Soul through our Consciousness Soul, we just can't as yet, live in such an Aware State permanently. What also comes with this peak, is the potential to accelerate our personal and collective evolution right now ... and strengthen the Human-self to house all aspects of our Spirit-BEing-Self within it. At this point in time, it is our Spirit-Self's organ of Awareness that we can now develop and use in conjunction with the development of our Consciousness Soul. The grounding agent for grounding Awareness into the Consciousness Soul component of our human ... is our Will. The Will is a muscle of our Consciousness Soul, which once developed sufficiently, makes it possible to bring and hold the Spirit-Self into our Human. It is from a lack of development of the Will, from the weak Will of an under-developed Consciousness Soul; which has most people flipping from Awareness to attention ... from sensory to super-sensory ... and back again ... unable to stay conscious, let alone *truly* Aware. We will talk more on this again in the following chapter.

So, to get a better feel for the force that is experiencing, let's see if we can get a clearer feel and understanding of what Awareness is and its relationship to experiencing. Firstly, there is a difference between Awareness and attention. This always gets confused and miss-interpreted. Let's see what our Wiki has to say again.

- **Awareness** is the ability to perceive, to feel, or to be conscious of events, objects, thoughts, emotions, or sensory patterns. In this level of consciousness, sense data can be confirmed by an observer without necessarily implying understanding. More broadly, it is the state or quality of being aware of something. In biological psychology, awareness is defined as a human's or an animal's perception and cognitive reaction to a condition or event.

Did you notice they call it an ability? The confusion here though is that it is spoken of as an ability of consciousness, rather than an ability of Spirit. This is notable. Hopefully, from our new understanding of consciousness with respect to the Soul and Spirit Self's of our BEing; we can see that it's our Intellectual Soul that rationalizes that it is our Consciousness Soul's ability. Our Intellectual Soul mind extrapolates, because it has no true *experience* of Awareness, but only a formed perception that Awareness comes from or within itself ... being conscious. From within an under-developed Soul, the Consciousness Soul component of that Soul-self, doesn't have the capability ... yet ... to be fully *conscious* of the Spirit. Becoming conscious of Spirit is indeed a mission of this Consciousness Soul age. Consequently, because we haven't as yet completed this spiritual mission; through the Intellectual Soul <u>mind,</u> which gives us the capability of conceptualizing and rationalizing ... anything; its concept of Awareness can only be attributed to consciousness. This is again because the Soul is not conscious ... yet ... of the Spirit. This however, can be overcome in this present time with reverent and committed esoteric training. Here lies another stimulant for the question, "Are you out of your mind … yet?"

Awareness is an __ability__ of my Spirit-Self aspect of my BEing-Self.

Attention is an __attribute__ of the Intellectual Soul component of my Soul-self.

Attention defines and describes etc., what is able to be seen by consciousness through the senses, of what exists in my linear world of Body and Soul.

Awareness *feels* that which exists in my non-linear world without descriptions. Attention is unable to see or feel this domain. Your Intellectual Soul uses attention to direct energy, to direct focus of mind via your Consciousness Souls attribute of Will. Have you ever heard the saying, "energy flows where attention goes"? This is a statement from a Spiritual Science understanding of how creative forces act within the human structure. This is what is meant by the viewpoint of the power of projections onto others or out in the world.

Let's have another look into the Wiki definitions.

- **Attention** *is the behavioral and cognitive process of selectively concentrating on a discrete aspect of information, whether deemed subjective or objective, while ignoring other perceivable information. Attention has also been referred to as the allocation of limited processing resources. Attention remains a major area of investigation within education, psychology, neuroscience, cognitive neuroscience, and neuropsychology. Areas of active investigation involve determining the source of the sensory cues and signals that generate attention, the effects of these sensory cues and signals on the tuning properties of sensory neurons, and the relationship between attention and other behavioral and cognitive processes like working memory and vigilance.*

- *The relationships between attention and consciousness are complex enough that they have warranted perennial philosophical exploration.*

From looking at these standard definitions, we can clearly see that attention is understood to be very much a human attribute but, specifically, it is an attribute or as it states above, a process of our mind. From our new perspective of the Soul's contribution through our Intellectual Soul, it takes on a different understanding. Because of this link to your Intellectual Soul and because your mind is incapable of feeling anything, it is the rationalizations of your Intellectual Soul mind that mis-interprets attention as Awareness. Your mind through reasoning and rationalizing etc., creates reference points for itself. These reference points become the default definitions for the mind when it comes across something it doesn't know. Do you know the times you say "ohh yeah, that's like so and so" or, "yeah, that's the same as … "? Because your mind at this time has no reference, definition or conception of Awareness, it will often confusingly use attention (which it already has a reference for), as a substitute for Awareness.

Because Awareness is a _spiritual ability_, it is difficult to accurately define for you what it actually is and its function, so don't be too linear with your thinking as you go further here. Stay Aware rather than attentive and allow the _experience_ of Awareness to enter your Consciousness Soul. The Sentient Soul element of our Soul-self makes the Soul capable of sensing the physical human world and the influences of physical, etheric and Soul elements that make up our human events and subjective experiences. So too, does the Spirit-Self of your BEing-Self, give you the capability of _experiencing_ your Human-self realities through its spiritual nature, via as we showed earlier, the _observer experience_ received through your Spirit-Self's Awareness.

Awareness is a spiritual ability to _feel_, ... but from a much more _super_-sense-ability. It is this super-sense-ability through which the _force_ of "experiencing" works. Your Spirit-Self is the component of your BEing-Self that makes it possible for your BEing-Self to be ... Aware. This _Aware of Self_ state is an integral part for your Spirit _within_ the Divine Spiritual Realm, but also makes your Spirit capable of being Aware of ALL parts of the Divine also. This includes of course, all aspects of your Human-self. Because of the enormity of the capacity of Awareness to take in so many subtle elements of creation, it is beyond our Intellectual Soul-mind at this point in our evolution, to be capable of accurately or completely describing, defining or judging it all. This incapability is because we are still in the development stage of our Consciousness Soul. As our Consciousness Soul develops, it develops within it a spiritual Will strength that provides the linking faculty which facilitates the bringing of our Spirit's Awareness into our human Soul. Ultimately this faculty will evolve our Human-self into an Aware Human BEing. At our present level of consciousness collectively, we _are_ able to bring Awareness into the Consciousness Soul, but we are unable to hold and fully integrate it there as a permanent human attribute. Remember, it is our strength of Will that is necessary to ground our Spirit in your human. The development of the Will of your Consciousness Soul go hand in hand with the grounding of your Spirit-Self in your Human-self ... and are in-separable. We will discuss how to do this and more in the following chapter.

When you put your Awareness on something, you naturally and automatically _notice_ all of the non-linear as well as all the linear elements, of the forces and spiritual elements ... and it happens within a moment. You just simply become aware of it, get a super-sense of it, but of its totality and completeness, of its "IS-ness", of simply what it is without any preconceived ideas or concepts.

**Awareness doesn't define or describe or judge or emotionalize or any of the things my Soul-self does. Awareness notices by feel, by a super-feel in fact, without attaching to any specific element of what it is noticing or rather ... what it is feeling.**

This term "feel" needs to be looked at here, because it is not what your Body or Soul-self 's would conceive of. This *super-feel* if you like, is beyond our strictly human-self reality of physical or Soul sensory existence. The depth and parameter that is this super-feel, is extremely difficult to describe obviously, but relatively easy to access, and is overwhelmingly distinctive once experienced. Actually, experiencing this difference is what I call, *stupidly simple*. You will hopefully see this in the future chapters also. The difficulty or hurdle to *experiencing* this super-feel of Awareness, comes from blocks created by the Intellectual Soul mind's limited conceptual vision of reality, stemming from the fact that the Intellectual Soul component actually can't feel anything and is trapped in the realm of the Soul. Believe it or not, it is the higher thinking capability of the Higher "I" Ego, that ultimately will be the savior of our Soul's release from our present material plane of existence. Our Ego is the link, through the developed Consciousness Soul's capacity to facilitate higher thinking, of which can re-connect the Spiritual Realm to our Human Realm of existence. More on that later also.

For a lot of people on this planet at this point in our Human evolution, the Intellectual Soul mind is incapable of *feeling* with Awareness, from this super-feel sense. Remember, it is through our Sentient Soul that *sensory* ability is possible within the Soul-self. Our Intellectual Soul gives us the ability to rationalize, extrapolate, to explore through thinking and defining, it is not a *feeling* organ of the Soul. Our Intellectual Soul, through its identities and emotional creations that permeate through our Body-self, manifest into our physical reality subjective experiences. This creates *feelings* of which our Sentient Soul then senses again, as they reverberate back to it from our outer reality. Our Consciousness Soul then becomes conscious of this, relaying it as a *conscious perspective* back to our Intellectual Soul yet again, for it to rationalize and define through as ... a subjective experience. If you look and feel into this cycle, you may notice there is actually no true *experiencing* going on here, just reactions and responses from one component of Soul, to Body-self, to external creation and back into Soul-self again and then the whole *process* is rationalized and conceptualized into what appears from our Intellectual Soul's perspective as ... an experience. The flaw in this cycle is, that nothing is actually taken in to the whole human; meaning Body Soul AND Spirit, as an experience that transforms the Human or transmutes the human energy form in any way. This cycle is a regurgitating form of one component of human-self receiving an aspect of reality and then passing it to another component of its human-self as a different form and so on and so on ... but it all continually happens within the realm of the material physical human reality it exists. ALL of this happens void of spiritual expansion or growth. As we will see later, Life is a continuous flow of experiential creation designed for us to experience, grow and evolve from. Without true *experiencing* however, Life's flow is stagnated and blocked, creating all manner of dis-ease and dis-harmonies. This cycle of conscious creations being regurgitated within consciousness only, is a hidden cause for most ailments in our world right now.

This cycle, if left to its own existence without any spiritual input, would eventually become so implosive and condensing, that humanity would densify to such a degree, that it would become too solid to change or evolve out of its materialized self. From that state, we could never spiritualize our human form and free it from its material existence. If this were to happen, it would remain trapped in the consciousness cycle of our Body and Soul creations. We, as a humanity, have previously come to this very dark place in our evolution.   Rudolph Steiner has given us great detail of the higher spiritual perspective of what happened to circumvent humanities complete solidification and densification into purely physical matter, without any spiritual content at all.   This circumventing event was the Christ event, what's called "The Mystery of Golgotha". The Christ BEing entered our Earth's Spiritual Body to permeate it with a spiritual impulse that now allows EVERY member of our Humanity without exception, the possibility to gain access to the Spiritual Realm again. However, although this is possible, it requires us as individuals, to do the inner work of spiritualizing our Human-self first, to be able to tap into the power of this Divine impulse and continue Humanities evolution out of the density of its current materialistic existence. This work here you are doing now, is but a stepping stone on the path to this end. This however, is a topic for a whole other book then this one here.

Have you ever had what seemed like a stimulating intellectual conversation with another person, and yet it didn't seem to get anywhere? I get this a lot through Facebook interactions with certain people. I actually love Facebook for providing me access to so many people, but more so because it is a perfect opportunity for me to truly experience this purely Human-self interactions. The way we regurgitate information and our identities disguise it and try to own it as a new thought or concept just fascinates me. I love it because I not only get to see through others the traits and mechanics of our Soul-self intellectualizations, but I get to intimately experience these machinations within my own Soul. BEing as human as everyone else, there are always times when my Spirit's Awareness is pushed out by my Soul's identities, and all of a sudden, I find myself in the grip of react and defend, doing battle with the other in the throes of survival, who has now become an opponent, rather than a like-minded explorer of consciousness. I consider these moments, the jewels of Life, as they bring out the elements in me of the limiting and destructive behavior's that I need to spiritualize to grow out of.

An enlightening moment came for me one time when a friend and I entered this Facebook battleground. Both having strong wills and sharp Souls, we challenged and volleyed back and forwards for quite some time. The occasional stab from his dagger of invalidations, that wounded and destabilized my self-righteous identity's rigid standpoint, would then trigger my victimizer identity to retaliate with a thrusting spear of undermining intentions to his heart. I would do this with statements along the lines of how I thought much more of him than this and our friendship was bigger than his mental resistances to feel and share. Of course, from this, the occasional stab and thrust inevitably turned into a regularity of stab and twist, thrust and rotate from both of us for maximum damage, purely because we had both allowed our Intellectual Soul to push out our Spirit-Self's Awareness ability to super-feel ALL of what was going on and not just our mental resistances.

As happens with Facebook conversation streams, our external world would press on the internal world we were attempting to share, making our conversation take interludes of work, family and partner needs etc. It was in these interludes that I would again reground my Spirit and tap into my BEing-Self's Awareness, able once more to see the damage I was doing from being trapped in the dense human consciousness of my Soul-self. Through my Awareness; which had stimulated me to go back through the fifty odd comments we were sharing, I was able from the *observer* this time, to have a truly *observer experience* of them as they are, without my subjective Intellectual Soul mind's blind reactions and judgments filtering them. What became experientially noticeable to me, was not just the denseness of our interchange, but the way that the Soul without Spirit, doesn't feel anything and simply regurgitates its own emotions and reactions, judgements etc. to try and save face, or rather, to not admit to IT's self its own limitations and falsehoods. I noticed that when I re-entered the battleground from Awareness, I was not so reactive to the still deliberate, or maybe even unconscious jabs from my friend's protective identity. From Awareness, I could stay in touch with a much bigger picture than what my Consciousness Soul was conscious of. My friend however, was obviously still not grounding any Spirit Awareness, as he would come back seemingly more peaceful, rationalizing through his minds Spiritual identity, but the jabs and stabs were now simply more covert and behind the back.

Ironically, the topic of our conversation battle, was about this, about the difference between the experiencing Spirit and the non-experiencing subjective creations of the Human-self. As always happens when we deliberately explore spirituality, a Divine Orchestration is always in play to bring about experiences for us of what we are exploring. What was beautiful for me, was by experiencing through feeling with my Awareness, I gained a super-sense, a super-feel into my friend's consciousness. I was able to see and have a sense of where he was at, rather than where I thought or wanted him to be at. I felt so much more experientially connected to him and noticed that I was no longer reacting to what he was posting, but instead, I was responding more in alignment with his Spirit's necessities for truth, rather than his human desires to be right. As my battle-friend's viewpoints were coming from his Conscious Human-self, his identities could not concede to anything about Awareness, Spirit or experiencing through feel. I was shocked by the revelation that my friend, who I had considered to be quite a spiritual person and advanced thinker, was most definitely existing as his spiritual identity, shrouded in the self-created limiting beliefs of his Intellectual Soul.

My spiritual identity is my Intellectual Soul's interpretation of my Spirit-Self; of which it is incapable of experiencing.

I was now becoming fascinated by this interaction with him. I noticed that as I would ask him for his *experience* of these matters, of his *experience* with Spirit etc., he became more and more defensive, attacking, invalidating and dismissive toward me. What brought a smile to my face was how his Human-self became incredibly allusive to ever answer questions directly and experientially. I was amused by our Soul's ability to twist and mis-construe and manipulate statements, just in order to avoid actually sharing a true experience. Eventually, after meditations on this event and into the structure of our Human Consciousness, it was revealed that when the human has no Spirit elements grounded in it, when it has no higher guidance from the Higher "I" Spirit-BEing-Self, it will draw into its self; like a turtle draws into its shell, to avoid exposure of its self-made falsehoods. My friend shared with me at the end of our crusade, that he had gotten insight into a very long-term issue he had been struggling with. He still has never shared what that issue was or his experience of it to this day. As I said earlier, some people are not yet capable of _feeling with their Awareness_, because of the extreme parameter of experiential ownership Awareness brings in.

By "feeling" with my Spirit-Self Awareness, my True BEing-Self is able to "fully experience" BEing human, through my Human-self.

Hopefully from here, you may start to see or get a sense of the difference between the _subjective/objective experience_ of your Human-self and now, the _observer experience_ of your BEing-Self. This is why I call our Human-self creations _events_ rather than _experiences_, because they are created over and over, but never actually end by completion through the real experience. From this subjective regurgitation, consciousness remains within the human paradigm. This effectively creates a state of Consciousness Coma, that can block out the Spirit ... even for life times. It is through your Spirit-Self's Awareness, through being Aware, that your _observer experience_ is able to spiritually nourish your Soul. Awareness gives your consciousness the ability to feel and experience more deeply and completely into your human events, because it super-feels all of the other elements that are outside of and beyond what your subjective consciousness is conscious of. The _observer experience_ of your BEing-Self is only possible, because of your Spirit-Self's ability of Awareness to super-feel the human event of your Soul as an _object_ of reality. Awareness is how you get _super-sensory_ input into the Spiritual Realm from your seemingly separate external world reality of your human. This done by transmuting it into an experiential effect on your Spirit-BEing-Self.

My observer experience is a super-sensory, super-feeling effect on my Spirit-BEing-Self.

TRUE _experiencing_ as a function, as a spiritual force, is how your BEing-Self; through its ability of Awareness, is able to be intimately involved and fully immersed in more than _just_, the _subjective/objective experience_ of your Human-self's events, but in the spiritual nature of your Human-self within its spiritual realm as well. Awareness is not the experience we have within our Spirit-BEing. Awareness is the super-feel conduit that draws in ALL the effects, influences, subtle contributing elements etc. that come from the events created in our human reality ... along with the spiritual reality creations of karma, intentions, purpose etc. etc. All of these elements, both subjective/objective and observer, is the _true experience_, that is carried out and integrated by your True-Self ... your Higher "I" BEing-Self. It is true your subjective experiences are in a sense experiences, but you are not _experiencing_ them through your Human-self of Body and Soul. You are _experiencing_ your subjective human experiences through the Awareness of your Spirit-BEing-Self. Your Human-self is the creator of your _human events_, of your reactions and interactions, your emotional responses and judgments from your different identities and all of their aversions etc. etc., that you have mistakenly called subjective experiences. True _experiencing_ is not a function of our Human-Soul-self at this point in our human evolution. Until we are capable and willing, to integrate our Spirit into our Human, then we remain mis-identified AS our Human-self, rather than through it. To simplify it again, when you spiritualize your Human BEing, your human will become a consciously experiential Human-Spirit-BEing.

Experiencing is feeling with my Awareness, but without any definitions, judgement or descriptions of what I am feeling.

As a final perspective of experiencing for this chapter, it is a force we each have access to equally, that transmutes reality from a human creationary state ... into a BEing state. _Experiencing_ is a spiritual force we use to bring the human physical linear world reality into our Spirit's non-linear super-sensory Divine reality. Without this force, we are not able, it is not possible, for the physical world of our human form to re-enter the Divine Realm of Spirit. You already have glimpses of this force in action within you when you walk in Nature and feel its presence, feel its state so to speak and feel relaxed and yet maybe energized at the same time afterwards. You are using this _experiencing force_, when you enter a room and get a sense of something wrong, or something so great and uplifting in the environment and so forth. There are many moments of Spirit Awareness in use throughout the everyday life of many of you right now. As you read this book and you get a sense of it making sense to you, even though you may not fully understand it all, this is your Spirits Awareness in use, here now, present time. It truly is this stupidly simple. This is because, the potential for us all to ground the Spirit in our human Soul at this time, is at its greatest potential than it has ever been. Ironically, because your Consciousness Soul and its _Will muscle_ is still young and weak; through your Intellectual Soul mind, your Spirits Awareness is simply pushed out of the human that you are. Ironically again; as we will discuss later, when you strengthen your Will and use it to consistently ground your Spirit Awareness in your human, your Intellectual Soul mind will also transform into a spiritual organ of the Higher "I" Ego, manifesting a new and higher spiritual quality to your thinking. There are massive benefits to human health and wellness of Body and Soul, when you consciously use your force of experiencing; when you embody experiencing as a force within your human BEing. We have now been given the opportunity to Quantum leap evolution and accelerate our human self-transformation into a truly Spiritualized Creator Human BEing.

So, now that we have an idea and hopefully a feel for what experiencing actually is and where it comes from and how it is used, let's explore in the next chapter how we can use this _experiencing_ ability of Awareness deliberately. As we will see in the later chapters also, and from what I have experienced through my Conscious Bodyworks, the power of deliberate experiencing to discharge dis-ease and sickness is profound and direct, to say the least. I have found the function of _deliberate experiencing_, profoundly transformative in maintaining an exceptional level of wellness and health in the Body Soul and Spirit. Through _deliberate experiencing_, through feeling with your Awareness without any definitions, judgments or descriptions of what you are feeling, you can heal old conditions of ill health and disharmony within your whole BEing. Learning about these intimacies; practicing their use on a daily basis to the point of Living in Awareness, is preventative medicine for your whole BEing. A profound and Self-empowering wisdom awaits you ... when you get out of your mind ... and experience your true Spirit-Nature within you.

Understanding Life is a good practice for my Soul-self's mind and intrinsic in its design, but it is a far cry from the experiential <u>wisdom</u> unleashed from Intuitive knowing, derived from experiencing Life through the Awareness within my Spirit Nature.

Chapter 6

Life's Purpose for the Human Experience

In 2009, my sensual cowgirl partner and I from my previous story, had a visit from her daughter. Their relationship was and is, one of close support and companionship. After her first marriage had broken up, they had lived together off and on for quite some time since her daughter was sixteen. Although the daughter was now a grown woman, they both still had a good degree of co-dependency with each other. Mum being mum, she would like to fix the problems of her daughter, so her daughter didn't have to suffer unduly. Daughter being daughter, in this situation, she loved mum fixing her problems and bailing her out. Of course, the ole control identity can't lose face by being bailed out all the time, so it would still have to make mum wrong for bailing her out. Even so, she would still create new situations for mum to bail her out of again and again, through her "unloved" identity. The rational of this needy identity is that if she bails me out, she must care and love me.

My identities are the costumes of human-ness I get to use to play out the experiences I need to evolve through.

This relationship was always challenged of course, whenever the mother would have a new personal relationship. The daughter would feel dis-connected and even abandoned by her mother, who was not giving her the attention she was used to getting. Actually, her *Victim Poor Me* identity would create very believable stories and feelings of being abandoned by the mother, to blame her and make her wrong or guilty to get her attention back. This is how the identities of our Soul-self will do whatever it has to, to get the attention it desires, or to just simply feel like it's in control or loved. Its viewpoint here is that any attention is good attention, even if it is drama filled. These Soul-self identities perspective is, the more drama the better. Being trapped by identification as your drama, is a great way to be disempowered by your identities. It weakens, confuses and undermines the resolve of the self and the other person, so it can keep the self-deception of control running. The Victimizer identity likes to hold the upper hand by attacking with some well-timed and delivered button pushing, guilt triggering and heart wrenching statements that would wipe the floor with any world class debate team. This particular daughter's identities were masterful at this and I have to say, a guilty single parent identity is an easy target for such a master. I know that guilty parent identity well from being a single parent to my three teenage daughters as well.

Now my relationship with my then partner, really intensified this interplay between mother and daughter, because all my work is about expanding our awareness of these patterns and identities and to experience them fully to integrate them, before inflicting them onto others. Taking full ownership of our identities can be challenging at first but is truly a most liberating experience in the end. As my partner began to own her "fix-my-daughter" pattern coming from her guilty "Victim" identity, she stopped fixing her problems and moved to trying to empower her daughter. Of course, this sounds great but, if the daughter is still stuck in her "You need to fix me, so you can prove you love me" pattern from her Victim identity and she doesn't have tools to integrate this then, drama will prevail...and it did.

So, she came to visit us for two weeks with her mum alone, while I was on a trip to my kahuna in Hawaii. I showed up the third week after returning from O'ahu. The two weeks together went really well, and they were in a great space when I came home, but I could feel some underlying tensions of unresolved judgments still running once I returned. My presence was most likely a silent, hidden trigger, as my partner now had to share her time with me also. At the drop of the wrong word or seemingly insignificant assumption of the other's feelings, the air would become so thick that you could throw an ounce of lead between them and it would never hit the floor.

It's amazing how the air, or space between two people changes when they disconnect from each other. Actually, what happens is, that although our Spirit-BEing-Self is permanently connected to all others; in the moments when our identities take control, our BEing-Self is pushed out by our human-self's consciousness. Consciousness remember, is conscious of self as separate from its environment, so in these moments of identity created crisis, our consciousness Soul-self, is back in its own space and because of the lack of Spirit guidance, doesn't and can't feel connected. Of course, it will always try to convince itself that it is and anyone around it's self as well. Back when I was parenting my teenage daughters, I didn't have a lot of tools as I do now to experience with and was *winging it* most of the time, as I'm sure most other single parents do. After spending thousands of dollars on self-evolvement courses filled with many drama-filled experiences of integrating resisted ownerships, at the time of her visit I had an arsenal of great, easy, simple tools. I was mercilessly relentless with my use of them. An attribute I'm sure my partner and her daughter were not always happy about.

Ownership is a form of integration and puts an end to suffering

So, the third week became a week of clarity and ownership of her daughter through our exploration into *experiencing* her identities and their inherent belief structures. For the first time, she was able to experience the simplicity, power and freedom that comes from *experiencing* with Awareness and integrating identities. To finally, *experientially* find that your beliefs are not your truths, but merely constructs of your identities, constructs that bring about your human drama events; is a major step toward the freedom and power that comes with experiencing ones TRUE and Higher "I" BEing-Self. My partner and I were both very proud of her, as she would hit that oh so well-known wall of resistance we ALL have and then, use her Will to experience the events of her Soul-self identities deliberately, allowing herself to be guided through it by her BEing-Self. As she integrated her old debilitating identities one by one, she gained more strength and courage to tackle the more solid patterns of belief that were deeply permeated within her Consciousness Soul. She was amazed at how easy and simple it was to do, as she began more and more to *feel with her Spirit's Awareness,* as her BEing-Self served its higher intentions. We all began to bliss from the experience, as the space between us all was blessed with real Love.

The greatest thing about ownership through my Awareness ability to Embody Experience, is that it reconnects my three-self's of Body Soul and Spirit together, effortlessly.

This is a natural phenomenon of my TRUE Spiritual Nature that brings my Human-self in harmony with Life's Divine Orchestration.

Now on the last night before she left, we were going through the gains of the week and there was obviously much appreciation and gratitude flowing between them both for the experience of their time together. We were talking about her commitment to continue the work of embodying her experiences and to use Awareness more deliberately in her Life. Having now had a real experience of her true Spiritual Nature and beaming with a renewed willingness to fully experience all aspects of her Self's, she decided she would continue. Now the key word here is DECIDED. When we TRULY decide something, it happens from the Spirit-BEing-Self and it will end something and begin another. Because they both had been in such a state of connection between their own Human and BEing self's, as well as each other; on becoming present with the fact they were about to leave each other again, their identities slipped straight into action to create yet again, another old pattern for each to integrate. I asked them both to express how they feel about separating again tomorrow and to share it with each other, so they can know what the other was really feeling. Now my mischievous Aware Spirit-Self was obviously in touch with their Spirit-Self's for me to ask such a sensitive question. You guessed it, the daughters "you don't love me because your sending me away" aspect of that same ole Soul-self-identity reared its enormous head again. Mums "dis-connected because I don't want to say anything to upset her" identity jumped into the swamp to play also. Frankly, I was a little shocked at how quickly her identity rushed right back in there again, after so many good days of ownership. This IS the intensity of our identities and their function for us.

To bring anything into my Awareness, doesn't get rid of it, but it does dis-empower its influence over me.

It was a nano-second jump from bliss, connection and being in Awareness with each other, back to un-Awareness as the Soul-self identities again pushed out the Spirit and created *feelings* of being disconnected and abandoned. To justify the dis-connect and prove its point, this re-ignited Victim identity would pull out of the etheric Life-Body, a remembrance of a time 6 months prior and then another incident that was 2 years prior to that. It would have gone further back into the memory banks of discouragement and discontent, but it couldn't get past my safety net of Awareness to bring it back to present time. Resistance to experiencing this present moment of farewells and goodbyes triggered both their Soul-self identities to push out their Spirit's Awareness once more. The lower human consciousness patterns of blame and attack from that old familiar Victimizer identity, would grab the opportunity of a Spirit-less human consciousness, to disempower the other to make them feel bad. These resistances created by our human consciousness identities, push out the Awareness of our Spirit-Self, which inevitably pulls us out of experiencing, connection and alignment with our Body Soul and Spirit self's. All of this, locks us back, smack bang in the Soul-self zone of denial. One breath, I'm all three selves in harmony together and the next breath I'm just human consciousness again. Without Spirit, we're just our poor human-self, drowning in the inabilities and dis-empowerments that come from the co-creations between my Body and Soul human reality. Void of Spirit, we're just locked into yet another dense mode of survival.

Now the really interesting thing here with the daughter's identity was that, even though she had embodied a number of identities using Awareness and the Virtue Embodying technique throughout and she knew it all worked rather effortlessly, she couldn't or wouldn't go there with this one. In her words "this is a big one." This *poor me* Victim identity viewpoint has run this program for such a long time with such great success, that to just experience it and have it discharge, was not an option for this blame and suffering identity. Her words once more were "I can feel it, but not quite put my finger on it."

This particular "artful dodger" identity, was masterful at staying undetected. My personal guideline for these undercover identity marauders, is that if I am looking for it and can't find it, then I can be sure that I'm in it.

Integrating identities and experiences can <u>only</u> be done from and through your Spirit's BEing-Self ability to experience, by feeling with your Awareness, but without definition, judgment or description of what you are feeling. This daughter's defiant wounded child identity however, was not going down quietly. The more we explored together and exposed the deeper, more subversive modes of conduct from it, the more ridged the resistance to ownership became, and the more attached to not feeling dug in. This one has had many years to perfect its strategies, but in the light of our combined Awareness and intentions to integrate, it had to pull out all of its stops to hold on. This identity is a master manipulator and likes to pull others in to play with it and sets *them* up as the reason for her/its failings. All of this, just so it doesn't have to complete the experience. This manipulator identity has the ability to control all of the other identities, like a stage manager controls his props and actors on stage, to set the appropriate environment for its hidden agendas. Unfortunately for this identity and fortunately for my partner's daughter, I know this identity very well also, so I could see, most of the time, its acts and strategies coming.

With Awareness, I finally caught myself being pulled along this very subtle, but powerful "save me" tractor beam from her Manipulator Identity element. It was craftily dragging me in so it could manipulate me into getting off the track of getting her to embody her experience. It was much like a skilled fisherman pulling in a 1,000lb shark on a 10lb trout line. Slow and calculating was this identity's way. With just enough enticing Sentient Soul *feeling* tugs of attachment here and a seductive Intellectual Soul perception of letting go of resistance there, always however its hidden agenda was to always resist through distraction.

Our "I Consciousness" comes here into this life, to bring our human into the experience of being a separate BEing, motivated by Life's purpose to create individual subjective human events to experience. To do this, it must have a system of resistances and attachments that create an atmosphere of conflict, with which it can flip from one paradigm of resistance, to the other of attachment. When viewed with Awareness, this consciousness system provides unlimited events of dis-empowerment, which of course, provide us with equally unlimited _opportunities_ to embody experiences for empowerment and embodiment of our Spirit's _higher virtues_.

My present-day hurdle for consciousness to evolve into its spiritual state of Consciously Aware Spirit-Self; is to integrate and discharge the human reality dynamic of resistance and attachment.

The truth of the matter is that I really enjoy these interplays between the consciousness identities of others and the interactions and reactions we create together. I always gain new levels of awareness of our identities, our Higher "I" Ego and our Soul-self dynamics through these moments. It moves me to immense appreciate of how amazing the Divine's human creation is and the opportunities it gives us all to grow and learn new life skills and embody higher virtues into our human Soul-self. The Intellectual Soul element of our Soul-self is the master of reasoning and rationality. It is after all ... our Intelligence. It truly has an impeccable talent for putting the right combinations of beliefs, emotions, judgments and feelings etc., together, with the right identity at just the right time to create just the right experience for me. All of this to create an opportunity for me to embody the perfect virtue for that situation or human event experience. Of course, this doesn't mean I always integrate it, but it _always_ ... gives me the right opportunity. Our Intellectual Soul is so good at it, that it can do all of this in a blink of a thought and then change it all in the very next thought. Some call it split personalities, but I rather believe it to be masterful identity flipping and there isn't a person on the planet who doesn't have this ability. Maybe against popular belief, this capability comes from the successful evolution of our Consciousness Soul.

There are some very elaborate _consciousness systems_ on the planet now, that delve into the intricacies of Identities and our ability to flip them from one to the other. This flipping is not the ability of our Ego, as a lot of these intellectual spiritual salespeople would love you to believe, but purely the ability of consciousness. Specifically, it is the identities of your Intellectual Soul element. It loves to keep a good game or identity running for as long as it can, even after the game's expiration dates have well and truly passed. This is what it is designed to do; to create human events for your Spirit-BEing-Self to experience. Can you see any other way for us to create enough human events for our BEing-Self to experience?

The end-game for any human event, comes with experiencing, from _feeling_ with your Spirit-Self's Awareness, without any definitions, judgments or descriptions of what you are feeling/experiencing. In a nutshell, the Divine's intention for giving us our Spirits Ego Body, is so it can transmute higher thoughts into experiences … and vice-versa. This is our opportunity for our human to ground higher Spiritual virtues in our human-being. This is manifest for us to become an experiential Human-Self that takes command of its own evolution back into Spirit. If you can BE Aware of the experience and fully experience it before the Intellectual Soul mind flips identities, then the game ends so to speak. Resistance is a strategy of the Soul-self to _not_ complete an experience … because at this point in our present level of consciousness … consciousness is not an experiential existence. Resistance is how consciousness justifies identity flipping before the experience is complete, to successfully sabotage its own evolution back into the spiritual realm.

> _**Ironically, resistance and attachment are empowering tools of Divine Creation, creating opportunities for me to strengthen my Consciousness Soul's Will, enabling my Spirit's higher Awareness to function within consciousness.**_

I love the statement "it's too big to experience" or "it's too painful to go there" or as the daughter said, "this is a really big one." These are gigantic red flags that she was right smack bang in the identity, with all its stops out to not experience it. When you get pulled in and engage with another's identity like this, you give your power away to it. You give _IT_ power to continue the game and you diminish your _ability_ to end it. To not react or engage in the others attacks or questions, of which are intended to confuse you, stops empowering the others Soul-self identities. My strategy with the daughter was to stop her identity getting power from me, so her Spirit-BEing-Self's higher Will, can regain control and move Awareness back to experiencing again.

> _**Truth is that my creative power doesn't lie in the power of the conscious mind, but in the power of my Spirit's Awareness.**_

This is what I did on that eventful last night stand of her wounded child identity. The expression of shock and bewilderment on her face was worth a million dollars as I declared, "You could always stay in the identity if you want, or you could decide to integrate it,". "If it's comfortable for you, then just stay there." I suggested. I slipped in again before she could reply with, "You don't have to shift; nobody here is making you change or even needs you to change for that matter. You decide what's right for you and I'll support that,". I slipped this in just as her conscious mind was about to try the "you're abandoning me" identity on for size ... yet again. I must admit, I did have just a little compassionate sarcasm in the energy. This cloaked question that triggers a response to *feel* what's right, always works. Those seconds of shock for her Soul-self were enough for her BEing-Self to jump back in as she went off to bed to do some more Experience Embodiment.

The next morning as I was greeted by the sun's nurturing rays beaming through the windows of our breakfast room, I could feel there was a shift in the night. I could feel the inevitable wave of change that each and every day has brought to every one of us since the beginning of this earth walk called time, but this day had a difference to it. Today, there seemed to be an extra glow in those sunbeams. As I blissfully gazed out the window, I noticed the daughter coming toward the house from the detached apartment at the back of our house where she was staying. My mind's judgments wondered what drama she might have in store for us all today. Feeling her space however, through the connection of our BEing-Selves, I could tell that Awareness spent a lot of time in her human overnight and some further deep integration had taken place. As our eyes connected through the glass panels of the back door, a smile the size of the Gulf of Mexico exploded across her face. I knew I was in for a tale worthy of an Agatha Christie who-dun-it novel ... only we all knew who did it.

"WELL," she started "what a night! I've only had a few hours of sleep with these identities running in and out all night!". There was a sigh of almost excited exhaustion and an opposing scowl on her face, as she explained her journey. I could sense her next comment to me as she said, "what have you done to me by making me see these things?". I jumped in straight away to catch her before she fell into her identity slide of doom into what's wrong with this. I shared that it was her Awareness that see's everything and all I did was help her to become aware of her Awareness. My mischievous reply to her thoughts was, "Aren't you glad you can see them now and isn't it a great feeling when you fully experience them, and they discharge their energy?" "AAHHH ... yeah ... I guess, but does it have to be so hard and dramatic?" she replied. I couldn't help myself. I return volleyed with "Which self is making it hard and dramatic though?" We could hear the digital clock tick as she formulated her response. "Yeah, yeah ... my Soul-self," she knowingly replied.

The <u>experience</u> I am resisting, is far less painful and dramatic than the resistance I set up to avoid it.

I asked her if she had been able to embody a virtue for her "you don't love me because you're sending me away" identity and she said yes, but it was the other one, the Undecided identity that she had exposed the previous day that woke her up at 3am. So, to empower her with the tools she now has available and to validate the work she had just done in the early hours of the morning, I asked her, "When you experienced that identity and integrated it, was it hard or dramatic?" She replied "Well … no … it was easy … eventually once I could _feel it_." "So, would you say that it's actually effortless and drama-free to just _experience,_ by feeling something with your Awareness, from your Higher "I" Spirit-BEing-Self domain, as opposed to the draining and drama-filled consciousness of your Soul-self domain and its identities?" At last, her Soul-self acknowledgment and submission, combined with her BEing-Self appreciation converge and she has her glorious, AAHH …HAAA moment of fully experiencing what she had resisted most of her life. Ironically, her resisted experience was the power of her Awareness to simply feel and experience.

For me, these moments are Divine blessings of consciousness. This is the powerful force driving my intention to empower others with these tools for _their_ self-empowered evolution of their Soul's consciousness. Anyone who has been witness to another's _self-_ realization and integration of their experiences and identities, can attest to the indefinable glory in these moments. In that moment of her ownership, full alignment and harmony of her whole BEing of Body Soul and Spirit was achieved and true self-love experienced. The grounding of this love in this person's reality, was experienced as an all-encompassing connection of oneness to her Higher "I" Spirit-Self and all those present. In these moments, these connections are felt and returned by sensitive Aware others at the same time. I have been in courses of hundreds of people when this has happened, and sensitive Souls all the way across the other side of the ballroom have felt the energy shift and connection from these spiritual warrior's experiential victories. Ownership of our Human-self through Awareness, harmoniously aligns and embodies all three aspects of Body Soul and Spirit, of which make up our Human-BEing. This is Life's purpose and who we truly are. This harmonizing of our Self's is why we came here to fulfill Life's purpose for this human experience.

Now I know that this sounds simple and so easy that every single human being should already be doing this. In actual fact, it is surprisingly easy, and every single human being IS already doing this—or at least partially experiencing life, but very few are doing it deliberately, consciously or completely. If we were all doing this all of the time, then there simply wouldn't be any drama in our world at all? Indeed, the sad reality is that there are simply far too few beings in the world right now deliberately experiencing by _feeling_ with their Awareness. This is not to say that it is impossible for anyone to be consciously feeling or rather—deliberately experiencing their life situations fully.

In actual fact every single human being on the planet no matter race, creed or color has experienced some aspect of their life fully at some time or another. Very few are doing it most of the time and even far less are doing it all the time. It is not a secret method or ability that can only be taught by special sects and organizations. There are no 5 magic keys you need to acquire, to gain access to this supposedly exclusive club of successful CEO's and entrepreneurs, or the everyday Joe next door that seems to have such a great perspective of Life. He may not be a millionaire, but he is surely abundantly rich in feeling and experiencing his life fully. The natural consequence of someone that is feeling with their Awareness and experiencing their life with little resistance, is the appearance of very little drama in their life.

It isn't that I don't have drama in my life; it's that because I allow myself to feel it fully through Awareness, it discharges and doesn't get stuck, it doesn't create a loop of drama in the conscious Life of my Soul-self.

I think it's ironic that we can spend thousands and thousands of dollars on motivational self -development courses over years and years looking for this answer. Ironically, at the end of these spiritual salespeople's courses, we all get to the same place where all our answers come from. It is our own personal *ability to experience* our fear and do it anyway. I have found it actually has nothing to do with fear either—as fear is just another form of resistance. It's all just about *experiencing* through our Awareness. Once again, experiencing is feeling, without definitions, judgments or descriptions.

From this, the underlying principle for your experiential existence as a Human-BEing, is that the primary purpose for everything created in your world reality ... is simply to be fully experienced. This is a Divine Law created specifically for this reality of BEing Human and its evolution of consciousness back into its Spiritual Nature. Once any event of consciousness has been fully experienced, its primary purpose is fulfilled, and its creative energy will naturally and effortlessly dissolve or discharge back into the source that created it. That source is the consciousness that is ... YOU. Your Soul-self minds identity *drama* is just blind resistance to allowing this natural cycle to complete itself. Although this sounds negative or bad, it is actually a blessing for us, because it gives us an opportunity to use the Will of your Consciousness Soul. This is done to strengthen your Will and use it to direct and hold your Awareness on the experience. Every human experience, every resistance and attachment dynamic are all opportunities for you to use and strengthen your Will and of course, to bring Awareness into your human consciousness. This cycle of discharge from experiencing is on automatic, and if we just allow ourselves to experience all of life without definition, judgment or description, all resistant dramas would just dissipate like the fine droplets of a summer's misty rain being vaporized by the hot scorching summer sun. Experiencing resistance—dissolves resistance.

If I have come here to have a Human Experience, then............ why do I resist being human?

Life's purpose for this human experience is designed to offer the most comprehensive opportunities for spiritual evolvement and karmic integration available to consciousness within a physical reality. Why is most of the planet happy to stay small and hang out in a delusional fearful consciousness void of its true Spiritual nature? Why do we avoid the powerful experiences for change that Life presents us?

Now I know that this question of Life's purpose for our human experience can be a massive question to answer, especially if we come at it from a purely human intellectual approach. As we have seen above, Life's purpose for our human experience may well be the harmonizing of our Body Soul and Spirit, but I feel there is a purpose within that purpose. What goes hand in hand with that harmonizing purpose is also a higher purpose for the spiritualization of our human consciousness. I doubt I will be able to give you a complete answer to all of the aspects involved with this question of life purpose, let alone a comprehensive answer for Life's purpose for the human experience ... but that isn't my job ... it's yours. Find your answer for your Self. Your answer lies within the domain of your Spirit's domain, and it is free to access, but you need to embody your Spirit into your Human Soul-self to get it. I will however, do my best to support and challenge you to find it, but like I said earlier, enter into this deeper discussion without being too linear in your thinking and allow possibilities to *talk to you*. Allow your Self to get a sense of the things we are going to cover here, and let that sense permeate your consciousness. BE Aware throughout, of the many filters of pre-conceived ideas, definitions or judgments you may have and of which we all inevitably have. See if you can feel how these examples and concepts work in *your* everyday life. I would like to lead us into this as a continuation from what we have been discussing through the previous chapters already with respect to the relationship between our Human and BEing Self's. Firstly, let's get another deeper feel for what the human experience exactly is and hopefully clearer on where it happens.

Remember as we discussed earlier, our human experience is actually the regurgitating event created by our Consciousness that we call subjective/objective. So, let's just clarify for descriptive purposes, that our subjective experience is our dramatic human event created between our Body and Soul self's as they relate to the external world of form. However, this is not actually being *experienced* by either, yet created by both in conjunction with the external world. The daughters subjective experience was all her identities drama relating to the world around her and in particular, her mother. Her objective experience was her being conscious of herself in the event. These are all *doing* or *action* elements of react and response mechanisms within human consciousness. This is what we can term ... "The Human Experience", however ... the pure human Body and Soul coalition is not *experiencing* any of it. It was when the daughter was finally *experiencing* with her *observer* Awareness, that she could feel the experience that was actually happening behind the event her identities were creating.

Just take a moment right now and look at the human experience you are having in this moment, as you sit here. More than likely, you are probably "looking" for the first signs of an experience through emotions, reacts, stimulants etc. that may be going on in your body. This is your Sentient Soul at work sensing as your Consciousness Soul stimulates it/you to look. If you found some, then you may notice you then went into analyzing and rationalizing and even labelling what those emotions etc. are and what they feel like, as you have now become *conscious* of them through your Consciousness Soul. The analyzing and rationalizing is your Intellectual Soul at work. If you found them within your Body sensations, then your Body-self is at work manifesting the feelings etc. directed by your mind in the physical world, of what your Intellectual Soul mind has stimulated via its identities. Your Soul then passes all of this to the etheric Life-body, which in turn is how it gets to manifest out into the world reality again through the physical Body. From this observation, you may notice that all of this takes place within your Body and Soul, within your everyday Human-self, within seconds. As such, we could comfortably call this your subjective/objective human experience. It is without question full of everything you know to be human in every form of emotion, intellect, physicality and materiality etc.

Now take another moment while you sit there again, and this time, let your _Awareness_, gently move out from you in all directions. Not looking for anything, not trying to find anything, not describing defining or judging anything. Just get a sense, get a super-sense without descriptions or definitions of the space around you. Without describing these senses etc., simply notice the _differences_ between your body and the chair you are sitting in, the desk and the walls, the difference between the space you occupy and the space within the room. Allow your Awareness to _feel these differences_ as it passes through and touches each. Now recognize the _differences_ in these things around you, or as your Awareness touches them, and just get a _sense_ of the _difference_ between them, again … without any definitions, judgments or descriptions. This is an Aware sense of the differences without focusing on them. Continue to do this for a few seconds on five or so different things. Just get a _super-sense_, of the space you occupy within the space you are feeling differences in. Now recognize with your _Awareness_, what you are experiencing within your human-self, right now. See if you can feel how you are BE-ing … in this present moment. What is your state of BEing? Without looking for anything, sit with it for a minute or two and BE interested, in whatever you are feeling, without attaching or focusing on any one piece of it. Can you tell a difference between the human experience you previously had as opposed to this one? Just notice the difference without describing them. Did you notice any more details in your Aware experience compared to the human experience? I know that it is subtle, and your mind will want to discount it, simply because it is too vague, too subtle for the mind to grasp and of which it has no reference point … as yet. Never the less, it is there … there is a difference. You may have recognized that through the Awareness experience, you could also have a slight sense of the air around you and its influence of heat, cold, wind, etc., or the sounds or other subtler influences as it all added up to the experience you were having of that present moment and how you were BEing in that moment.

> _My TRUE experience at any time throughout my Earth-walk, is how I am BEing in any moment … not what I am doing, or what is happening to me._

As we have learned earlier, your human-self creates the events for your Spirit-BEing-Self to experience BEing human through. Your human event is the _doings_ of your Body and Soul self's creating all of the reactions and interactions within your human reality. Experiencing, by _feeling with your Awareness_, without any definitions, judgments or descriptions of what you are experiencing, is how you BE with it, it is the BEing-ness of all of your Body and Soul creations … as well as any and all external and internal influences that have an _effect_ on your BEing-Self. I know I seem repetitious about this human experience thing, but it is important to get the distinction between the human event and the Aware Spirit experience. For far too long we have been miss-lead by wondrous spiritual salesmen into all sorts self-development courses etc. professing all forms of enlightenment enticements, yet never venturing out of the human consciousness domain, let alone actually, truly experiencing the Human Spirit Nature or the Spirit of Self. I know, I too have travelled to my Spirit's remembrances, on many a deceptive path through the intellectualization of spirituality by modern day spiritual salespeople. I have also been seduced by their skillful rhetoric and promise of peace, stillness and *the life I deserve*.   At the end of ... *that long and winding road* ... at the point where Divine intervention slapped me with the insight that has led to this work here now, I got to experience that it is at the point of fully experiencing anything, that breakthrough and integration happen. Throughout all of the systems of supposedly self-empowerment or meditation techniques or consciousness exercises of tapping, twirling, dis-creating, standing on your head or cry like a banshee; that point of "AHH HAA!!!"; that point where you actually fully and completely experience something, is the shift point. This is the point of healing when it no longer has a hold or influence over you anymore. This "AHH HAA" point is not a point of learning something new—it is the point you just remembered something you already knew ... from a past Life where you had integrated that thing.

The primary purpose for everything created in my reality ... is to be experienced ... fully.

It is through Consciousness that we create this Human Reality. Any viewpoint of "I" comes from the singular separation by your Soul-self-consciousness from Divine Universal Consciousness.   Any viewpoint of "I AM", comes from the connected experiential nature of your Spirit, which has come here now into your Human-Soul Life to expand and evolve the Human Reality system. The deception is that we are here to evolve our Eternal Spirit-Self, or some call it our Authentic or True Self. Although our True or Authentic Self is already evolved and present in the *spiritual realm*, it does most definitely still learn and evolve from these human experience adventures into the physical realm of consciousness.   Its intended evolution however is not of Self or human, but of the whole Spiritual Realm. The even greater mission though, if you would, is for us to evolve the self ... specifically the Human-self and expand the Human Reality to a point of it being able to ground and integrate the Spirit in human form ... permanently. This is the stage of Spirit Man I mentioned earlier.

More accurately, is that your Spirit, once fully grounded in your human form, will be able to transform the physical human into a non-physical form again; one more suitable for permanent Spirit occupation. This is the full spiritualization of the human. This is moving our Human fully into the Spiritual Realm as an integral Creator "I AM" BEing ... in the Divine Collective. At our present point or level of consciousness however, this current Human Reality is unable to permanently sustain the Spirit in it. This is why, when all of the Masters throughout time have been granted Enlightenment by the Grace of the Divine ... they leave the Planet.

Self-Realization comes about through the final self-development and mastery of my "I Consciousness" within the Human-Soul.

Enlightenment is granted through the spiritualization of my Human via the Higher "I" Spirit Ego-Body ... after it has been embodied and mastered.

Enlightenment is not something attainable, or a goal that can be aimed for or even achieved ... it is "granted" when one *lives* in every moment in integrity to ones Highest Self, through non-resistance to the Human form of existence and its congruent experiences. Therefore, there is a saying that, "Life is the same after Enlightenment" and stays the same, because you were already in a state of non-resistance to Being Human before you were granted Enlightenment. Being Human will continue as it was before Enlightenment, just now you have married Consciousness to Awareness, and become truly *consciously aware*. Enlightenment is really the granting of an expansion of your Human-Soul with your Spirit's Awareness. This state of existence now bridges beyond the Human Reality to a full *experience* of the TRUE, spiritual non-definition and non-separation between the Spiritual and Human Realms. The granting really comes about through the grounding of your Spirit within your human, through the spiritualization of your human as an integral part of the whole of which we can then call ... the Human BEing. Awareness is a key piece to this evolutionary path we are all on right now, in THIS present time.

Awareness is the first true self-empowerment spiritual organ I am assimilating into my human-self.

Awareness is the first of the Spirit organs for us to integrate as an essential instrument, which will enable our human to BE Aware and become consciously experiential. This new state of existence for our human form will transmute our consciousness state of doing, into a TRULY Consciously Aware state of BEing. It is through your Spirit-Self's organ of Awareness that the astral-body of your Soul-self begins its spiritualization journey, allowing your whole human-self to become a fully functional *Consciously Experiential BEing*. Put simply, this means that you will no longer just be conscious of Life and your existence in it, randomly *experiencing* it through your Soul's unconscious intermittent allowance of your Spirit-Self's to enter your human. From this higher state, you will now be able to fully *experience* Life through your fully developed Human Consciousness impregnated with your Higher "I" Spirit-Self. Through this first mastery of human spiritualization, a solid foundation is set for the next development and integration of your Ego's Life-Spirit transformation of your existing etheric Life-body, into a spiritualized Life-Spirit Body. This spiritualized Life-Body will enable us to consciously tap into Spiritual Creator Life Forces from the spiritual realm. These forces are capable of transforming our etheric field that sustains our present physical form, into a force capable of creating and manifesting instantly and deliberately in the physical world through simple word. This spiritualized Life-Body or Life-Spirit, is the link for how your

Spirit will be able to be fully <u>infused</u> into human consciousness. Just as consciousness creates through your physical body into your physical world through your etheric Life-Body, this new spiritualized Life-Body resulting from the infusion of your Life-Spirit into your existing etheric, makes it possible for your Spirit to manifest directly into your physical world via your Physical Body. From there, the foundation is set for your Spirit-Man's development into a fully creator BEing, that will ultimately transform and change forever your human form, to never again be materially physical in nature. At this point, this Human-Spirit-Man will be able to change the structure of the environmental BEing that is our Planet, because our present environment will no longer be suitable for this Human-Spirit to exist in. To keep things in perspective however, here now in this present moment of our evolution, we are here, to bring ... to our Human ... to give our human the ability to TRULY *experience* Life as an "I AM", fully immersed consciously and experientially not just in human creation, but in Divine Creation ... period.

When the Masters were granted Enlightenment, they didn't say deny your human mind or the human form, they simply said to understand that it is not your True and Highest Spirit Nature. For them, at that point, this planetary human reality was unsustainable for them to stay here. For us, at this point, we are here to be the <u>first</u>, of future man, to be able to stay and exist as a Self-Realized Consciously Aware Human form, in the New Earth of an Enlightened Human Reality. Although our planet BEing is still evolving also, it is, already capable –thanks to the Christ BEing's sacrifices as I mentioned earlier—of sustaining this higher level of spiritual existence for us to stay here as an Aware Consciousness. None of this however, can happen without your contribution and participation. It is through <u>*your*</u> embracing of the *subjective/objective experiences* of your Human-self *without resistance* to it, that allows you to apply your Higher Spiritual Virtues in it. Awareness is not the end game nor a WOW moment, it is simply a Higher attribute of your Spirit that allows your Spirit, to experience the fullness of this Human Reality Paradigm ... and ultimately beyond it.

It is the simple application of THIS one attribute of Awareness, that is the anchor for ALL the other Virtues that will facilitate the final expansion of my individual consciousness, along with our beloved Collective Human Reality.

We are at an exciting time right now, because the Human Reality is at the doorway to being able to ground the Spirit ... your Spirit ... in this Human Reality ... for all future. The Being that is our Mother Earth, has already altered its frequency via the Mystery of Golgotha, to facilitate this grounding. It is our time now to evolve it all further by the application of our Spirit's higher virtuous attributes into the Collective Human Reality via ALL of us. This is made possible by our ancestors who have come before us and laid the path for all of us that are here now ... and those still to come. Applying Higher Virtues and attributes into *every* present moment human experience, is much like downloading new software into the Collective Human reality, via our personal input server that each of us are, as humans ... BE-ing. It doesn't happen by a single application, but by continuous applications throughout your whole life, that become integrated as your complete Human existence. Embodying these virtues needs to become a natural and effortless application beyond *thought intended action*. It is our Mother Earth that "manifest" the spiritual fabric of our Human Reality; from which we all exist in. ALL of this is created by Divine Spirit for *your* Human Consciousness to grow and evolve back into the Spiritual Realm. This includes all aspects of the Body/Soul co-creation that is your individual Human-self and personality. There is a paradoxical truth stated by many of the Masters who have come before us, that is ... *your human form is an illusion to be realized and released from.* Ironically however, it is also real. While we are here, it is the form of your existence here as a Human; through which is the ONLY way that we can ground Spirit in this Human Reality and apply *our* Spirit's Higher Virtues into it. The experience of being human—is a path of evolvement that leads you to human-self-realization of the *non-human* aspect of the true Spirit Nature of your BEing-Self.

It is ONLY by embracing my human-ness, that I can embody my Spirit, reuniting ALL with the Divine Space that creates and connects all things.

The human consciousness subjective *doing-ness* path is designed for us all to evolve our "I Conscious" human. The Divine intention for creating this Earth plane, is to prepare and develop your consciousness to make it capable of integrating the higher states of Spirit-BEing, the higher *virtuous* states of Spirit, into our Soul Consciousness. This is done through the experiences our human frailties provide for us. Some spiritual teachings hold the viewpoint, that we do this in order to become one again with The Creator, The Universe, Source, God, Brahma, The Divine, The Supernatural Creator, Allah, Yahweh, Vishnu or whatever other name may have been used to describe the indescribable Creation of Existence. This indescribable power is the fabric of existence itself and is what I simply call the *Divine Space that creates and connects everything.* It is Life ... the space and energetic fabric onto which anything and everything manifest in any dimension. This Life-force has a Divine Orchestration to it that brings together all of the elements. These elemental BEing's if you will, bring together whatever is necessary to manifest what we need for the humans here now creating this human-experience, so we may be able to have the opportunities to download our Spirits virtues into our Human-self. This Divine Orchestration is motivated and energized from Life's higher *purpose* for our Human experience.

What has been revealed to me through my Conscious Bodywork is a pattern, of life becoming complex when we resist the experiences that Life is flowing to us. When this happens, this Divinely Orchestrated stream of Life Force is interrupted and restricted, resulting in bad health, chronic body conditions, failures of relationships and business, etc. etc. These human *resistant complexities* are created from the collection of your beliefs, judgments, choices and decisions that you make, via your Intellectual Soul creation of identities for you to be human through.

We have been deeply miss-lead and disempowered to believe that these identities and their structures of beliefs, judgments etc. are actually elements of our ego and need to be got rid of. They are in fact, creations of Consciousness, your consciousness, designed to manifest human consciousness events, here in your human reality, for your Spirit to experience. The uniqueness of your identities are designed to give YOU the appropriate life experience opportunities for what your Spirit Nature intended to integrate for this Life-Walk. The subsequent Life Purpose for these opportunities of experiences … is to infuse your specific human with an appropriate virtue specific to that experience. It is these embodied virtues that can then *transform* your gross matter conscious human, into a virtuous Human BE-ing of Spirit. This is how you will transform your identities etc., not by trying to get rid of them. That is just another form of resistance.

These same beliefs, judgments and decisions however, are also the filters that block and limit the amount of Life Force entering your being in your everyday lives. Even perceived "bad" influences, if seen through their Spiritual Nature with Awareness, are creating highly advantageous experiences for you to not just learn from, but to remember and bring into play in the here and now, the fruits you have gained from your previous lives. These human-experience moments bring with them even greater opportunities to download YOUR Spirit's virtues into your human-self. You evolve by learning yes, but more correctly, by gaining the fruits of what you learn, the fruits of which are these new attributes and virtues previously acquired … and then *applying* them into your present-day lives. When we take up the opportunities presented to us, to embody these virtues through the almost infinite array of experiences offered from Being Human, we naturally and effortlessly expand our consciousness. By doing this, we make it more capable to embody a greater parameter of that virtue the next time another opportunity presents its self. Therefore, I believe we are all one Human Family, without definitions and separations of culture, country or creed. Even our identities have a common core to them, we just get to personalize them with our own belief structures etc., so they serve our higher individual need for our very own unique and particular experiences. Your identities have a very specific function with respect to Life's purpose for your human experience. Let's look at identities for a moment.

Identities are an essential and an intrinsic creation of my Intellectual Soul.

Their first basic function is to provide you with different human events of emotional react and response. This then creates certain interactions with other humans or the environment; all ending in a subjective human event for your Spirit-Self to experience. Prior to us coming here for each life, we choose our human form and each and every one of us have a common blueprint and cache of identities to choose from, that go with this human form. These are all optimal for this particular stage of human consciousness evolution at this point in time. They are also uniquely designed relative to the level of *your* particular Soul's Consciousness and the karmic necessities of your Spirit True Self … for *your* present life time.

A sample of what identities are, is our victim and victimizer identities, which I'm sure we have all more than likely had an experience of … more than once no doubt. In actual fact, these are really just opposite ends of the one Avoidance Identity, as they work in unison together flipping from one to the other and back again whenever necessary to generally *avoid* ownership. Our victim identity side will create the human circumstances of being powerless to change, of feeling attacked and unimportant or devalued. It can create a feeling within the Soul, of everyone and everything being against it and never being able to change anything. It will construct all the relative and effective beliefs necessary to stimulate within your Physical and etheric Life bodies the appropriate sensations to muster *feelings* ... of shame, doubt, fear, dis-empowerment etc. Beliefs are *not* the creators of your experiences, as some would have you believe ... they are the creators of your human events.

Beliefs are merely the way my Intellectual Soul creates sensations within my etheric Life-Body, which then stimulate sequences of emotions, judgments etc. within my physical body; from which then bring together actions resulting in human events coming together.

Beliefs don't create experiences ... they create *conscious* human events ... that you, your Spirit-Self ... can then experience. As we covered earlier, the true *observer experience* is how you BE, within that event. Can you see for example, when your victim creates the event of being powerless, that it has as a motivating belief, "I am powerless", but the belief is not creating the *experience* of powerless-ness, it is stimulating <u>actions</u> within both your etheric-Life and Physical bodies. These then manifest in your *conscious physical world* as NOT speaking up or NOT defending yourself. The actions of backing down, of shutting up etc., etc., are the human event, while the whole time your actual *experience*; how you are actually BEing within this event is more of being internally frozen, immobilized and even in the deepest depths of *avoidance* of all feeling, willing or thinking. This is an opportunity for the *experience of avoidance,* to be manifest through the physical world *events* of being a victim, through beliefs, judgments emotions actions etc. etc., of which your true experiential Spirit-Self is truly experiencing. Do you get the picture? Can you feel these elements in you? Can you see how at some stage throughout your life you have deeply experienced this victim identity play out its role for you ... as you? No doubt, if you are feeling with your Awareness and honest with your Self, there have, no doubt been more than one event. Can you feel now, how you may have in that moment, actually been *avoiding*? This is the subtlety of the <u>TRUE</u> experience being offered by your *conscious human events*. This is how, from the countless spiritual salespeople around right now, we are being deceived to believe that our emotional and dramatic human events are our true experiences ... and we need to get rid of them. Of course, this is just more resistance loaded up on the event again. They deceive you with this, because they profess to have the solution, the answers, the techniques, the meditation practices and the five secret keys etc. etc., to freeing you from this drama filled life that is continually regurgitating its self. You pay them to keep you disempowered and reliant on them for the answers, rather than empowering you with *your own ability* of Awareness, to access the truth of your TRUE spiritual experience. There is no end to these streams of human events being created throughout your whole life time here now, but there is most definitely a continuing growth and strength in your ability to experience them and discharge them ... when you live in

Awareness. The true healing element that comes through living with in your Awareness, is that you no longer block life's creationist force from flowing through you, from which your Body Soul and Spirit is realigned and enlivened.

My Awareness is the only true power for healing ... and it is already naturally intrinsic in my Spirit's Ego BEing-Self.

Awareness is the preventative medicine of my Spirit, for my Body & Soul disharmonies.

The victimizer is equally effective; as is ALL of our identities, in their creation of human events. The victimizer will kick in generally after the victim, or even during, depending on your Intellectual Soul's expertise in avoidance and ... lack of Awareness. This is the one that my Facebook opponent was operating through during our crusade together. The victimizer will attack and invalidate its opponents, or rather, what it perceives as an opponent, for the victimizer is also an expert judgmental individual. It will calculate its response before its opponent has even finished what it is saying. The victimizer is a defensive and blaming individual adept in avoidance of any ownership or responsibility. It is a great one to use when we don't want to accept responsibility for what we are creating and deflect attention to someone else to take the blame or responsibility. You see, it's another facet of avoidance again. It has some extremely effective traits for very subtle and covert forms of emotional abuse etc. as well. It is also a good one for dis-empowering another and divert attention off your lies and pretenses. This is the identity responsible for most of our emotional abuse and passive aggressive behaviors etc. This Avoidance identity can flip from victim to victimizer in nano-seconds. It does take a good level of Awareness to catch these two guys at play, as they effectively *avoid* all sorts of maladies of ownership, by flipping from one to the other. Can you feel how the flipping from one end to the other of this Avoidance Identity through its Victim and Victimizer poles ... effectively avoids the Soul being seen? The Soul is avoiding being seen and accountable.

Another identity example is our Powerless Identity. This one is also a dual sided identity like the avoidance one. On one end, it is control. On the other end, it is chaos. The control side has a need to manipulate others to get its own way. Whether it is right or wrong, it really doesn't matter, except what it chooses to believe. This one is bossy, is disconnected and un-compassionate. Its covert side can be a form of passive aggressive, but it is more inclined to be dismissive, arrogant and ignorant toward others. This one has the attribute of the perfectionist, that identity that nothing is ever as good as when one does it their self. This is a fantastic one for simply not feeling, not acknowledging self. This one is the fanatic on the attachment end of the Powerless Identity. The irony of this identity is that it never actually achieves control, it never has true power. The control side needs to deceive itself that it is in control, by trying to control everything and everyone around it, everything it looks at. Can you see how this control end is an attachment side of powerless?

The other side of the powerless identity is the chaos end. This side creates confusion, disorder, frantic indecision, uncertainty, indecisiveness and unable to focus on one thing or finish another. Do you notice here that all of these attributes have a resistance stimulation to them? This is the resistance end of the Powerless Identity. This chaos end has beliefs like "I can't", "I can't find what I need" and "nothing fulfills me". These forms of beliefs create actions of flipping from one thing to another, of not finishing, of never feeling complete. Hands up who knows what chaos feels like in your life. Can you feel the powerless-ness of chaos? At first appearance, it seems a little victim, but chaos is not victim avoidance, but proactive chasing its tail from one crazy unfinished experience to another. Chaos isn't motionless or disempowered by its environment etc. as is the victim identity, it is hyper active, creating the appearance of doing a lot, but completing nothing. It is chasing a perception of power, but with no intention of catching it.

Resistance and attachment are the opposite sides of every identity, from which all conflict arises from.

From this you may see how the Powerless Identity creates the human events of not creating or finishing anything we participate in, as it flips from one side to the other, from chaos to control ... and back again. From resistance to attachment ... and back again. If you feel with your Awareness the Powerless Identity within you; and trust me, we ALL have one, you can feel the resistance and attachment sides to it, as they play out of these control and chaos elements. The dynamic human life events we are all involved in all stem from the storehouse of identities we all have, which are lying dormant within the Intellectual Soul component of our Soul-self. These identities are conscious, they are conscious of their self and their reactions to and separate from the environment around them and the environment that impresses on them. This is what makes them appear so true as your nature, but although they are in fact true of the nature of your *human* for this life, they are not true of the spiritual nature of your eternal true Spirit-BEing-Self. Every identity has a suitcase of <u>specific</u> beliefs it operates from and through. It is the beliefs that make up the *individuality* of the same core identities we all bring with us into this present human lifetime. When we come in contact with another identity of one of our human co-inhabitants on this third rock from the sun, it is the identities belief structure that stimulates the actions we call triggers, through our human Body and Soul creation.

Once again, my identities are not really aspects of my true spiritual nature, but creations of consciousness, specifically my Intellectual Soul component of my Soul-self and are necessary tools through which my human events are made possible for this life I am living.

The environment for deep diving into identities is in a workshop. There is not enough space between these pages to cover identities successfully. It is best to discover the specific identities you have created for your unique Life Walk here through meditation yourself. I recommend you use identities as a topic for the meditation style I give in the Living Exercises chapter at the end of this book. I must however give a special mention here for the Spiritual Identity. This identity "looks" so pure and righteous, but in fact is extremely contradictory and covertly judgmental. Of ALL our identities, it is the greatest pretender and deceiver. The Spiritual Identity is almost the final frontier, the last hurdle, the greatest block and covert "self-deception" personality that prevents us from TRULY "experiencing" the realness of our true BEing-Self, of our Spirit manifesting through our Human-ness. It is the Spiritual Identity that prevents us from being the true and real expression of our Authentic Human Being-ness. If you are not identified as your Spiritual Identity, then you will embrace this statement as truth. If this truth is challenging (which is my intention) then it, the Spiritual Identity you are covertly identified as ... will react. The density and conviction of your identification AS your Spiritual Identity, will determine the intensity and severity of which your identity will respond with attack, invalidation and accusation to defend its self. This identity can become extremely indignant when its self-important deceptions are exposed to the light of true Awareness. This is the entrenched identity of many of the common spiritual salespeople we see throughout our western spiritual community in these times. Oh, and by the way, this identity is non-denominational.

Of course, I to have my own Spiritual Identity and of course it judges ... just the same as yours may be doing now. I am INTIMATELY Aware of my identity and when I have "completely" integrated it you probably won't hear from me again. The whole point of this human existence is to share, learn and grow through the reflections of our Self through others in the world. This happens for us to become so Self-Aware, that there is no longer _resistance_ to experiencing ANYTHING ... especially what others reflect of me. Imagine the infinite potential of having NO resistance to experiencing ANYTHING. It is this non-resistance to Life's experiences that will bring in a new way of BEING Human. From this, a new Human Being-ness will then exist for us all and all who come after us.

I have a saying that, "True freedom is the willingness to experience ANYTHING ... and at which time, I will no longer have to experience everything".

If you are watchful you can see examples of human identities all around you. We are all too quick however to pass them off as personality traits and characteristic's, but with a little Awareness, we can easily _feel the difference_ between our identities and the truly personal traits of our "I Consciousness" Soul-Self. I have even had a number of clients get totally spooked, when they experienced the difference between their True BEing-Self and their identities. From the wealthy patron sitting at the table beside you, who asserts his importance through his control identity by making the waitress wrong about the state of his soup; to the defiance of your teenage daughter through her victim identity demanding you have no idea what she is feeling. From her Soul-mind-self viewpoint, she probably has no idea of what she is really *feeling* either, because *consciousness simply can't feel*. It only creates *feelings*, because at this point, it is only conscious. Coincidentally, through Rudolph Steiner's work in the book "Biography"; in which he clearly shows the development activation stages of all of our Bodies we are discussing here: that it is only at the age of twenty-one to twenty-eight that our Higher "I" Ego Body is activated and developed to work with. So, our teenagers really don't have any real or true *observer experience* of what they are feeling. This is partly why it is such a conflicting age period in our development.

The Intellectual Soul-self mind is incredibly adept at creating *feelings* via the brain that manifest as real stimulants of the physical body and the space around the physical body; which is the etheric Life-Body. The sensations in the space that seems to be around or outside of the body are actually being manifested in this Life-body via the brain. This is why they appear to be coming from our BEing-Self, but in fact, they are just *feelings* created by our physical and etheric forces. This is also why we perceive our feelings as being so personal, so intimately individual and separate to anyone else's feelings. Again, they *are*, personal to the dense human-consciousness you are right now, but it is your human personality, not the TRUE Spirit Nature of your Higher "I" BEing-Self, that which is truly experiencing this human life.

> *With Awareness training, I am able to clearly distinguish the difference between my consciousness created "feelings" ... and the <u>results from the</u> ability of my BEing-Self to "experientially feel".*

The Intellectual Soul-self is so masterful at creating these effects that, because it can't feel yet, it logically fools itself into believing the *feelings* are real experiences. This again; to give consciousness the ability to truly *experientially* feel, is another aspect of Life's purpose for our human experience. The Souls identities will defend, even to the death, those *feelings of beliefs* it believes to be of itself. Many wars since the beginning of the Human Consciousness Experience are the result of these *mind generated feelings of identities*. Ironically, when the mind shifts its attention to something else or gets a good problem to solve, the feelings go away. From this simple fact, we can see that the *feelings* we have are not exactly real, although they seem very real to the identity that is creating them in that moment. If you are identified AS your identities ... then you will take those *feelings* created by your identity as real, and thus be highly attached to them. The *feelings* created by that identity are a necessary part of that particular identity and together with the Body-self is how they bring about the events your Spirit-BEing-Self experiences. If you don't have *feelings* of abandonment, you can't <u>create the event</u> of being ignored, to experience being abandoned and dependent on someone else. If you don't have feelings of rejection, you won't create the event of being alone, for you to experience separation.

My identities provide me with endless opportunities for countless forms of experiences through an almost infinite range of consciousness interactions between each other ... and my environment.

I once did an embodying experience exercise called "belief inventory", on my Unworthy Identity, with the topic of money. What was revealed to me was a cache of eighty-seven beliefs, ninety percent of them being perceived as limiting. Feeling with Awareness and embodying ALL of these beliefs together revealed the experience of this Unworthy Identity and how it was/is creating in my life. My Unworthy Identity still exists, and it will till I leave this planet, but now that I have intimately experienced it fully and ... its belief structure, it no longer has a debilitating effect on me. When it shows up now—because of my Awareness, I am able to *FEEL* it immediately. Through this Aware feeling ability, my Unworthy Identity is no longer a limitation to me, but is now an asset, a red flag for me, a sign for me to BE something else in that moment, to be more virtuous and embody a specific virtue appropriate for that present moment experience I am having there and now. You see, with Awareness, my "Unworthy Identity" to this day, still gives me opportunities to embody more and more virtue in my Human-self. Life is this continuous flow of Divinely orchestrated events that brings us together with others, from whom I am able to bring forth the appropriate identity within me to manifest exactly the right experience. This provides the perfect opportunity for my Spirit-Self to download an appropriate virtue into my human-self. As personalized individual consciousness, we can't possibly set up or orchestrate the necessary connections and interactions to bring about the right person at the right time, with just the right identity needed to trigger my own specific identity, to create the perfect experience I need to have ... in that moment. There is a Divine Orchestration of spiritual beings bringing all of these elements together for us ... in every moment of our existence here. In a nutshell, we could almost stop right here and say that this, is Life's purpose for our human experience—to fully experience what life serves us. But wait ... again ... there's more.

Life's primary purpose is to impregnate my human-self with Awareness, so it may embody the higher virtues of my Spirit-Self.

The further purpose for my Human to become virtuous, is to be spiritualized and co-exist experientially in both the Human and Spiritual Realms.

Consciousness creates my human life events and circumstances and attracts other players for me to experience things, so I can learn, embody more virtues and evolve. How could you experience being a victim if you didn't wear the coat/identity of victim along with all of its beliefs and believe that everyone is out to get you and you can't defend yourself and you're powerless to change anything and all the other necessary beliefs and judgments that make up a victim identity. How could you learn to stand up for yourself and NOT be a victim if you have never been a victim? How can you learn to be self-empowered if you've never been dis-empowered? How can you learn to let go of control if you have never needed to be in control?

My identities are my friends and when I <u>don't</u> resist the lessons and opportunities they provide me; the experience flows through me effortlessly and I am energized and rejuvenated by Life. When I <u>resist</u> experiencing my lessons and opportunities, Life resists back and creates an endless loop of suffering and discouragement until life's intended experiences for me are fully experienced and ideally …. I have consciously embodied another virtue. Once it is fully experienced, Life's creative energy naturally returns back to consciousness…effortlessly.

Isn't it ironic we have never been taught how to *experience* something…until now?

I feel the Soul is the student to the lessons through my human-ness. Life is the teacher and Love is my Spirit-Self's ability to learn.

When I was young, I had a fear of heights that would make my belly spin and turn in a knot. My feet would tingle, and my limbs would feel like they were going to explode. One day in Australia, on a trip to the Blue Mountains when I was not so young anymore, I was walking along a path that led out to the outermost edge of the cliff face. The valley floor was some 1,000 feet or so of sheer drop below, which I had no idea about until I walked around the bend in the path and was overwhelmingly confronted with the enormity of its grandeur.

I was fine looking ahead at the awe-inspiring view of the far-reaching range some 20 miles on the other side of the valley, but when I came to the edge and looked down on the valley floor below, fear overwhelmed me. My *mind created feeling* was so strong from the perceived danger of falling, that my bodies limbs froze, and I literally fell to the ground. Although I was safely on solid ground a good 8 feet from the edge, my minds drama of the possibility of falling was creating all the appropriate body sensations and feelings to immobilize the entire body. My Intellectual Souls idebtity drama was so intense and energized that it had convinced the body that it was being pushed to the edge. My body was so convinced from this belief of the mind that it manifested the appropriate sensations of falling to support the identities drama. My Souls drama was so strong that my body collapsed to the ground. This is an example of the dynamic effect of the Intellectual Soul's effect on the physical body.

By *resisting* feeling the fear, I increased the intensity of my Soul's drama so much, that I literally had to crawl on the ground to back away from the edge, to get out of sight of the canyon floor below. I was embarrassed of course and tried not to show my fear to my girlfriend of that time. I failed miserably in that attempt. I remember being surprised by this reaction, considering I was still playing Rugby and surfing so much, where danger was common, yet fear had very little power over me. I would later realize that this was my experience of the power of resistance and how resistance actually empowers the thing I am resisting, rather than dis-empowering it.

By trying to not feel the fear, by __resisting__ the experience, I increased its intensity and felt unable to change.

The powerful influence of my Soul's drama became obvious when my partner, who was with me at the time, began to get scared also as she witnessed my debilitating sensations. My fear had become palpable to her, changing the expression on her face from concern to terror. Although she wasn't fearful of the edge or height we were at, she was more fearful for me and what I might do. She was now fearful of what might happen to me from my weakened state. As we slowly moved back up the path and headed toward the top again, she would keep looking behind at me to see that I was still coming and OK. Her fear, of my fear of falling—her Souls mind drama of the possible danger I was in—had now made her experience of this awe-inspiring environment we were in, uncomfortable and now, she too was disconnected from it. Our Souls drama doesn't just replicate in our own mind ... but will also infect the minds of others.

Fear is the minds drama, that's like a door that stops your power to change from entering. With the door firmly shut, all the energy creating the fear swirls inside the mind and feeds the virus as it replicates throughout the whole body. As long as I kept looking and thinking about what could go wrong while I was standing on that path a thousand feet above the valley floor below, my drama increased, and my body became weaker and weaker. I became powerless to change.

The debilitating effect of resistance in my story above, shows how powerfully these forces manifest in our world through our body. As we explored earlier, resistance and its corresponding attachment, are the opposite sides of our identities. If we look at these opposites of resistance and attachment as forces, then we can start to see where the space between these opposite forces is where *all conflict* within our human-self originates from.

If I am resisting one thing ... then I will always be attached to something else.

If I am resisting being self-sufficient, then I am also attached to having someone else provide for me. If I am resisting taking ownership for my life, then I will be attached to having other people take responsibility for my actions and life. When you explore with your Awareness and feel into the identities that live within you, you can feel the conflict that each and every one of them harbors within their dynamic nature of resistance and attachment. Without Awareness of our identities, we exist in a constant state of subtle and covert suffering, caused by ironically, these mindless creators of our human events. You see, although our identities are created within our Soul-self mind, they are their self, mindless. They exist and operate through specific belief structures unique to each specific identity. These belief structures are what trigger the human actions that bring about our human events. Identities are the same for each of us when we "take them off the spiritual rack" so to speak, as we ready to come here for this specific lifetime, i.e. Victim, Control Powerless etc. You design your identities with individualized belief structures to react and respond to external and internal stimuli, within *your* own specific parameter of experience for *your* life here. These belief parameters are determined by a much higher spiritual intention for your present life than what your Human-self can create. They are however, structured specifically to support the evolution of your individual consciousness and its karmic requirements ... for this life-Walk. Identities are NOT self-determining entities of your Soul's human-self, but automaton elements of your consciousness. This is why, when we are blindly identified as our identities, through the reacts etc. of our identities, we are blind and powerless to the triggers that the influences our outer world places upon us. Add to this, being lost to the influences of our *inner* indoctrinations of how things must be, and should be etc., and you may see where our mastery of BEing human is sadly and naturally inhibited through a *lack of Awareness* of our identities.

So, my identities are an automaton design of consciousness, of my consciousness, to bring about the human events I call subjective/objective experiential events.

My identities are NOT ... my True Self ... but their collective could be termed my human personality for this Life-Walk.

If this is the case, then how do we become free of our identities and their covert and constant influence of drama? What happens to them within the context of evolution, within the evolution of human consciousness? Do our identities evolve also?

It is really superfluous to be concerned about our identity's evolution, because it is the evolution of the consciousness Soul-self as a whole that is important, not any individual part of it alone. At this point in our evolution, Mastery and development of consciousness is automatically facilitated by the *Aware* experience of the *dynamic* between the parts of consciousness. Automatic Mastery of these dynamics is what comes about through simply *experiencing with our Awareness*, the identities and their *dynamic forces* that bring about our human events. Through Aware experience of our identities, we bring them into the light of our Awareness, we bring them into our Spirit-Self, where they can no longer covertly or sub-consciously affect us. Understand that the creation of our identities came about as a natural development of the density of our Intellectual "I Consciousness". As we spiritualize our Soul, as we spiritualize "I Consciousness", it will become less dense and more fluidly pliable then it is now. As this happens, and we move more into a complete experiential state of an "I AM ... Consciously Aware BEing", then we will no longer need the dense individual identities to interact with and participate in Life as a separate "I Consciousness" entity. It is our identities that help create the separation element of our "I Consciousness" from our "I AM ... Spiritual BEing". When you explore identities experientially with Awareness and not just analyze the concept of them intellectually, you will notice that they are the elements of consciousness that are most separate from their external environment. This separation is a great assist for BEing an "I" in this present reality, but it is also a great inhibitor of our Higher "I" Spirit's embodiment in our human-self.

Right here now, in this present time of my human evolution, spiritualizing my human comes about through infusing the "I" Consciousness of my Soul with Spirit, by embodying the higher virtues of my Spirit-BEing-Self into this Soul Consciousness.

It is through experiencing with my Spirit-Self's Awareness that I am able to achieve this here and now.

Life's purpose for our human experience … is to spiritualize the Body and Soul Consciousness of our human-self, by embodying the higher virtues of the Spiritual Realm into it. Each time we simply BE … the virtue of compassion or forgiveness or humility or courage or understanding or empathy or any of the other higher virtuous states of Spirit, we change the frequency of our human consciousness, of our Soul … directly. This embodiment however, can only be effective if we BE the virtue … without any attachments or resistances to it, or for it to do anything or change anything.

To BE the virtue … is to simply exists … AS that virtue.

If we can understand that our Soul's consciousness is not yet developed sufficiently to be able to house and ground the Spirit into it entirely and permanently, then we can see how we are unable as yet, to also be able to download the <u>full parameter</u> of any higher virtue into our present consciousness completely, in one single download. It is through the continual and consistent downloading of virtues as I described above into our Soul's consciousness, that we gradually, expand and strengthen our Soul's capability to house more and more of any virtue. Gradually, the more times you grab Life's human event opportunities to experience fully and then embody the appropriate virtue that specific experience demands, you make your Human-Self more virtuous. EVERY Awareness experience derived from any human event … is an opportunity for a very specific virtue, relative to that specific human event, to be downloaded into your human-self's consciousness. EVERY time you download a virtue, your consciousness expands and becomes more capable of an even greater amount of virtue to be embodied into your Soul's consciousness next time. This potential to BE come a more virtuous human, is available *every* time Life orchestrates another event opportunity for you to experience. Piece by piece, experience by experience, one virtue at a time, gradually a virtuous state increases within your human-self until ultimately, your human-self is capable of housing your Spirit-Self completely, harmoniously and permanently in your new human reality. The <u>ONLY,</u> requirement of you to make this happen in your life is … to live in Awareness.

Life's purpose for the human experience reality ... is to spiritualize the human-self, through the experiential opportunities that Life itself, is giving me in every human event brought about through the identities of my consciousness.

Now you may be going "out of your mind" right now thinking this concept is beyond your reach in this present chaos reality we all live in right now. Let me reassure you unequivocally *and* experientially ... it is <u>FAR</u> easier, simpler and achievable than your mind may ever want to believe.

Life supports me to embody my Spirit.

Since the Mystery of Golgotha, the environment, the spiritual fabric, upon which our human reality manifests and is completely reliant; has changed and is continuously changing to facilitate the spiritual embodiment of our human-self. We are at the peak of this spiritual intelligence development along its densifying evolutionary journey, which has brought us into our current and densest form of "I Consciousness" we have ever been right now. Without the infusion of our Spirit Nature at this time, into this extraordinarily intelligent consciousness, we will continue to densify pass the point of no return, becoming more and more materialistic in our existence. Unfortunately, some of us may have seemingly already passed this point. If you can see selfish abuse and disconnect due to egoistic materialism around you in our world relationships right now, both personal and environmental, then ask your Self how much worse it could get? If humanity continues to push out the <u>true</u> Spirit-Self of its BEing and densify even further into materialistic greed and self-satisfaction, then it will miss the turning point, the sign posts to an alternate path to its true Spirit Nature. It is your Spirit's embodiment—and <u>ONLY</u> through your Spirit's embodiment, that will reconnect your human-self back to the truly loving spiritual realm from whence your Spirit Nature came. No "spiritual salesperson" can facilitate this for you or give you the tools, exercises or technology that will <u>do</u> it for you or ... "get you there". Our evolution has brought us to exactly this point in the greater Cosmic creation we all exist in right now ... for a purpose. That purpose is ... now that we have become a <u>new</u>, individually independent "I Consciousness" Cosmic species if you will; as a now Self-determined individual "I" consciousness ... it is time to spiritualize <u>It-Self</u>. This is *your* <u>responsibility</u> ... here and now—because we, as a humanity, have ALL come of age. The in-definable number of benevolent spiritual BE-ing's that have been together with us throughout the millennium of this evolutionary journey; who have been assisting and developing our "I Consciousness" state from its *formless* beginnings to its present-day physical *form* and who have been with us all along ... have already stepped back. They do this to allow us to take charge of our own spiritual evolution back to the Brotherhood of the spiritual realm, as a fully experientially integrated and harmonized individual "I AM" BE-ing of spiritual light.

They are there waiting, to welcome us back into the fold, not with trumpets blaring and banners waving, or any of our current small ego mind created forms of "WOW !!" exaltations and aggrandizements. They will be there for sure, but with a simple expression of the most expansive Love and Gratitude, of which is _FAR_ beyond anything you may think you have already experienced through your present state of consciousness.

Their Love will be for _your_ successful achievement of transforming your human-self into a truly Human-Spirit-BE-ing existing as Love, free of all lower influences that destroy, inhibit and diminish Life. To BE a BE-ing in full experiential Awareness of one's co-creating relationship with The Divine Principle.

Their Gratitude will be for the massive expansion of the Spiritual Realm, of which will be a direct result of _your_ successful participation and contribution into the full transformation of your dense human through its spiritualization. Again, the benefits to the Spiritual Realm from the spiritualization of our human-self, is beyond ANYTHING your present extraordinarily intelligent <u>mind</u> is capable of comprehending.

So hopefully, you are little more <u>_out of your mind_</u> right now and less identified as your identities, but still appreciative for the role they play in _your_ journey along Life's purpose for the human experience; this journey toward the spiritualization of your human. Having insight and knowledge of these principles and dynamics of consciousness is great, but the actual living of these with Awareness in your everyday life, is what will free you from their subtle and debilitating influences. Let's move on now to see how you can apply this more extensive knowledge and wisdoms of the many components of your conscious existence right now. To be able to live these principles in a way that enables you to deliberately spiritualize your human ... without your minds dramas, nor alienating it from the rest of the world, is the result I am striving to for you. Through the next chapter we will explore how simple it is to accelerate this journey to spiritual embodiment and free you in this lifetime, to free you from your lower human nature influences, through simple Awareness of your Higher Spirit Nature.

Are you out of your mind ... yet?

Have you freed your Human-self to fully experience its Spirit-Nature ...yet?

Chapter 7

Ho'oponopono for the World

In 2009, I did another of my Hawaiian Bodywork trainings with my Kahuna, Kai Po Kaneakua, in the Hawaiian Islands, but this time it was to the island of Molokai. This trip and training was different to the rest, because Molokai, being the island of the Kahuna's, was where *my* Kahuna grew up and where most of his Kahuna training happened. In his time on Molokai, he was fortunate to be trained by no less than eight different Kahuna; which makes him a rather gifted student of any time. In true tradition of Kahuna training, you don't choose the Kahuna you wish to train with, as often happens now days, but rather, the Kahuna would pick the suitable student. This system of training, which goes back thousands of years, ensured that only the best equipped student was chosen; one capable of taking in the immense knowledge and wisdoms the Kahuna had to share. Most important however, was that the integrity of those wisdoms would be best maintained by the choosing of such a worthy student. This form of acceptance ensured the truth of the practices and traditions would not be diluted or destroyed and the appropriate reverence for them would be around in its full integrity for centuries to come. This system of conveying these wisdoms intact, had been tried and proven correct for thousands of years. From this understanding, you can see the caliber of Kai Po, as he had been accepted by not just one, but eight different Kahuna, which gave him an amazingly broad spectrum of knowledge and wisdoms, ranging from agriculture through to healing, Lomi massage, plant medicine, spirituality and more. I have always felt so blessed to have been able to train with him, even for the limited time I have had with him. The wealth of knowledge he has shared so willingly discreet with me, remains reverently integrated into my Soul. This particular training trip however was a little different, because it was an "Ancestral Journey" training, to connect myself and the other students with the Ancestral lineage of the practices Kai Po had previously been sharing with us.

At first, I was a little disappointed when he announced that we were doing it. I have always tried to satisfy my Soul's insatiable thirst for remembering ancient wisdoms and advance my healing massage skills, but this time however, my arrogant mind didn't see the value in simply having a history lesson about it all. As typical with spiritual trainings, Spirit has a very different intention for our human experiences than what our Soul-self mind perceives as valuable or not. Of course, here was yet again another of my Intellectual Soul mind's identities disappointed with what it couldn't understand. On stepping up the Awareness from my Spirit-Self a little more, I exposed my arrogant "Deserving Diva" identity and embodied the virtue of humble surrender once more. Within minutes I was back present again and in awe of Molokai's unique and very spiritually charged environment; of which I was now experiencing ... for the first time ... this lifetime. I say *this* lifetime, because I have a huge rapport with everything Hawaiian and know that I have been involved in that culture more than once before this present life. Throughout my Lomi training, I consistently had waves of knowing remembrances of the techniques and wisdoms being shared with me. Feeling with your Awareness, you can *feel* the difference between a *memory* of a past ancestral experience and new information or skills being learned for the first time. An easy test is to simply ask your Self if what you are receiving makes sense. I often ask this of my clients after sharing a concept of consciousness with them. I find it truly amazing how much we already know, and yet we often refuse to recognize it as previously self-acquired knowledge and discount it as something new. Even more often, we even judge it as unworthy of experiencing. If the answer to your question of making sense is a yes, then you can be sure it is something that you already know but are just *re-membering* within your etheric Life-Body in this present life time, in that moment of hearing it.

If you didn't know it already, it couldn't make any sense to you at all ... could it?

So, as I was at that time, trying to raise my courage to start teaching my Lomi massage, I came prepared on this ancestral journey with a small movie camera and a large intention, to capture every word I could that came out of my teacher's mouth. I did this, so I thought, so I could study, interpret and duplicate what he does and says, hoping to be, or at least appear, as good and credulously authentic to *my* students, as he was to me. Of course, this was now my Intellectual Soul's *inadequate identity* stepping up to the plate here again, trying to hit a home run with feelings of unworthiness and incapability of being able to teach from my own experience. I was already working my massage practice with my Conscious Bodywork techniques of experiencing through Embodied Awareness, with fantastic success. My confidence however in the responsibility of teaching it to another person correctly, was still a massive stretch for me.

When I asked Kai Po about teaching and if he thought I was ready to teach yet, his only advice was that I would know when I was ready. At this point in time, through the eyes of my inadequate identity, I felt I was definitely not ready. At the time, I felt I should just leave it to my Soul's conscious intellect of its identities to learn a perceived new way of working and teaching, rather than access my Spirit's Awareness of the appropriate way to deliver knowledge intuitively. Ironically, I had strategically forgotten something from a previous course with Kai Po some years prior, when he frustratingly raised his voice to the class shouting, "Don't show me what I've taught you ... show me how you _use_ what I've taught you." At that time, this was a surprisingly liberating humiliation for me. From that moment on, once I stopped trying to <u>be</u> my Kahuna, my connection to my clients went to a whole new skill level and their healing results took a quantum leap. Allowing the Kahuna student within my Spirit-BEing to come forward and show its skills of how I could *use* what my kahuna had shared ... thoroughly transformed my practice. Realizing that I was *re-membering* and not learning ... transformed my human-self's

Soul also. Again, it was through the use of my Spirit-Self's Awareness, that brought me to "the alter of ownership" of my limiting identities. It was from this ownership through Awareness, that I was empowered to apply what I was taught and blend it with what *my* Spirit-Self was continually trying to reveal to me.

Wisdom cannot reveal its Self to my Soul's consciousness, without <u>ownership</u> of the experience vehicle that is, my human-self.

My Spirit uses my Soul, to bring higher wisdoms into my human existence so as to ground <u>them</u> in Humanity …for us all.

It was only when I was willing to own my Soul-self's sabotaging identity and its insatiable need to stay small, that I was then able to infuse my human-self with the virtues of courage, surrender and vulnerability. It was these virtues that ultimately discharged the resistances and attachments that were limiting my human-self-development. Through these discharges my <u>Will</u> strengthened, so I could hold and trust my Spirit's intuitive guidance to direct my bodywork sessions more than ever before. This grounding and use of my Spirit-BEing-Self's Awareness in my bodywork practice, is how I became able to communicate with the relevant human-self components of my clients. Through this communication I could then locate the correct "body", that was creating the dis-harmony or dis-order within my client's physical Body and BEing.

The miraculous and often amazing healings that came from this level of communication, more often than not and still to this day, would stun me in AWE of what is possible through the simplistic power of a spiritualized human.

The more that I lived this level of Aware-ownership, the deeper my communications became in every session, not just with my clients, nor with the world I exist in, but especially with my BEing-Self particularly. What revealed ever deeper within me, was that I *can't* teach what I am *not* living. It just felt wrong or dis-harmonious and dis-integreous for me to teach what I had learned, without first living the experience of what I had learned … AND … re-membered it into my etheric Life Body. Our experiences need to be fully integrated and membered into our etheric Life Body, before they can be recalled correctly by our Consciousness Soul to be teachable to others. If what I learn is not transmuted into experience and thus re-membered into my etheric Life Body, then the learning is not integrated into my whole self and will get stuck in my Intellectual Soul and its rationalization of Life. This is what has happened for many of the spiritual salespeople that proliferate our world now. Their knowledge of spiritual things is stuck in their Intellectual Soul and has not been integrated through their whole human-self through true Self-experience. Their teachings hence; although *seemingly* spiritual in content, is mentally transmitted and as such, you get a deceptive teaching that is actually quite void of Spirit. It was at this deeper level that I uncovered my own *spiritual salesman identity* for the first time. It was a shocking and yet humbling revelation for me, as I always had such distain for the spiritual salespeople I had come across throughout my own spiritual journey. Another example of Life reflecting those elements of myself that I resist owning.

The thing I see in others that I resist the most, is the reflection of the thing I resist the most ... about myself.

I often see behind the "*good for the student*" facade of these spiritual salespeople, to what covertly mattered for them is simply the next million-dollar year. My distain came from seeing the subtle manipulations and deceptions by these salespeople of their students, of whom most were duped by the impressive righteous robes in the form of deceptions, woven into their spiritual rhetoric, worn posthumously by these salespeople's spiritual identities. This was also a massive pivotal turning point for me into the deeper experiential understanding of the realm of possibilities which come from a spiritualized human, living with true Awareness.

So, it was with these insights and communication skills, that I came to Molokai, on what was to be an extremely intimate journey of communication with Spirit, through so many mediums as it turned out; most of which I had no initial awareness of. It was quite funny from one contradictive perspective that, being someone who was committed to living from experience and *present* moment Awareness, yet here I was trying to record everything to watch and study at a *later* time. This was my spiritual salesman identity in its glory, trying to blindly justify plagiarizing my kahuna's life passion. Once again, this covert identity was trying to discard any true respect or reverence for my teacher and the spiritual wisdoms he had already bestowed on me, by disrespectfully stealing his teachings from behind his back. This identity was so covertly active in my Soul, that the Spirit of the Hawaiian ancestors had to get dramatically abrupt with me in their intervention, to bring these hidden agendas into the light of my Awareness.

We really are an arrogant consciousness, when we delude our Soul-self that we can outsmart the super-sensing Awareness ability of our Spirit-BEing-Self.

My BEing-Self spoke VERY loud on day two of the trip. After having had recorded some three hours of the most intimate record of Kai Po's life training and teachings, I got back to my hotel that night and found that I had recorded over the most relevant and poignant parts. I remembered at the time I was recording, acknowledging to myself that I didn't need to be totally present with what he was saying, even when I couldn't understand it, because I was recording it all and I could go through it again later, on my own. Sometimes my Soul's arrogance totally shocks me to my core. I eventually realized that this was the disgraceful disrespect of my Intellectual Soul's spiritual salesman identity yet again, which thought it could deceive not just *my* Spirit-Self but hoodwink Kai Po's Spirit as well. The intention of this identity was just down right insane. Although I would have liked to be more *out of my mind* in that moment ... I was definitely out of my mind insane for trying this hoodwink. Eventually, after *experiencing* through the shock of losing the recording, I became present with my Awareness on it once more and got the message that the experience to be had, is the one happening in the present moment it originates in, not the intellectualizing of the recording of it after the fact. From that moment on, my heightened intention was to be extremely present with everything he shared. It was time for me to heighten my Awareness to a new level.

As if this episode was not enough, at the end of the very next day, as I was driving back to my hotel on the other end of the island, Spirit had another very loud message for me to take notice of ... again. There were no subtleties with this one either. Obviously, from my deaf and dumb arrogance of not being alert or listening to Spirit the day before; Spirit was not going to leave anything to chance this time. About a half mile from my hotel, driving through an undeveloped part of the island; which most of beautiful Molokai is by the way, my Sentient Soul *sensed* the Spirit of the ancestors sending their subtle whispers of wisdom toward me. As I turned a corner, my Sentient Soul was stimulated by something white taking off from the open ground about 100 yards off to my right. "Oh wow" I thought, "it's a white bird". As I drove and obviously slowed down to check it out, this bird flew straight toward me. As I slowed even more, it turned right in front of me and flew straight along about 6 feet off the road, at the very same speed I was driving and just 12 feet in front of my windshield. Jaw droppingly stunned, but in immense AWE at the rear view of this *huge* majestic white bird in flight ... *with me*, with a wingspan as wide as my car, I noticed it was not just a white bird, but a huge white owl. My snowy feathered messenger did this for about a hundred yards or so, long enough to glue *all* of my attention on this present moment flying just twelve feet in front of me. Almost as if it knew when my Soul was totally locked onto this intimate moment with it, it flew off into the bushes just fifty yards to my left. I stopped of course, to watch this majestic white messenger a little longer, but to my shock, by the time I had stopped ... I couldn't find it anymore. It was like it just vanished into the tree. I even got out of the car to see better, but to no avail. I mean really, a huge white bird in a green tree just fifty yards away should be easily seen ... right? Well, apparently not if it simply doesn't want to be seen ... I guess. My Consciousness Soul, having been tapped on the shoulder by my Spirit-Self, immediately got the significance of this large bird disappearing so mysteriously. The impact of this moment was in order to intensify the ancestor's message for me to *take notice*.

At this point, I was now shaken to my Spirit, as I couldn't deny that this was not just a chance encounter of a white bird flying across my path, but a huge *white owl* no less, flying <u>with</u> my path and for enough distance for me to not be able to deny the significance. This was surely an omen messenger for me to take entrancing notice of. At my Spirit-BEing's core, I knew instinctively that this was a direct notice from the Spirit of the Hawaiian ancestors and that they were *with* me. Also, there was no denying that this was a time for me to be exceptionally alert with my Awareness. Typical of the Soul mind however, as soon as I returned to my hotel, it needed to google the totem meaning for white owl. Although our Intellectual Soul is brilliant at creating identities and managing and coordinating them to give us the optimal human event for our Spirit-Self to experience, it is a complete invalidating dead-head, when it comes to spiritual insight. After nearly an hour of multiple searches to get a more rounded view of its meaning, my Intellectual Soul finally accepted that my owl messenger was telling me to be very alert for what Spirit is bringing to me. How clever is this mind of mine? What took an hour of google searching for my mind to get this message, my Spirit *felt* and fully experienced into my Consciousness Soul with this same conclusion ... in the very moment my messenger first flew in front of my windscreen. Spirit was giving my Consciousness Soul a "heads-up", to make sure I, my human-self, got what was about to come, the very next day as it turned out.

Apparently, this message coming from Spirit was meant to permeate my whole human-self and not just get stuck in my Intellectual Soul's spiritual salesman identities back pocket of hidden agendas. As I never blindly believe *everything* I read on the internet, the next day I told Kai Po and he confirmed all that had been received the previous day. He said, white owl is a VERY special and rare messenger, to be seen *only* by those whom Spirit has something extremely important to deliver, directly to *that* person ... for them to take in and act on. He said, "Spirit is with you now and has something *extremely* important for you today. You must stay *very* alert." Of course, hearing all of this, my spiritual identities head exploded the longer it lingered on these thoughts, and its self-importance went through the roof. With another loving slap to my Soul-self from my Spirit-BEing, I was quickly brought back to Earth with a shattering blast from my etheric Life-Body, of re-membrance of my previous day's arrogance. I recalled what happened from not being present and respectful with the message the ancestors were trying to confer to me that day through Kai Po and my vow to not repeat it this day. I thought to myself, "seriously Pete, I am on Molokai for my Kahuna's ancestral journey, the ancestral island of not just my Kahuna, but the island that has for thousands of years, traditionally been the *Island of the Kahuna's* ... and I didn't think that the ancestors were going to try to talk with me?" If they can manifest me taping over my video after not listening to Kai Po, then what might they manifest if I don't listen to the messages from Molokai's ancestral Kahuna Spirits trying to communicate with me now? Molokai has always been the island for most of the Kahuna training, and it was because of the Kahuna there, that Molokai was the only island never over-taken by the many would-be conquerors attempting to take unjustified possession of the Hawaiian Nation throughout time.

Well as it turned out, this day to be Aware and alert, was ironically the very day for the history of Ho'oponopono, which also *originated* on Molokai many thousands of years earlier. Ho'oponopono is the traditional Hawaiian system of both self and collective conflict resolution. Prior to just a few hundred years ago, from before the visitors from the Tahitian Islands came back to Hawaii, there was never any wars throughout the Hawaiian Nation for thousands of years, because of the principles of Ho'oponopono. The underlying principle of Ho'oponopono, is to *make things right with self* ... first, before you can then make things right with others. In our western terminology and intellectual understanding, this could simply mean ... to own one's own stuff ... first. This principle however, much more than any westernized mediation concept, is steeped deeply in full *ownership of self* and its relationship to the Divine ... into the deepest and most intimate levels of Body Soul and Spirit.

The ancient Hawaiians believe that everything in one's environment that one would see, hear, taste, touch or in any way experiences, is one's responsibility, simply because it is in one's life.

So, as it turned out, this day was Ho'oponopono day, and as we went from sacred site to reverent space over the island, Kai Po's sharing's would continually be explaining things about Spirit and Soul and Human-self etc. All of this kept reaffirming for me my work with experiencing and Awareness and embodying virtues, of which I had been using extremely successfully with my clients for many prior years. At one particular moment, when Kai Po was explaining about the animal totem for Ho'oponopono being the octopus, a loud and strong voice echoed throughout my human-self-consciousness, saying "experiencing with Awareness and virtue embodiment, is Ho'oponopono for the world." I was filming Kai Po's sharing at the time, so I was looking through the lens when this imposing Hawaiian accented voice spoke. It shocked me, as I thought and felt there the presence of someone standing beside me, talking to me. As I took my eye from the lens to see who was there, it spoke once again, "experiencing with the Awareness and virtue embodiment, is Ho'oponopono for the world." I turned to look around, but no one was there. Of course, this spooked me further, but I was fast becoming used to being spooked now on this spiritually spooky island of the Kahuna's. Things appearing to be there and then disappearing was fast becoming a spirit message trademark for me. As my Soul-self-mind; which is so "sense-less", started to make excuses for the voice and again try to invalidate the whole experience, the voice spoke for the third and last time with, "experiencing with the Awareness and virtue embodiment, is Ho'oponopono for the world." Even my mind shut up this time and I think it was also in a little shock at the deep experiential impact of this message. This message didn't just penetrate into my Soul mind this time but resonated through the whole BEing of all my three self's of Body Soul and Spirit. I sensed that was why the ancestors spoke three times to me, so that the message entered all three components of my Body Soul and Spirit Self's.

Once again, the ancestors had spoken ... and I was shaken to the core of my whole BEing. The message itself was powerful, and I knew within my BEing that this was what the Spirit of the ancestors were wanting to convey to me this day. As if the voice wasn't impactful enough, this message of the importance of the Awareness embodiment work was confirmed and consolidated by Kai Po's sharing's throughout the rest of the day as well. I tell you, when Spirit decides you need to get a message ... you're going to keep getting it ... until *they* decide you've got it. I have since, experientially come to realize that if we stay in Awareness and not just get, but *fully experience* the message as quickly as possible, then the circumstances for the delivery of the message doesn't need to dramatically escalate. As the day went on and Kai Po would explain more and more wisdoms about the relationships between our Body Soul and Spirit, I began to see the importance of my earlier message regarding the Awareness embodiment and virtue relationship. I always sensed that the experience work and its particular use of the embodiment of *true* Awareness to experience with, which had already been revealed to me, was important for any individual in discharging any conflict. Now however, the ancestors were beginning to show me an even bigger picture application for *experiencing, Awareness and virtues,* as a resurrection of the Aloha Spirit, within the whole of Humanity.

There is an ancient prophesy in Hawaiian culture that the Aloha Spirit of the world of past times; the true loving and deeply experiential connection with the spiritual realm and each other; would be lost and humanity would be consumed by materialism and selfish intellectualism. This time of materialism and intellectualism also aligns with some of the teachings of Rudolph Steiner as well. I think if we look around us as we speak, we can clearly see that this part of the Hawaiian prophesy and the time that Steiner talks about, has already come to fruition. The Hawaiian Kahuna and Kupuna; the Master's and the elders respectively, and holders of these traditional wisdoms, saw this prophesy many hundreds of years ago. They knew that they needed to protect these wisdoms. From that time on, they made their Spiritual World Wisdoms secret and inaccessible to the invading cultures of the world—especially the western Intellectual Soul minds. The second part of the prophesy however, foretold that there *would* be a time when the Aloha Spirit would again rise up in the Spirit of Man, and Humanity would again walk hand in hand as a brotherhood with the Spiritual world, embraced in Love with all. I was now beginning to see where the dynamic of experiencing with Awareness could have a significant part in this latter prophesy coming to pass. When we look today at the resurgence of the Hawaiian Nation's independence and its cultural ways coming back into use throughout the islands again, then we can already see the first sparks of resurgence of the Aloha Spirit. I can see now however, how the Embodying Awareness work ... *IS* Ho'oponopono for the world, because it is an every-moment, in every day, every Nation, every BEing, simple application for the deepest intimate ownership of Self, at every level of one's existence of Body Soul and Spirit at this present-day consciousness level. It is through the Embodying Awareness exercises that we can ground the Awareness of our Spirit-Self into our Soul-self, into our very consciousness and bring about this deep and intimate level of virtuous experiential ownership. This level of ownership lies at the heart of Ho'oponopono, and of which our western intellectual humanity has never truly experienced to date.

Embodying true Awareness, is preventive medicine for the Soul.

What is even more interesting here, is that through the wisdom of Anthroposophies spiritual science, it is also known that the point of our evolution we are presently at, is the turning point for the completion of our Consciousness Soul's development. As we explored earlier, a healthy, fully developed Consciousness-Soul is essential for the grounding of Spirit into our human-self. Of course, with every ending there is always a beginning. In this case, with our beginning of the human embodiment of our Spirit Self's development, comes firstly its ability to *experience* at a much more intimate and all-encompassing level, by super-feeling with Awareness ... but without any definitions, judgments or descriptions of what the experience is. This is not possible with a weak, unhealthy or underdeveloped Consciousness Soul. A healthy Consciousness Soul is simply one that is conscious of the Spiritual Realm as a force greater than one's human-self, even though it may not yet be fully experience-able.

Simply put, it is the time for the development of the super-sensory ability of your Spirit-Self's Awareness, to start to be grounded in your human Consciousness Soul.

This is our first step in truly spiritualizing our Human-Soul-self.

The other thing about a message from Spirit for your Self, is that the message is for *you* and not to be gloated to the world for your small egoistic fulfillment. Just as on day two's wiping of my recordings, on this day's recordings, there was a wind howling, and apparently, when you face a camera microphone *into* the wind, all you get in the recordings is a very loud whooshing sound. Yes, you got it, everything Kai Po had shared about the octopus totem for Ho'oponopono, was just a lot of rushing wind on my recoding. Actually, I think the ancestors moved the wind around to face me, because there wasn't any of that session that was audible. Also, when he talked later on the Body Soul and Spirit relationships, I had run out of battery, so I was unable to record any of that as well. Of course, this was yet another message for me, <u>within</u> the message of *Ho'oponopono for the world,* of the importance of using *Awareness for the embodiment of an experience.* Unfortunately, I didn't get this embodiment message within the Ho'oponopono message, until a little after my Molokai trip. While I had attachment to the recordings and using *them* to learn more and integrate my Molokai experiences, I was potentially missing a lot of the *actual experience* being presented to me in the moment it was presented. By going over and over something with our Intellectual Soul mind, we push our Spirit-Self Awareness further out of the picture and as such, disconnect our Soul from the *actual experience*, from the *BEing* state of our Spirit in the experience. All we end up with most times, is the sound of the rushing wind of our mental interpretations. This rushing wind is a good analogy for our Intellectual Soul's mental interpretation of an *event*, along with all its perceived emotional dramas. Think about all of the mental drama that goes on within any experiential human event. This *mental wind experience* however, is NOT the BEing *experience* itself. Without our Spirit-Self's input of feeling with Awareness, there is no *true* experience to be had. While I was analyzing what Kai Po was saying, I wasn't present for the <u>experience</u> I was *having*, for how I was <u>*BEing*</u> ... with what he was saying.

I wasn't *experiencing* how what he was saying was stimulating an affect within me ... I was mentally intellectualizing what he was saying and creating a reference point my mind could refer back to later.

How can I own my actual experiences ... if I'm not actually <u>experiencing</u> how I am <u>BEing</u> in them?

Merely intellectualizing of the human event around me—that I am dramatically participating in ... is not ... contrary to popular belief ... <u>experiencing</u> it.

If I am not *aware* of how I am BEing in any human event, then am I really *experiencing* the event? If I am not Aware of what I am experiencing, of what I am feeling as the Being within the event, can I ever truly take any ownership or responsibility for what I am creating, let alone the effect I am having on others or my environment? This covert and often blind non-ownership is why so many people live in resistance to their Life. I was present with my Self when I got the voice message about Ho'oponopono for the world, but the depth of spiritualizing my human-self by using the embodiment of Awareness to experience with, only came sometime after I had learned and worked with Ho'oponopono a number of times. I came to *know*, that it is through a deeper level of *feeling with my Awareness* which brings about true ownership of my experiences. It is only when our experiences are fully integrated into our etheric Life Body, that they can then effect change within our human-self of Body and Soul. When our experiences are mentalized or processed through our Intellectual Soul, then they get stuck in our Intellectual Soul, losing all power to effect any real change or growth within our human-self.

Even though I had previously been involved for over ten years within an intense self-development organization, supposedly based in *feeling* and whose premise was grounded solely around our beliefs create our experiences and hinged totally on the mind and consciousness; I eventually came to realize that this whole system was in fact, Spirit-less. Consequently, what I had been indoctrinated into believing of what was ownership from this self-development system, was in fact only addressing the identities within consciousness, and ownership was really a game of hit and miss self-deception by the mind ... with itself. Remember, the perception of the mind of the is simply the creation of your Intellectual Soul. What trapped this self-development system in the Intellectual Soul was the self-deceiving *mind game* of the Intellectual Souls spiritual identity. What they professed was the *experience* they were supposedly *dis-creating* through its belief structure, was actually only the human event happening within the Intellectual Soul. This mental treatment of experiences, never got to the realm of the true experience, through which the Spirit was trying to embody virtues into the human. At best, the dis-creating techniques they used were only happening within the Consciousness Soul and rarely accessing the Spirit BEing-Self's experience through Awareness.

The true experience is what is happening within your Spirit-Self's Awareness, of how you are actually Being, not the doings of mental and emotional creations of the identities of your consciousness. This organizations focus was on beliefs, which, because our beliefs originate within our Intellectual Soul level of consciousness, effectively trapped them *in* Consciousness and pushed Spirit out of the equation all together. I always felt there was something off with the fact that the trainers and even the creator of this system himself, would never allow any talk or reference to Spirit in anything they or we did. It was all about the mind and consciousness and now I could see why. There are plenty of other affirmational belief-based modalities of healing and other self-development systems based on belief management etc., which *can* definitely help to intellectually understand consciousness. KNOW this however; these systems will never be able to spiritualize your human-self or get you to the truth of *true experiential ownership* of your *experiences*. It was only through the deeper experiential ownership of

Ho'oponopono that the even deeper spiritual truth of Awareness eventually fully revealed itself to me. I came to *know experientially*, that it is through feeling with Awareness which truly discharges resistance and attachment, revealing the *stairway to heaven on Earth*, through true experiential ownership.

TRUE Awareness is the conduit, which facilitates and accelerates the Spiritualizing of my Human-Soul-self.

So, my message of Ho'oponopono from the Hawaiian ancestors, had been delivered to me and had integrated deep into my Body Soul and Spirit. Now, it was to be implemented into this world reality ... through me ... apparently. I struggled however, to see how this insight was meant to strengthen my intention to teach or lighten my load, when now apparently, I was meant to teach the *whole world* ... and not just a small class of five or so students; of which by the way, I was already struggling to come to grips with. On leaving the island, somewhat shell-shocked, but definitely spiritually altered, I was in a whirlpool of mixed emotions of exaltation for being given this honor to teach ... but overwhelmed with how I was meant to pull this thing off. Through meditation, through more ownership from a more heightened Awareness, it was revealed that there was more information and skills to be had yet. What was revealed through a deeper and more intimate experiential understanding of Ho'oponopono, was that the use of Awareness Embodiment, would accelerate and simplify its powerful result and make it more accessible to the westernized intellectualized consciousness. So, began my spiritual scientific research into this ancient power of Ho'oponopono to heal the materialistic Intellectual Soul and find what role the element of our Spirit-Self's Awareness has to play in the re-grounding of the Aloha Spirit in the world ... for us all.

Ho'oponopono has been the traditional way of conflict resolution in the Hawaiian Nation for generations, but this system is so very different to the way we in the west might negotiate an agreement to resolve a conflict. Ho'oponopono is not concerned with the two parties in conflict to just come to some agreement. Ho'oponopono is intended at the deepest intimate level, to realign the three "self's" of Body, Soul and Spirit we have been learning about, or in Hawaiian terminology, unihipili, uhane and Aumakua respectively; which make up your human BEing. Ho'oponopono's dynamic nature, reconnects the individuals Body Soul and Spirit, through full ownership of their actions, thoughts, feelings and deeds, of which the dis-harmony with others and their self has been brought about. It was only when both individuals had got to this deep, spiritually *Aware* level of personal loving ownership, that they would *then* be able and allowed, to move toward finding an agreement, of which <u>both</u> were *completely* aligned. This would have always been facilitated by a suitable Kahuna of Spirit; one that lived in Awareness and could *see/feel* into the individuals whole three Self's of Body Soul and Spirit. Through this super-sensing of the whole Self of each individual, the Kahuna could guide and assist each to their full and deepest self-ownership and re-alignment of their three self's. The Kahuna understood at an incredibly super-sensitive experiential level, that our three-self's become disconnected when we are in *any* conflict.

Any form of conflict creates a fragmented and mis-aligned human-self, disconnected from its spiritual roots. This renders it incapable of TRUE higher insight or intuition and without which, true ownership is extremely difficult ... if not impossible.

Now from hearing this, one might think that it is ownership that may well bring the three self's back together again, but ironically, it is in bringing the three self's back together, that ownership becomes possible. A lack of experiential Awareness results in a state of conflict as a consequence of the opposing forces of resistance and attachment and is what creates the fragmenting of the Body Soul and Spirit components of the whole Self. Ownership doesn't bring the three self's together; it is the natural and effortless end result of the three-self's coexisting and co-creating in harmony together again. It is the discharging or dissolution of conflict, which naturally brings the three self's back together again. Do you remember in the previous chapter, when we talked about conflict being the result of the opposing dynamic forces of resistance and attachment created from our identities flipping from one side to the other? It is by *experiencing*, i.e. by *super-feeling with your Awareness*, but without judgment definition or description of what you are feeling; by which resistance and attachment can be brought together to reveal the true experience being avoided. As I said earlier, experiencing discharges conflict. Experiencing with Awareness results in all three-self's coming back into alignment and connection and communication with each other again. From this re-connection of the three self's, ownership results. Although Ho'oponopono in its original form wasn't known through this *detail* of the dynamic of Awareness and experiencing to discharge conflict, it is non-the less *the* dynamic. This dynamic is what has always achieved Ho'oponopono's mystical resultant healings within the individual Self, along with thousands of years of harmonized living together as one Nation.

So, the truth is, that it is simply <u>experiencing with Awareness</u>, which brings the three self's of Body Soul and Spirit back together again.

The practice of Ho'oponopono comes down to a seemingly simple application of a sequence of statements. The thing with these statements however, is that they are not just statements of words or affirmations of intentions, but true and real experiences meant to be *fully embodied*, as they are being stated. The statement is simply the access point to stimulate the individual to TRULY <u>experience</u> the <u>consequence</u> of their actions thoughts intentions and judgments etc. This stimulation however, only happens when the individual embodies the statement through experiencing with their Awareness and NOT the mind of the Intellectual Soul of the human-self's consciousness.

***The statements of Ho'oponopono, is to say, "I'm Sorry - Please forgive me -
Thank you - I Love you."***

The catch is however, that I am saying it to my Divine Higher Self, not to the other person. When I say each, I am allowing all three bodies of my-Self to "feel" the relevant charge and connection to the present event of conflict within each. This deepest level of ownership is not directed at the other person, or even just at the event I have been involved in and the actions carried out in that event. Although these areas may well be the entry point for this exploration, they are not the focus point of the exploration. Remember, it is the *experience* that is important ... not the event. The REAL power of Ho'oponopono is in our ability to TRULY and Self-HONESTLY "*experience*", each phrase as we speak it.

- *I'M SORRY* ... is to "feel" truly sorry for the *event* and everything "I" have done (without drowning in thinking about what that is but allowing what it is to reveal the true feeling of the experience of its self to me ... from within me). This is the area where the *resisted* experiences of my Human-Soul-self have been suppressed and have been buried deep within my Intellectual Soul, away from Consciousness. I'm sorry is true remorse; which is an experience in itself of the disharmony I have caused and created to my Self and all those who exist in my environment. At the deepest level of this step is the experience of the affect I have had on the other, of what *they* might have actually experienced. This step is the extensive exploration and ownership of all my resistances and the consequences of my actions etc., to any and all those living in my environment. This step is completed by the fully experiential embodiment within my Human-self of the *virtue of humility*. Embodiment of this virtue has no attachments to being humbled by anything, but simply the state of BEing Humility.

- *PLEASE FORGIVE ME* ... is from this new space of humility integrated from embodying the previous virtue, to "Humbly"; truly ask for forgiveness of the Divine Source for what has happened by what I have done and how I have been. This is asking for forgiveness for my failings where I had not been more virtuous and rejected my Life's opportunity for higher embodiment. This is done without ANY blame of the other OR Self. This is the forgiveness step ... to "feel" humbled by the experience and the place I play in this bigger picture. This humility grows deeper the more I am able to forgive and experience my place in the greater Divine Orchestration that I am participating in and co-creating evolution with it. The completion of this step comes about with the true embodiment of *forgiveness* of. If I need for that person ... *to forgive me* ... then I am still incomplete in this step with my own Ho'oponopono. This step is completed by the fully experiential integration within me of the *virtue of forgiveness*, which also means forgiveness of my human-self. Forgiveness has a consequential result of non-attachment. Embodiment of this virtue has no attachment to any person place or thing outside of self. It is simply the state of BEing forgiveness.

- *THANK YOU* ... is to "feel" TRULY thankful and grateful for the experience and the opportunity it provides for me to learn and apply something new. Thankful to the Divine Orchestration that has brought about the sequence of events that created the opportunities for these experiences and for the other person showing up *for me,* to play the hard role of Liar or abandon-er etc. Thankful for the opportunity to expand the virtuous state of my Souls Consciousness through these experiences. Probably most importantly is, thankful for my human-self and all its components within the Body and Soul. This step is completed by the fully experiential embodiment within my human of the *virtue of gratitude.* Embodiment of this virtue has no attachment to any person place or thing outside of self. It is simply the state of BEing Gratitude.

- *I LOVE YOU* ... simply becomes a natural "*Response*" after having "*FULLY experienced*" the above steps and is the one that finally dissolves any residual charge toward everything external I had at the beginning. I Love you is particularly directed at one's own self also, and Ho'oponopono is not complete until one can truly love one's own self. The first steps clear the space within me, which leads to this place of "making things right with Self." Embodiment of this highest of virtuous states for this stage of our evolution has no attachment to any person place or thing outside of self. It is simply the state of BEing LOVE ... free of influence and embodied with complete Willingness.

This last stage dissolves the barriers and disconnections between my Human-self and ALL others, not just the one that I have perceived as having lied or abandoned me etc. within this current event. By this stage it is understood that that person was merely the catalyst or trigger to give me the opportunity ... in this moment ... for me to clear my space of anchored negatively charged Chi or Life Force, that has been blocked within me, and of which I have been storing from *previous* events as well, or even previous life times. Rudolph Steiner so precisely puts it in his description of what Love truly is, when he said that, "Love comes about, when one is so openly honest, clear and fully Aware of one's self, free of all internal or external influences upon one's self, to the degree that one is capable of *experiencing* the whole and true BEing of the other. It is within this open space thus created by one in such a state of open self-honesty, that the gift of Love flows in and creates such an intimate connection and bond between one's Self and the environment it exists in ... including all those existing in that environment." This step is completed by the fully experiential integration within my human of the *virtue of Love* and its consequent intimate connection.

I do not create Love, but Love has been granted me by the Grace of the Divine Spirit, when I "BE" the space of pure openness, in which Love can enter into me as a Divine expression.

From this understanding of what *state* is necessary for true Love to come about, we can also see how TRUE Self-Love, can only exist within a BEing, who has achieved this state of full and total open honesty with *one's self* ... on all levels of one's existence, with intimate experience of all of its components of Body and Soul. Have you ever met the Dalai Lama for example, or any *true* Spiritual Master, and been fortunate enough to have felt the true Love that seemingly emanates from that BEing? You may see now from what we have just covered, how that Love was not created by the Master BEing but is a gift of Grace to that BEing's complete open honesty, not just with the world around them, but more importantly with the inner Self that they BE. Their level of self-ownership and self-realization is evident by the space they create, in which Love can exist. It is *this* state of TRUE Love, which the last statement of Ho'oponopono refers to. This state is only achievable, after the deepest and most intimately open and honest experiential ownership of one's human-self. In days of old, each of these steps were guided so lovingly and compassionately by their Kahuna, all the way through surrounding both individuals in this same highest open space of Love in which the Kahuna occupies. The Kahuna thus creates a safe space for them to explore and own their human-self in. Imagine two human-BEing's coming together from this level of ownership, BOTH in this state of TRUE Love; BOTH now willing to find an alignment together to resolve the disagreement they first had. Ironically, one of the many meanings for Aloha in the Hawaiian language is ... Love.

It is through Ho'oponopono, that the Aloha Spirit of Love can be resurrected into all of Humanity via my Human-Soul-self, as a Phoenix transforming my "I Consciousness" into an "I AM consciously <u>Aware</u> Human-Spirit-Self".

Ho'oponopono for the world, is the simplistic version of this level of ownership by experiencing one's life through the embodiment of Awareness. An underlying covenant of the TRUE Hawaiian spiritual philosophies is that, "we are ALL equally responsible for all who exist within our environment and everything that happens within it". You can see how this state of ownership through Ho'oponopono, easily made this philosophy achievable and livable as an everyday existence for the original Hawaiian Nation. Maybe you can get a sense, or *super-sense* of how living from this resultant state of Love, coming from a constant application of the principles of Ho'oponopono, naturally made responsibility normal. Unfortunately, in our materialistically intellectual world consciousness of today, this level of responsibility has become rare and abnormal. In the time when this original pure form of Ho'oponopono existed and was practiced, the consciousness of the people was much finer than ours is today. This practice was simply felt within the Soul and experienced through the Spirit as much more of a natural effortlessly flowing spiritual experience, than the materialistic intellectually conscious one we might expect to have today. The results back then always created profound reconnections and alignments; as is still possible today when done correctly. Throughout the development of our current egoistic intellectual consciousness and its inherent intellectualization of spirituality, certain Hawaiian Kahuna, have until recently, kept knowledge of these truths of the use of TRUE Awareness safe and pure.

I know that this is what the Hawaiian Kahuna ancestors on Moloka'i were telling me, when they slapped me with my message of Ho'oponopono for the world. The *embodiment* of Awareness to experience with, had already revealed its Self to me and I was already practicing it. Because of this, I could experientially see how the correct use of Ho'oponopono produces the true powerful effect of harmonizing back together again our Body Soul and Spirit; our unhipila, uhane and Aumakua. Still today, this power of true ownership with Awareness is being devalued, through the western intellectualized exploitation of Ho'oponopono by yet another long line of deceptive spiritual salesman, one of whom first became famous as a Law of Attraction "guru". His version, like the practices of many other present-day salesmen and women, is based and focused on the benefits to <u>self</u>, totally missing the full responsibility to the whole Spiritual Realm, let alone the correct and respectful use of Awareness to *FULLY* own one's experiences. This is where the true power to heal, harmonize and transform all of the selfs of our Body Soul and Spirit lies.

The underlying principle of Ho'oponopono is, "one must make things right with "self" first … before one can make things right with others and the world one exists in". Awareness and its inherent *requirement* for responsibility, is the key ingredient in this Soul and Spirit healing harmonization. Without this level of experiential ownership between the Soul and Spirit through Awareness, there can be no TRUE physical Body healing. Ironically and contrary to most current indoctrinating self-development systems of spiritual salespeople, ownership is NOT just recognizing, acknowledging and letting go of, or getting rid of, ANY elements of self. These are all mental processes of which darker forces have influence over, so as to actually exclude and push out Awareness of Spirit. TRUE ownership is bringing in and FULLY experiencing, all of the elements of self, particularly what one is denying or *falsely* believing that one is NOT.

True Awareness gives me the ability to easily bring in and take full ownership and experiential integration of my darkest self … and transmute it … into a more virtuous Self … if I choose.

In past times, the Kahuna, who would be living in Awareness, would always be the one facilitating Ho'oponopono for individuals and groups. Because of the Kahuna's level of Living Awareness, he/she is the one observably capable of seeing the truth behind and within the self-deceptions of the human-self's identities resistance and attachment flipping. This flipping of course, creates the very conflicts with self and others in their world. Of course, the Kahuna could only do this because they had already taken full responsibility for their own self-deceptions and hidden agendas. Particularly relevant to Awareness, the same applies today also, although rarely practiced, that a teacher cannot teach the integrity of what he is trying to teach others, if he hasn't experienced it FULLY within his self. Mental concepts are not experiences until they have passed through Awareness and experientially fully integrated into the Soul through Spirit, from which may then be fully integrated into the Consciousness Soul of the Human. A major part of the completion of our Consciousness Souls development, is brought about through the depth of ownership we have just explored. This ownership lies within the *living* practice of the principles of Ho'oponopono applied through feeling with Awareness.

To recap on the 4 steps of Ho'oponopono.

1) I'm Sorry .... Ownership and responsibility for what I have been and done. This is for the experiential embodiment of the virtue of Humility. This a pre-requisite for all further intentions of ownership.

2) Please forgive me .... True Remorse for what I have caused and done to others. This is for the experiential embodiment of the virtue of Forgiveness and its inherent state of non-attachment.

3) Thank you .... Gratitude for the opportunity to grow from this and the opportunity to correct my wrong doings. This is for the experiential embodiment of the virtue of Gratitude.

4) I Love you .... Willingness to BE completely open, honest and compassionate to self and others. This is for the experiential embodiment of the virtue of Love and its inherent state of non-resistance.

Obviously when you look at these steps from the understanding of the proper use of TRUE Awareness, we can't deny that this depth and level of ownership can only come from our Spirit's ability and not the self-deceiving mind or any component of our human-self's consciousness. For us all today, we are moving into the time of having to be fully responsible for our human-self, on all levels of its existence and for everything that we create through thought and deed in this human reality.

It is time for me to BE ... the Kahuna facilitator of my own Ho'oponopono for this world I co-exist in.

The simplest way to do this now, from our presently evolved state of "I Consciousness", is by learning a new way to experience our Life fully, using our Spirit-Self's Awareness to embody virtues. To get to this new way of experiencing, we must first *Willingly* come to be fully present with where we are at right now, in our present state of human conflict and its resultant physical inflictions. Although we have just discovered the *true* use of Ho'oponopono and the power from its correct and complete application to transform, reconnect and align our Body Soul and Spirit, there is a simple way to use the *principles* of Ho'oponopono in an everyday, every moment application that can circumvent having to deal with conflict resolution ... before it originates and needs a resolution to be facilitated.

As we found from our discussion in the previous chapters, all conflict is the resultant experience of the opposing forces of resistance and attachment, which are intrinsic in our current state of human "I Consciousness". So quite simply, when we are trapped in between the throes of resistance and attachment, we have not just entered into a state of conflict, but we have also effectively disconnected the three self's of our Body Soul and Spirit from each other. The consequences of a prolonged state of this deepest disconnection within one's BEing, can be profound and physically devastating. At the heart of nearly all ill-health and lack of wellness within your Body Soul and Spirit, is conflict. Within the Human-Beings of our today world; this state of which I would call BEing-less, is the dramatic result of this covertly deepest level of inner conflict and disconnect between ones three self's. At the highest level of truth; existing in this state of simple conflict from unresolved resistance and attachment, is at the core of almost all sickness and illnesses on our planet right now also. Countless times throughout my Lomi Conscious Bodywork practice, Life confirmed to me these facts of illness, sickness and un-wellness, being the direct result of this experiential void resulting in the disconnection between our Body Soul and Spirit. Countless times, unbelievable healings were bestowed on those clients, who trusted in their own ability of Awareness and Willed their courage and vulnerability to truly _feel their experiences_ with their Awareness, to the point of virtuous embodiment.

Ironically, whenever we move through evolution to a new state of existence; in this case moving from a state of Soul Consciousness to a state of a Spiritualized Soul Consciousness, then everything that inhibits that transition, everything of human consciousness that has been resisted up to this point of change ... will be brought to the surface to be cleared and integrated fully. Ther is no movement passed these points without Spiritual integration. NO amount of avoidance, pretending, letting go or trying to move on will bypass self-ownership at this time. If we understand that all physical disease and illness is the result of resisted experiences etc., combined with this point of transition, then we may get a glimpse of why there is so much chronic disease in our world right now. Disease can be a way of burning off old systems, of changing the physical structure of our human form to make way for a more evolved form, one more suitable for the new level of consciousness to occupy. This is why also, that the experiencing through embodied Awareness technology, has been brought to us now, to facilitate this transformation through the embodiment of the higher virtues of Spirit.

The embodiment of virtues is the TRUE preventative healing force within Humanity.

It is time to understand that the body is the *last manifestation* of our experiences in this physical human reality ... not the beginning manifestation. It is only through the body its self, which all experiential events are able to manifest in this material human reality. There is a flow of creative experiential Life Force that is Divinely Orchestrated, enabling our human events to become manifest as our personal reality. It is through *experiencing*—of feeling with our Awareness—that our human events become a stream for this same Life Force to heal if you will, the disharmonies and imbalances of our human existence. It is through these experiential streams, that we are able to bring our Body Soul and Spirit back into an aligned and harmonized co-creating space once more. Understanding this, we can start to see why the physical body *breaks down*, as a result of the *prevention* or *interruption* of the flow of these Life Force streams. This breakdown effectively stops our experiences from completing. Divine Orchestration will not just continue to manifest but amplify the events we need to embody the Life Force of spiritual virtues necessary for our individual's development. The Body will breakdown when Life Force is denied its flow through us. Through the Soul's resistance or attachment to the events of our human Life, it effectively interrupts this flow of Life Force by way of avoidance and non-ownership of our experiences. This breakdown is the resultant symptom of the interruption of the dynamic flow of Life Force between our Body Soul Spirit. Through this dynamic, the manifestation of the *experience* we have at any given time are all made possible.

When I disconnect my Body Soul and Spirit self's, through the simple act of non-ownership from non-Awareness, I prevent the flow of Life's empowering <u>*experience streams of Life Force*</u> *...from flowing through me.*

If we look at nearly all the health and nutrition research that abounds throughout our information services these days, we will notice a common thread stating that all high Life Force potent foods, heal the body. Even though traditional intellectual science can only *interpret* the physical world needs, they still see the massive benefit that Life Force, or live food ... has in our body's healing and maintenance. The only way this science can interpret and quantify Life Force intellectually, is to define it in a category or form of physical nutritional elements and chemical reactions. The fact is however, that it is Spiritual *Life Force* ... not purely physical nutritional chemistry; and that not just the physical Body, but in a sense the Soul and Spirit bodies all need this Life Force to thrive on and grow and evolve from also. If this is true, and Life's experience streams are the carriers for this Life Force; then can you see the damage you do to your whole BEing, when you resist experiencing ALL of your Life and disconnect the three component parts of your Body Soul and Spirit from each other? Effectively, you are disrupting and blocking the flow of Life Force that is meant to heal and enliven you ... ALL that is you, as it is meant to stream through all three-component self's of your Human BEing. All nutrient and organic produce has this Life Force within it, and yes, there is a degree of truth in the fact that you can affect healing and strengthening of the body through nutritional methods, but nutrition alone may heal the Body, but it can't truly heal and enliven the Soul or Spirit, which is where all originations come from. Ironically, it is the lack of *Life Force* in the Soul and Spirit, that trickles down into the physical body, resulting in the very symptoms of dis-ease and illness we see in the physical Body and of which, we are mis-guided in trying to heal solely through physical means.

Now you might be thinking then, that an overabundance of Life Force may be a good thing and maybe somehow, we need to build it up or store it or hold onto it within the systems of Self's. Well when, through resistance or attachment, we disconnect and block this flow of Life Force, it does indeed back up within relevant regions of the human-self, within the *identities* realm particularly, where all resistance and attachment originate from. This blocking or backing up of Life Force is what actually creates the disharmonies of illness etc. Life and its Forces are meant to flow through us, not to be horded stored or especially blocked. Life is a mobile and fluid dynamic stream of *creative* Divine forces. The rhythms of Life are a flow of these Life streams in and out of our BEing, just like our breath into and out of our body. These rhythms are essential in the discharging of conflict and the harmonization of our three self's. Similarly, experiencing is also a rhythmical process of energy out and in. When your human is participating in the manifestation of your *human events* with others in the environment it exists in through your identities via their intrinsic emotions, reacts and judgments etc., then you are expending energy out into and onto the fabric of reality you exist in. This is an *outflow* of energy, of creative Life Force from your human consciousness into the physical world. By super-feeling with your Awareness, this *outflow* of energy is easily experience-able. When you truly *experience*—by super-feeling with your Awareness, but without any judgments, definitions or descriptions of _what_ you are *feeling*—then this flow of Life's energy is returned to your consciousness, to your whole Soul, building up your Soul forces. Remember what we said in earlier chapters, about anything created in your reality is only created to be experienced?

The primary purpose of any event manifested by your human-consciousness ... is to be fully experienced by your Spirit-Self, to the point of the embodiment of spiritual virtues within human consciousness through your Human-Soul-self.

Through this form of experiencing, you are able to spiritualize your human by the embodiment of spiritual virtues appropriate for that particular experience. When an event has been fully experienced, and its appropriate virtue embodied, it no longer has a purpose for existing, as its primary purpose has been fulfilled. At this point of fulfillment of the event, all creative outflow of energy will return to *your* consciousness, along with the spiritual energy of insight and more importantly ... the additional spiritual energy of the specific virtue you embodied through the experience. In simple terms, this is when you get that "AHHH HAAA !!!" moment of realization of something when you are experiencing an event etc. Do you know those moments of "AHH HAA", when the light goes on and you get an insight into the situation you are involved in? This is a moment of fully experiencing that allows the spiritual realm to reveal something to you. *This* is the health giving, enlivening flow of Life Force I am talking about that energizes and rejuvenates your human-self and its physical body. You can see by this, that if you don't *fully experience* your Life streams through the events you are continually co-creating together with others, then your Life Force will become diminished rather than replenished, as your Life Force continually flows out, manifesting and co-creating your human events. If you are experiencing an overwhelm of events and drama in your life and you see others around you participating with you in this continually dramatic life, or you react to these conditions with resistance to self-ownership of what you see in others as a reflection of you, then you can be pretty sure there are experiences you have not completed, and there are virtues *pressing in on you from your higher Spirit Self,* to be embodied in your life.

Dis-harmony and dis-ease, along with the breaking down and separation of all the systems of Body Soul and Spirit, all come about from this simple interruption of the rhythmic cycle of <u>manifesting and experiencing</u>.

Sometime after my Molokai trip, life shared the truth of the affect Life Force has on the physical body, through an event I had at a clinic I was working at. This work was for one day once a week, for the members of this clinic to have my Conscious Bodywork sessions. They had a microscope there for blood analysis that I also had access to. This particular day was just after I had come back from a Qi Gung workshop and learned a new breath-work technique for raising the Qi energy in the body system. Because I was only working there one day a week, I had to take my own massage table etc. and set up each time I went there. On this particularly revelatory day, I wanted to see what the state of the blood cells are like in mine and my client's body, before and after the bodywork session. My Intellectual Soul-self wanted to see if there is any significant change to the health of the blood system from my bodywork. Unfortunately, my client didn't want to participate in my little research expedition, so after rushing to get set up, I had the technician quickly take my blood sample to see the state of my blood. The result shocked me at first but was washed away as curiosity began to flow over me.

My cells showed a structure called Rouleaux, which is a state of flattened cells all joined together in one continuous trail, like a worm. Rouleaux is a medical term for a condition wherein the blood cells clump together forming what looks like stacks of coins. Medically, this is considered an unhealthy state, because the cells are not *free* to absorb and carry oxygen. It is seen by the medical profession as a precursor to many serious diseases. My spiritual identity was mortified by this structure. My human-self's spiritual identity reacted with invalidations, because it arrogantly believed I was above this level of ill-health, because of my physical work regime and all the consciousness practices and Qi Gung I was doing for my self-development at that time. As I began to feel with my Awareness what I was experiencing, my Spirit was able to subdue my raging consciousness identities indignant self-importance and I thought to try the new breath-work technique I had learned from my workshop, to see if that made any difference. This new technique was a process of nine very large, full and loud breaths in continuous succession and then holding in on the last large breath for as long as possible, followed by as slowly as possible, releasing it out. Although this whole process only takes maybe two minutes, it is quite a volatile process. The results of this method throughout the workshop was usually a kind of heightened invigoration of the Body and Soul components of the human-self, so I naturally expected some kind of change in the blood structure.

When we checked the sample after my nine-breath method, the cells had most certainly changed for the better, but there were still somewhere around 60% of them still attached together, but now they were in smaller clumps, rather than in a continuous line. Although I was happy to see a change, I could feel that this was definitely a physical response to the increase in oxygen throughout my body from the excessive breathing I had done. I was a little discouraged by the lack of dramatic change I was expecting, of which I realized, the expectation was the transmission from the subtle indoctrination of this particular Qi Gung spiritual salesman running the workshop. He had a lot of hype about the supposedly HUGE spiritual and physical benefits to the body from this form of breath work. My Spirit's *Awareness experience* throughout the workshop however, kept his covert projections of these high and mighty expectations in check, but my spiritual identity obviously became attached to some of them. I had to leave my little research experiment for the time being here, as my client became anxious of our time together and we had to get the session underway. I thought I would just see what my structure was like after the session, to see if my Conscious Bodywork has any effect.

Well once I finished the session, I was told that the office had some major phone issues and that some phone tech guy was needing to work in my space immediately. This ended up being for nearly two hours. This was VERY frustrating to find out at the last minute like this. This meant I couldn't do my follow up blood test and that I had to cancel my next session as well, then live in hope that he finished in time for my following client. Fortunately, he did finish just in time for my next client, but I was then rushed to get my blood test done again before starting the session. The results this time shocked me even more than the previous one in the morning. This time, the worm structure of my cells weaved about three times across the screen with a kind of lethargic motion. This time, I felt into the experience I was having at the time I had taken the test sample and realized, I was still quite stressed from all the alterations to my schedule etc. Now, experiencing this stress reaction going on within me, a flash of inspiration washed through me to use my Awareness Embodiment Living Meditation practice and discharge my stress experience.

The Awareness Embodiment Living Meditation practice is actually a short and simple present moment meditation I use it to simply tweek and ground my Spirit's Awareness into my human-self. It is a very brief and *in the moment* meditation and in *this* moment, only took about forty-five seconds to complete and to get to a deep state of simple experiential Awareness. I motioned the technician to take the sample as I stayed in Awareness, experiencing my Self without definitions, judgments or descriptions of what I was feeling/experiencing. The results this time didn't shock me at all, but totally dumbfounded both myself AND the technician. She commented that she had *never* seen anything like this kind of result before. Not only had all of my cells separated out singularly again, but they were now streaming across the screen at an incredible speed, of which the technician had never witnessed before and I had no idea was even possible. All the cells were so active, were so energized and moving so fast, that we had trouble capturing a suitable picture with a lot of cells on the screen at the same time. Although it only takes a half of a second for the computer to register the click of the mouse to take the picture, by the time the computer took the picture after the click, half the cells were already off screen. From this you can get a sense of how fast they were travelling.

Experiencing ... by feeling with my Spirit-Self's Experiencer Awareness, super-energizes the whole-body system, not just at the cellular level, but the whole space between the cells, the space I occupy as a unified Body Soul and Spirit.

Many times, I have heard people say that we need to raise our vibration, to increase our energy etc. Of course, there have been equally as many consciousness exercises like the breathwork one, all developed to facilitate this *raising of energy.* Who would have thought though that it could be raised quicker and more effectively by simply fully *experiencing* Life. To say we were both stunned by this result, is a massive understatement. I felt a flush of spiritual insight wash over me, cleansing my Soul's identities of any doubt of what had just been revealed to us. Clearly and definitively, this showed that *experiencing*, by simply super-*feeling with our Awareness*, we connect all three self's together and Divine Life Force flows through our whole BEing, rejuvenating and regenerating everything it permeates. My cells were reflecting to us both the result of a highly energized body system. Through meditation, insight revealed that the cells clump and stick together to share Life Force when there is an insufficient supply or flow throughout the Body, Soul and Spirit BEing.

When there is an ample supply of Life Force, the cells separate and become super active, transforming the body structure to a state of optimal health and function.

Experiencing by Awareness is not a function of just the Body, or the Soul, but is one of the Spirit. Although Awareness *is* an ability of your Spirit-Self, in its *application of experiencing*, it affects and incorporates all three components of Body Soul and Spirit that make up the Human BEing that you are. If any one of these components are left out of this dynamic incorporation, if any one of your Body Soul or Spirit components are disconnected, then true experiencing is interrupted, along with it of course, the flow of Life Force that comes with it linking them all. My cell structure transformation from the Roleaux state of ill-health, to a super-charged state of wellness throughout my whole BEing, came about from just *forty-five seconds* of a quiet, peaceful and relaxed practice of Awareness Embodiment. Ironically, this is not the usual intellectually known state of meditation of having to sit in a quiet space or under a Banyan tree to gain any results. This is a practice I have found that achieves this calm super-charged state of heightened Awareness every time, in *seconds*, in any moment, with your eyes wide open and consciously present in the environment you are in at *any* time. Imagine living in this state of embodied Awareness 24/7, rhythmically manifesting and experiencing life fully. It is this state of Living Awareness, which naturally invokes a complete willingness to experience all of Life. This willingness automatically brings us back into a rhythmic harmony with the Divine Orchestration of ALL of life for the highest good for all ... no longer just for self alone.

I consider true freedom, comes from the willingness to experience ANYTHING. Ironically, in this free state of willingness, I no longer "have to" experience everything ... yet, I AM Willing to.

The rhythms of Life are designed to support us to continue to evolve and grow for the good of all. Natures rhythmic cycles are another way in which the Divine is assisting us in the development of our consciousness also. Kai Po once shared with me the dynamic cycles of full and new moons, which will help us understand the effect of cycles for our higher good. In agriculture, the full moon is the time when all the minerals, all the earth energies of *form and structure*, are drawn up from the Earth into the plant. This is why a full moon is a harvest moon for certain produce, because all the goodness of the earth *forces* that support our human growth and development are up in the plant, ready and ripe for the picking so to speak ... and integration. Notice I am talking about *forces* here ... not nutritional chemistry. The *new moon* on the other hand, is the time when all of these same energies are now down in the earth, but it is also the time when the cosmic spiritual energies of creation are drawn down into the Earth as well. This is why it is a time to plant, when the spiritual realm's *creational forces* are present in the Earth, making it fertile ground to grow and bring new life into this world. There are also supportive truths that come from the practices of Bio-dynamic farming principles, as developed by Rudolph Steiner. One of the understandings in Bio-dynamics that has come from research of seed propagation, is that if you plant certain seeds at specific times of the cosmic cycle, they will propagate and grow up to three hundred percent faster and better than if sown at a time that is off cycle. This of course clearly shows, that there is a significant additional influence for growth exerted on our physical environment at specific moments in the rhythmic cosmic cycles, that continually affect us all.

This cosmic rhythm of above and below has great significance and effect on us all as well as the obvious ones of nature her Self. There is no separation within the spiritual realm. ALL separation is a construct of and only exists within ... the reality of human consciousness. Within this consciousness, when we understand this experientially, then this "crazy" *full moon* energy we often perceive manifesting chaos around us, can be utilized more correctly to harvest our *crop of consciousness*, and to thin out the weak, useless crops, from the strong and healthy ones. This means, that we can harvest the virtuous states of being we have embodied from our previous months journey and integrate all the resisted experiences we packed down and pushed aside throughout the month. It is these resisted experiences that become the growing weeds of conflict and dis-harmony in our lives. The *new moon* on the other hand, is a time to bring new ideas, concepts etc. into our individual reality, to plant conceptual seeds so they will grow and mature into a healthy physical manifestation.

The full moon in consciousness, is when all of the resisted elements of self, show up and are drawn up and out into the light of our Awareness. From there, they can be either harvested and integrated as new virtues and attributes of self or become opportunities to once again integrate the weak and resisted experiences of self, the ones that have been hindering and limiting the growth and development of your Human-Spirit. I'm sure you may have noticed the times when you felt a little extra crazy or agitated around a full moon for example, when you maybe felt a little extra resistant and reactive to your environment and the people in it. Did you notice also that it all seemed to be on automatic and you were reacting without any real conscious understanding of why you seemed more irritable than usual? Every full moon, emergency wards in hospitals report an increase in trauma through this period of our cosmic cycles. These are all responses to the _forces_ that affect us during these full moon periods. Through Astrology, it is also known that the position of other cosmic bodies, the planets that share our Galaxy at this time, bring about additional influences on our BEing also. These additional individually specific influences bring to the light of our Awareness, certain other specific traits and resisted experiences for us to complete as well. The most important element through our human life however is ... the integration of these resisted elements of our consciousness with their correlating attachments.

This is why people go a little wacky at the full moon. All of their resisted aspects of their self are being drawn to the surface of their Consciousness Soul, where they are now made _conscious_ of them. Remember, your consciousness can't really _experience_ yet without Awareness, so at a full moon, although they are affecting you, you have only become conscious of them, but not at that point, actually fully _experiencing_ them yet. With Awareness from your Spirit-Self however, these resurfaced resisted experiences can now be integrated, can be turned into fertilizer for the Soul by simply completing them and embody the appropriate virtue of your Spirit that these experiences are calling for. This is the time to bring them in from the isolation of your resistances and attachments, you have been trying to push them out of your Life for the whole month, or as is most common where for many years, you have tried to avoid and ignore ownership of your Life's creations. Each month is your opportunity to clear the ground after harvesting, so that the weeds of resisted experiences overrunning your Consciousness garden patch, won't strangle the new Life Streams trying to be established through your new moon conceptual plantings into your personal reality. This is the time of Cosmic support for us all to _own our stuff,_ to be brutally honest with our self and EXTREMELY diligent to NOT keep pushing our resisted self's out in the world ... again ... where we inflict them onto others, as we try to make _them_ responsible for our imperfections. When we do this, we simply foul our own space, stagnate our Soul's fertile environment, and create yet another dense layer of resistance on top of the ones we have already been creating for maybe most of our lives.

A stagnant Soul is at the heart of most dis-ease and illness in our present world.

Your full moon opportunity is ... an opportunity to embrace, integrate and bring into your Soul-self the resisted experiences of your past month. This is not a time to try and let go and get rid of them, which are just more covert forms of resistance. It is harvest time! It is time to harvest what these experiences have brought to your hopefully now Aware consciousness and integrate them through the embodiment of the appropriate virtue that reveals itself from *these experiences*. The full moon is not just a physical cycle of heavenly bodies shadowing each other. There are very specific forces connected to each heavenly body that trigger very particular and intimate elements of our human-self to the surface. Any good astrologer can confirm the effects of these cosmic stimulants on our state of BE-ing. It is these very same influences that Rudolph Steiner intimately recognized and researched to find the powerful influence for growth they assert on seed germination. Can we really believe that this undeniable influence on the growth of our plant kingdom has absolutely no effect on the growth of our own Body Soul or Spirit?

The full moon cycles are cosmic consciousness events, designed to assist all of our human creations. They are supportive forces to complete and discharge old experiences and make way for new experience streams.

It is in the following month where new experience-streams can then be planted into your healthy Soul's fertile space at the next new moon.

The new moon is the rhythm of new creations, of bringing in and planting new experiences in your human reality. This is the time to meditate on what new ideas, actions, thoughts etc., are essential to your highest good, to bring about a growth in consciousness and the embodiment of more Spirit in your life. A new moon is a time to make plans and set things in motion that will bring about an enhanced way of Life that will improve your existence ... preferably for the betterment of humanity. This is the time when the Cosmic forces of creation are drawn down into your BEing, into your human reality, where new life from your etheric Life Body can fertilize and energize your new ideas, concepts and inspirations. This is so your human seeds of reality can propagate and take root in your world reality. This is not to be mistaken for a time to just set new intentions for your outer world actions and creations solely for personal gain, as has been the case with the creation of the intellectualized version of Ho'oponopono from the spiritual salesman I previously spoke of above. These types of intention and goal setting play into the darker forces of intellectual materialism, which will ultimately trap you in the limited physical world and sabotage your access to the true Divine creative power that comes from a Spirit embodied human.

This is the time to plant the seeds of inner health and wellness, with ideas and concepts that align with a *higher* benefit for a greater good, than a purely personal one. This is the time to plant new reality seeds for your personal human experience—*which align with a greater good*—for humanity as a collective. This form of planting strengthens the power in your Soul forces, as you now gain access to the true *power* of higher Divine Intentions as well. To create for personal gain only—weakens the power of your Soul forces and its ability to overcome the influences from the *diverting forces* driving the lower intentions of our collective egotistic nature. This is where and when, healthy Soul Forces are essential for the propagation of new ideas etc. It is only through a healthy Soul that the Divine Cosmos is capable of bringing *higher* insight and ideals into the individual AND collective human reality systems; by which ultimately transforms both.

An unhealthy Soul lays itself <u>subject</u> to the darker diverting forces of materialistic and intellectually egoistic influences on the lower nature.

These diverting forces trap you in a process of densification of your Soul ... rather than an enlightening spiritualization of it.

When you plant seedlings in a garden, if there is a layer of crusty clay on the surface of your bed; of what could be potentially good soil to grow in, then the seedling will die. It will die, because when the clay dries out, it creates an impenetrable barrier on the surface that prevents life giving water from permeating deep into the soil and the plants roots. What *was* a good soil for growing, will now become dry, hard and too hot for the soft and subtle rootling's to take hold. Without the growth of these rootling's, the plant can't draw the appropriate supporting forces necessary for its sustained growth, into a mature and productive Living organism. These very same principles and effects hold true for your Soul also and its ability to nurture, support and contribute to a thriving and spiritually evolving humanity.

My Soul is but a rootling of the living organism, that is our collective humanity.

When your continued resistances or attachments to experiences becomes the crusty clay that covers your Soul's essence for growth and expansion of your consciousness, your human-self becomes dry, hard and hot, becomes decrepit, stiff and dense. The most obvious sign of this dense decrepit state of human-self existence, manifest as physical ill-health and dis-ease. This denseness is impenetrable by change through new ideas and higher ideals, let alone the embodiment of the Life-giving virtues of your Spirit. This is what is necessary for change to take root in your Soul and grow your human into a mature and enlivened BEing. This state can become so impenetrable, that the forces of Life's experience streams are unable to penetrate and flow through you. This contributes to the further breakdown of your physical body systems, along with the pushing out of your Spirit-Self's ability to experience with Awareness. A simple research into all those who suffer dis-ease and especially chronic dis-eases, could reveal the truth of how un-willing those individuals are to actually make real changes in their lives. For these individuals, to bring in and plant new ideas into their Soul, with <u>committed</u> intentions to do what it takes for *those* ideas and changes to grow to maturity and bear fruit in their Life, is extremely difficult.

To simply experience Life's experience streams fully, by super-feeling with Awareness, but without resistance or attachment, regenerates the Body, enlivens the Soul and embodies the Spirit in my Human.

Through my Conscious Bodyworks practice ... and of course from experiencing my Self with Awareness; the physical Bodies relationship to experiences has revealed itself, along with its ability to manifest dis-ease by storing and anchoring resisted experiences within its-self. Every function of the physical body structure has a correlating experience in the structure of the Soul. Every specific part of the *physical body* has a particular and unique function within the functioning of the whole organism acting as your physical human instrument. The function embedded in every intended experience, within the experience stream being Divinely Orchestrated to come your way, correlates with and is mirrored by, the function of a specific part of your physical body as well. That correlating body part becomes the *anchor* for that particular experience, enabling it to manifest its self in your reality. If you don't block or interrupt this orchestration, then the experience can flow through you and that particular body part remains open, healthy and functional. If you, or more correctly, your mind or Intellectual Soul, decide to NOT participate in the experience stream being presented to you, if you resist the intended experience for you that is embedded within that Life Stream, then that Life Stream's Life Force becomes blocked at the physical anchor point for that experience in your physical body. It is the blocking or interruption of this flow of Life Force that then creates a dis-harmony or dis-function within that *specific part* of the body, where the correlating *experience function* exists. It is these dis-harmonies, these dysfunctions, which then manifest as physical illness and the further breaking down of not just the physical, but the etheric Life Body also.

The ancient healing art of acupuncture confirms this as fact also, with the use of the needles on specific acupoint's; of which there are over four hundred throughout the whole body. The needling of these points is used to open these blocks of Qi, of Life Force, allowing Life Force to flow freeing throughout the Body and Soul once more. The healings achieved from acupuncture come about from the freeing up of this flow of Life Force through not just your physical body system, but your Soul system from which your emotional human events are created as well. What exists with acupuncture, is a clear understanding of the function of these points and the meridians they exist on. These meridians are like a map of lines for each particular system, which have specific names and functions for each, such as Bladder meridian or Liver meridian, Heart meridian and so on. Each of these meridians; of which there is 14 charted meridians, have specific correlating emotional states of the Soul associated with each. The Stomach meridian for example, when in balance, supports a sense of basic trust; but when its flow is impeded or blocked, its reactive emotion is obsessive worry. This has a proven link to stomach ulcers and indigestion.

I don't want to go into detail of this system, just to point out that acupuncture's wisdom of the correlation of the human experiences and their physical counterpart through the body, is ancient wisdom grounded in our human reality now, from over five thousand years of Chinese medicine.

The Awareness Embodiment technology that has been revealed for experiencing Life, does not in any way negate or invalidate this ancient form of healing through the harmonization of our Body and Soul, but in fact, they support each other tremendously. Five thousand years of proven treatment through acupuncture for the manifestation of consciousness related illnesses, is clear confirmation of the existence of this correlation between Body and Soul dis-harmonies I am sharing with you now. There is however a difference between these technologies. Acupuncture came about basically, for the treatment of consciousness related illnesses manifesting in the body. This system was first revealed for the level of consciousness our human BEing was at, five thousand years ago through to now. Acupuncture was not created to just heal the body, but to also understand the creations of consciousness as well. Although acupuncture can be self-administered, it is generally done on someone by someone else and the diagnosis necessary for the *correct* application, requires a trained practitioner. This form of treatment is an external stimulation for an internal response between both Body and Soul. The Awareness Embodiment system is different, because it is a totally internal self-administering treatment of which empowers the individual with the ability to become the diagnostic and administrative practitioner of their own treatment. This form not only empowers the individual to be their own practitioner and open the flow of Life Force throughout the Body and Soul, but it also embodies the Spirit.

The greatest self-empowerment that comes from the Awareness Embodiment system, is giving ME, the individual, the ability to not just harmonize and align my Body and Soul, but to embody and ground my Spirit, from which a resultant state of a harmonized Human-BEing is achieved.

Through Awareness Embodiment, it is now possible for you to be your own practitioner of your own consciousness healings and harmonization's. With embodied Awareness, you can use the Conscious Bodywork understanding of how the correlating physical body functions are connected to your Soul created human events. Just this Awareness alone, gives you the ability to now deliberately and fully, experience ALL of your Life through your integrated Spirit BEing-Self.

I AM my own practitioner of my own self-healing, using my body as the doorway into my Soul.

For example, if the intended consciousness experience for you, is to experience your resisted rigidity *of self*, and you resist owning and experiencing your rigid human-self in any and all of the forms it exists within you, then you will create a dis-function within the knees. If you look at the physical *function* of the knees, yes, they provide us with the ability to move, but more specifically, to be flexible and balanced in our stance, to be "bamboo like" and sway and bend with whatever is happening. I often tell my clients, our knees are how we surf with Life, it is our ability to be flexible with Life's circumstances and allow things to pass over and through us and not take the full brunt of the forces pushing against us. If you look at the great bamboo plant structure and its ability to bend and sway with the storm winds, you will see it will still be the one standing *after* the storm. The rigid Oak or softer wooded pine, taking a solid and rigid stance against the forces upon it, will often break and be damaged. So, this *flexibility* is the main function of the knees, to NOT be *rigid*, but flexible and bamboo-like.

If Life's intended experience stream for me is to *experience* my rigidity and I *don't* resist the experience and embody an appropriate virtue for that particular experience; which may be for example, but not limited to ... *acceptance*, then life will flow harmoniously through me, enlivening and aligning my whole BE-ing of Body Soul and Spirit. From this, no dis-functions of the knees would manifest. My whole BE-ing would be enlivened by not just the Life Force inherent within the experience stream flowing through me, but also the *spiritual force* of the now newly *embodied* virtue of acceptance as well. It is this embodiment of the spiritual force, through in this case the virtue of acceptance, which spiritualizes my human-self. This spiritualization expands my Consciousness Soul, thus developing my Soul forces further, making it sufficiently capable of embodying even more virtue of Spirit the next time. This correlation is present for every physical part of the body and their function within the whole.

Can you see here also the difference again between acupuncture and Awareness Embodiment? Acupuncture also understands the connection between body illness and experience, but it correlates with the *emotional influence* in the creation of the human event via the Soul. This is the state of your Intellectual Soul specifically, of your state of *Soul* wellbeing. Awareness Embodiment correlates with the Consciousness Soul directly through *experience* via the Spirit. This is how you are BEing within your Souls emotional state and its human reacts and creations of the human event created by that emotional state. This shows us not only the difference between these systems, but also the different level of consciousness humanity is at. The *Spirit Consciousness* we are rising into right now, is the right time for Awareness Embodiment to reveal its Self to us, to facilitate this rise and understanding of Spirit. Five thousand years ago, when we were rising into the level of *Soul* Consciousness, it was the right time for acupuncture to reveal its self to us, to help facilitate that rise and understanding of Consciousness through the Intellectual Soul.

The eyes may well be the window to the Soul, but I would suggest to you, that your whole physical body, is the doorway to your Soul.

A window only allows you to look in ... a doorway allows you to walk in and experience the room.

The window to the Soul makes it possible to *see* the correlation between the function of the individual body parts and the experiences being presented to the Soul by the Divine Orchestration of Life's experience streams.

The doorway to the Soul, makes it possible to super-feel with your Awareness, what the *experience* is, that is created; from which the dysfunctional body part is but a symptom of your resistance to the experience. The door is the dysfunctional body part ... the doorway is the *experience*—is how you BE with the dysfunction—is what you are experiencing through the dysfunction. It is through this doorway, of which you may choose to walk through and as such, allow you—your true *observer* experiencing Spirit-Self, to walk back into the room of your Soul and find the present moment experience being avoided or resisted in that room. Once you are in the room of your Soul, you can then re-decorate it with the appropriate virtue of which, will enhance this room that is your Soul. By choosing not to walk through this doorway, you slam the door shut on the experience stream, blocking the flow and consequently creating more *pressure and conflict* on the Soul to manifest the full experiential event the Divine is asking of it. This is what Life's experience stream has been trying to present to you. In the true sense of the word, your physical diseases are not purely physical creations.

Although some physical conditions can be the result of other physical conditions, the TRUE *originations* of the mis-alignments, dis-eases and conflicts manifesting through the body, come from a Soul and Spirit nature. These manifest physically as the body responds to these originating conditions by creating certain physical mis-alignments and conflicts between body parts. Let's look at the example from the previous scenario above of the knees and rigidity, and this time keep in mind what we learned from the earlier chapter on "Experiencing"; that for example, we can't integrate "empowerment", without first experiencing the opposite human event of "dis-empowerment".

My Spirit may be intending to integrate more flexibility into my Soul Life, to open it up through embodying the virtue of acceptance, into my human-self for example. This Spirit Intention then triggers in my Soul, the appropriate reactive and defensive "belligerent identity" that already exists within me as a creation from within my Intellectual Soul. This "belligerent identity" now reacts and defends itself against all external environmental triggers coming to it from the supportive Divine Orchestration of events. This Orchestration brings to my environment someone or something that challenges me to be more flexible in either my thinking, feeling or willing. From the resistance and attachment conflict generated by this "belligerent identity", my body responds with tension within the body system, creating a stiffening of the muscle systems. This stiffening is concentrated around the muscles of the knees, because this identity senses, as part of its belligerent rigidity, the need to protect itself from threat. If you super-feel with your Awareness, you may notice that the first thing you do when there is any *perceived* threat to your physical self, or even emotional wellbeing, is to bend the knees in a position to create a more solid and *rigid* stance, one capable of *resisting* any outside influences. Although the knees are about rigidity, there are very specific points on the inside of both knees that relate specifically to the *experience* of *protection*. Protection itself is actually a symptom and contributing factorial element of rigidity. I often use these points on clients for specific diagnosis of the experience of protection, so they may gain access through this experience doorway to their Soul, the condition of them *living* in this protective environment, of which my client is almost always unaware of.

In my case within this example, my physical body is responding with the muscle spasms of *protective rigidity* to a perceived threat. This in truth, my identity is although falsely created, never the less manifests this threat as my Soul's human-self reality through the belligerent identity of my Intellectual Soul. These physical muscle spasms now create a further *purely physical* response of compression within the micro muscular and ligament structures of the knees. Here is the *first* of our physically manifested conditions, created purely from a previous *Soul originated* physical condition. This condition created *physically*, is now the physical *compression* of the knee joint. From this compression, the inherent lack of blood flow and consequent lack of cleaning out of the lactic acids, salts and toxins etc. by the lymph system as well. This now creates a sclerotic and inflexible condition of all the muscle and ligaments connecting the soft tissue and bone structure of the knee together. What now takes shape, is another purely physical manifestation from this now toxic physical condition of the whole knee structure made up of bone, ligament and muscle. The result of these physical reactions ... is pain ... physical pain.

MOST ... physical manifestations, have their <u>true</u> <u>ORIGINATIONS</u> in either the Soul or Spirit.

Can you start to see how far down the creation line our purely physical creations are? How many steps and points of influence have taken place, before I actually had the truly observable physical "event" of pain in my knees show up? A friend for example, who is very rigid in his thinking, feeling and a gross lack of willing, had chronic knee pain. When an MRI was finally taken because he was experiencing pain, it revealed sever degeneration of the ligaments and separating disc between the bones. These discs are *divinely* designed to disperse compression and prevent the bones coming together. This of course, is the physical consequence of a *long-term* condition of rigidity originating *many* years prior to the symptoms of pain and degeneration being able to be experienced. Of course, all of that history has an origination in a lack of Awareness also. Consequently, the event of the pain he had been experiencing for some time before having the MRI, actually created even less movement. His Intellectual Soul logically justified his rigidity by it all now being too physically painful to walk or make changes in his life. As resistance, the physical pain was now an appropriate distraction from the experience of rigidity of his Soul. This then adequately moved ownership of his inner rigidity further from his Awareness. By this stage, Awareness and Spirit have been pushed even further away. The ultimate manifestation of his continued rigidity of his Soul, of the creation of being too physically painful to move, his lack of Will-ingness to change or do things and think differently, resulted in the final escalated condition of tremendous obesity.

From obesity, which of course is yet another now *chronic* physical symptom of rigidity; he now became even more incapable of moving. From this came the next inevitable physical condition of the breakdown in his heart and body, as it struggled to maintain circulation etc., to maintain any flow of Life Force through this now chronically rigid human system of Body and Soul. Ironically, the blood and its flow, are spiritual expressions of the Spirit Higher "I" Ego. The kicker here is, that the suppression of blood flow correlates with the suppression of his Spirit in his Soul, as he resists Aware feeling to take ownership of his Soul's rigid condition. Yes, he did end up in hospital, as he on one inevitable day, while trying to bend down to pick something up from the floor, fell over and severely damaged his knee and couldn't get back up. Are you surprised that it was his knee he damaged? Life continually tries to get our attention on the resisted experiences of our Soul life through our body conditions. Each time we ignore or avoid Life's "call to arms" to do the inner work necessary to virtue-ize the Souls condition ... the Divine Orchestration gets louder, and more intense events are created until we can't avoid it any longer.

The more I resist and ignore the doorway to my Soul opening via my body conditions, the more dramatic and chronically, Life slaps my physical body with increased ferocity.

Fortunately, he lived through this whole ordeal, as the hospital and traditional treatments went about as they do, dealing with the physical symptoms. Today, even after over 12 months of sever rehabilitation, he still carries too much weight and yes, he still carries and defends his rigid viewpoints vigorously, which ironically, is where his condition originated from. Still today, his friends and family shy away from bringing up anything of ownership with him, as all such conversations inevitably end up in denial and attacking rebuttals. Although his relentless search for that ultimate physical therapy that will finally change his condition *for him* ... and although he has most definitely lost some pounds through these physical treatments, he is still unwilling to dive into the depth of ownership of his Soul, of which his Spirit cries out for. Consequently, he still has a chronic weight issue that keeps him physically restricted and rigid. It is only by deep diving into true self-ownership of *HIS* creation of *HIS* rigid Soul, along with the experiences *HE* is creating for his human-self, that a sustainable change in his condition can come about. It is only through this level of ownership stimulating his Soul's embodiment of the virtue of humility and acceptance, that the physical condition of flexibility can once again enter his life. His physical condition as a result of this persistent reluctance is still an oversized reflection, of the conflict that continues to rage between his resistance and attachments. From this conflict, the chasm of dis-connect between his Soul and Spirit forever widens, as he resists being flexible or wrong and attached to being rigidly right. I still see the same behavioral patterns that originated his obese condition, running strong to this day.

How far from the true originating cause, are my actual physical conditions of ill-health?

Now ask your Self this question, "how am I able to truly heal my physical conditions to the point of freedom from their originating cause, if I only look at it and treat it from a singularly physical perspective?" There are so many treatments in our world now, for so many physical conditions of dis-ease etc. and they do most definitely create changes in the physical conditions created as reacts from physical conditions ... and yes, they can get us to a point of *pain relief*, but ... do they actual heal the true causes, the true originations of our physical conditions? How many treatments require you to be medicated for the rest of your life to keep your physical condition away? Is it really a so called "*healing treatment*", if you have to take it for the rest of your life? Or is it simply a *symptom management system* disguised as a treatment? Let's be real here, most westernized drug related medical treatments, are simply camouflaging the physical symptoms, so they are seemingly no longer overwhelming the body. What's worse is that these same medications push the Spirit out of the equation, along with the potential for true and sustainable healing. How many times have you heard of people being treated and then having to further medicate for the symptoms of that treatment? Look at the litany of symptoms and side effects of drugs being advertised on your TV etc. and try to truthfully tell your Self that these drug treatments are good for your Body Soul and Spirit. The most ironically mindless treatment I have noticed of late is chemotherapy for cancer. Would you believe that chemotherapy actually physically causes cancer? How mindless and disconnected from the true healing Life Force of Spiritual wisdom have we come, when we are treating the physical symptom of cancer, with a physical treatment that physically causes cancer? Even the medical field admit that chemotherapy doesn't even kill the *originating* cancer producing cells, but only the *symptomatic* cells created *from* the originators.

There is NEVER any true healing of ANYTHING ... without the removal or discharging of the Souls originating cause of that condition.

Some years ago, I had a couple of weeks of immersing my Self in this Collective Consciousness swamp of "death by cancer". I had just found out that I have skin cancer, which I had suspected for some year's prior, because of a persistent spot on my leg. Of course, out of resistance, I didn't do anything about it. Yes, I was in denial ... which is simply, resistance to experiencing. Although this was not particularly Life threatening to me at that stage, it did however thrust me into the whole cancer paradigm of unknowns, fear and suffering from regrets and sadness. Obviously, a lot of fear was generated as resistance to having any form of chemotherapy or other synthetic westernized treatments.

My Kahuna once said that the *sickness* of cancer comes from a deep seated, unresolved sadness, and having personally experienced that 2 weeks, I felt the truth of the experience he was referring to. Through experiencing with my Awareness Embodiment system and because of my now intimate experience of cancer, I spent a few weeks allowing myself to unearth all those areas of my Life that are still retaining any residual energy of sadness, attachment and resistance etc. and particularly abandonment. A fascinating exploration, for although I have done *many* explorations over many years of ownership in these specific areas, it was interesting now to just "allow" the residual energy still obviously anchored in my body, to surface for further completion. This was as you could imagine, both scary and liberating at the same time. Many insights revealed their self to me through this journey, along with countless surprises of how much energy was actually still trapped within me. These incomplete resisted experiences were still requiring a virtue embodiment.

One of the greatest revelations to me has been how cancer of ALL types, is the extreme expression of *resistance to sadness* and its inherent attachments to the perception of abandonment's in all forms. It is not just about where others had abandoned me, but much more particularly where I had abandoned my Self. My sadness from abandonment of which I was suppressing within me from previous and current human events, was the very same sadness I was feeling that was stimulated by having these cancers right now. The experience was the same, but the consequence of death here now was the extreme version of that sadness as apposed to the abandonment experience. This all made it impossible to avoid any longer. I could experientially see now what my beloved Kai Po was sharing with me. It is the resisted stored remnants that eventually and inevitably, manifested the NOW more extreme experience of sadness of which I had been resisting for so long. Yet here now, I couldn't avoid it any longer. This sadness IS the cancer, which had been silently eating away at me for years. The physical form of cancer is an uncontrollable growth that eats away and overwhelms the physical body. Ironically again, sadness when suppressed and pushed out of Awareness, becomes an uncontrollable malignant growth within the Soul, that ultimately also overwhelms the Soul's forces necessary to overcome it. Can you see again the correlation here between experience and body function?

One who lives in this state of deeply suppressed sadness, sows the seeds of terminal physical cancer, deep within their Soul.

If you super-feel with your Awareness, you may notice that all cases of cancer, inevitable invoke an experience of deep sadness, not just in the sufferer, but also those close to them. Isn't it ironic that cancer, being the result of a deep suppression of sadness by the sufferer ... inevitably invokes deep sadness in the very same individual that is trying to avoid experiencing it? You see here, an example of how Life's intended experiences and consequent opportunity for virtue embodiment ... can NOT be denied. If we avoid, push away, resist, deny, ignore or try to get rid of any experience, we create for our human-self, an escalation of physical conditions that will inevitable HAVE to be experienced. You see ... we ARE the Soul creators of our chronic physical ailments.

After two weeks of finally allowing myself to experience all that is connected to sadness and abandonment within me, I woke on a Thursday morning and was painfully looking at the large open lesion on my leg. This morning, I decided to allow my Spirit-Self's Awareness to enter my Consciousness Soul to intimately and fully *feel* VERY sorry and sad for my human-self. All of a sudden, I had a rush of spiritual insight. In a flash I "KNEW" and even stated to my Self, that I wasn't going to die from this as long as I keep "experiencing" the massive Life change this event of cancer was trying to bring to me. As I stayed in "super-feel" through my Awareness, within a half hour I was getting insight after insight of the connection between our Body and Soul and the power of this system of experiencing we have to work with, to neutralize and discharge these build ups of resisted energies.

I was laughing at my-self out loud, because of the simplicity of this Divine system that brings our deepest resisted experience and their inherent energy blocks to the surface to be cleared. I could see that this is a Divine Orchestration operating, so I may remain the most optimal Human, Spiritually possible ... in *any* present moment. I saw how from my experience of the cancers coming out on me when I would expose my body to the sun, that the sun was actually drawing them to the surface. This Cosmic intention is to draw the issue to the light, to be seen so I could connect with them and make things right within my Self. Nature and her cycles were reflecting to me and within me, an answer to the treatment of this *sickness*. Remember we discussed earlier the difference between a sickness being a disharmony in the Soul and an illness being a disharmony in the Body?

My Body had opened its physical <u>illness</u> doorway, to the <u>sickness</u> room of my Soul's resisted sadness experience.

By using my Awareness to super-feel again, this allowed me also to bring to the surface those associated and correlating resisted experiences still trapped in my Body. By allowing them to reveal to me, in the light of my Awareness, the very experiential energy that is contributing to my physical illness of dis-harmonies and dis-eases, blocks were being removed and I could feel my vitality increasing immediately. I could feel those resisted experience streams starting to flow again and Life Force starting to enliven my Soul once more.

On this insightful day, I was going to do some landscaping for my therapist friend, but with all of this happening, I decided to not work and try to write about this and continue my experiential discharging journey. When I called my friend to tell him I wasn't coming, his first question to me was, what have I done about the leg cancer? Before I could answer, he immediately started asking his other practitioners at his practice if they knew anything about how to treat it. Just as he was asking this, another practitioner who works there part time, was walking past and said "Ohh yeah, I've been treating them very simply for eighteen years now with an ancient American Indian herbal treatment with enormous success". He put her on the phone ... we talked ... I made an appointment that afternoon ... we began the first session. One application that afternoon of the worst and most obvious ones, of which I had over 20 on my chest apart from the large lesion on my leg and by the morning they were dead. We treated about five for the first treatment. At this rate ALL my skin cancers right now—and I had plenty of them, will be dead within two weeks without any dramatic rehabilitation's.

The *natural* physical clearing had begun so effortlessly I believe, because the space had been opened up as the healing of my Being was being completed. The more I moved diligently and honestly toward making things right with myself, the more my space opened up to let Spirit in and its intuition of higher guidance to guide me once more. It was from this open space of being right with Self, that allowed the Divine Orchestration to flow again through me, bringing to me the new experience of healing from the angel in my friend's office. The ongoing prevention will _not_ come in the form of resisting the sun, for it was resistance that created this cancerous event in the first place. It would come in the form of embracing a Life change of increased wellness on ALL levels of my Being through nutritional, emotional, physical and especially Spiritual practices that optimize the amount of Life Force flowing through me. This was an event that happened after the blood cell research I talked about earlier, so the insight into our BEing's need for Life Force on all levels of our existence, now sang a familiar and inspiring song of needs and possibilities for change.

I couldn't help but appreciate the Divine sequencing that once more brought ALL of this ... TO ME. This Divine Orchestration that had this angel walk past my friend just at the right time to hear the word cancer, without drama suffering and or grief attachment to any of it. My Will-ingness to experience anything completely and continually, neutralized any escalation of drama and resistance my Intellect would have loved to bring up. I know without doubt, that through further resistance and attachment, an escalation of the physical symptoms would have surely occurred, which would have also surely prolonged and no doubt intensified this whole journey of suffering for me. The truly amazing insightful result of this cancer journey into the depths of ownership of yet more sadness, was that after just two applications of the treatment, my body stopped reacting to the sun. This happened even though I hadn't treated every single spot on me. I no longer had the massive chest breakouts I had been having for the previous year. After only two applications and only treating about fifty percent of the remaining exposed spots, they all cleared up and never returned. This could not have only happened from the physical treatment alone, but because I had treated the cause of the cancers, the sadness itself, which is at the root of the condition. I removed the originating source, rather than just the manifesting symptom.

So, here is the full picture for you of what the Kahuna ancestors of Molokai were showing me, of how experiencing with embodied Awareness is Ho'oponopono for the world.

Remember, at the heart of all conflict is resistance and attachment? Well, sadness holds a deep attachment to something that has been perceived as lost or no longer obtainable. Through experientially understanding my Soul's components of Intellectual and Consciousness aspects, I was able to discover and become _conscious_ of this attachment within me. This particular attachment had to do with me being in the USA and my daughters and family still being in Australia. My _attachment_ was to have them close and being able to touch and hug and interact with them in any present moment. Although I had been in the USA at that time some six years or so and had done hours and hours of conscious work specific to this topic, through the Spirit-less belief system of that organization I talked about earlier, I was still deeply attached to and missing my family. Through that practice and many other cognitive ones, I have experienced throughout the years, the obvious virtue to apply here was non-attachment. The obvious resisted experience here was to be this virtue of non-attachment. The obvious solution to my _perceived_ problem seemed to be to simply become non-attached to my family. This solution however failed many times to free me from this attachment yet now was unavoidable, because in that cancer moment, I not only still had attachment to them, but

I now had cancer to intensify the issue for me even more. This solution failed, because it was a *cognitive* solution of my Intellectual Soul's rational and logical faculties. It failed to get to the real <u>experience</u> I was avoiding ownership of. Cognitive therapy is a thinking therapy created by the Intellect, for the concept of mind, but unfortunately, it is contained and limited within the Intellectual Soul mind. Because the Intellectual and Consciousness aspects of my Soul cannot feel or experience fully <u>without</u> Spirit-Self's Awareness, the mind of my Soul could only become <u>conscious</u> of the *intellectually rationalized* perspective of the attachment to my family and resistance to non-attachment … to letting go of them. You see, these solutions failed to complete a true caused based healing, because the solution of non-attachment, was only created by my Intellectual Soul as an action, of which my Soul's mind was falsely believing would bring about a change in my *state of BEing*.

Remember, a virtue is NOT an action … a virtue IS a state of BEing.

It is only through the <u>embodiment of a virtue</u>, that my Soul's <u>state of BEing</u> can be truly altered.

So, here's the kicker with experiencing with Awareness. Awareness will super-feel past the conscious Intellects rationalization and expose the TRUE experience being hidden behind all intellectual rationalizations. In super-feeling with my *TRUE* Awareness, I was able to experience, *not* the *attachment to my family*, but simply feeling the *force* that is *attachment*, the *force* that is *holding on,* the <u>experiential force</u> that creates and stimulates the Soul's Intellectual mind to hold onto and *attach* to a specific thing. You see, the Soul can be conscious of attachment as an action etc., it can <u>know about</u> attachment, but it can't <u>feel the force</u>. It is the force that is creating the effect of holding on itself. Your Soul's Consciousness uses attention to notice and acknowledge something that it can be conscious of, that it can learn and know about, but it is unable to <u>feel the forces</u> of the thing it is conscious of and of which are affecting it. Embodying the TRUE Awareness of your Spirit in your Soul's Consciousness, enables your Consciousness Soul to develop its forces sufficiently to the point of being able to super-feel … consciously. Just as embodying a virtue is the only way to affect a real and sustainable change in the state of BEing of your Soul, equally, embodying Awareness, is the only way for your Soul's state of BEing to become a sustainable, fully *experientially feeling* one.

When I embodied my Awareness in my Soul, the real experience being avoided is what was revealed to me, the one that is created from bringing both attachment and resistance back together again. Remember we spoke in the earlier chapters of resistance and attachment being the opposite ends of the experience, that the separation of them is the strategy of the intellectual Soul's identities to avoid ownership or rather, of avoiding the experience itself? So, the REAL experience lies in the rejoining of the FORCES that you consciously know as attachment and resistance. This once again, can only be done through your Higher "I" by super-feeling with your Awareness, but without any definition, judgments or descriptions of what you are feeling.

It is the super-feeling experience exposed from Awareness, in its pure and un- intellectualized form, that holds the key to the true and appropriate virtue being required for this particular experience.

In my case, after bringing the *forces* of attachment and resistance together and *super-feeling* the true experience of dis-harmony that revealed itself from this, I found the experience was one of great regret and self-condemnation. From this it was revealed that deep sadness, was but a symptom. I was covertly attacking my human-self from within, for leaving Australia and my family and friends and all the safe comfort zones I had created for myself while there. The avoidance of owning this experience of self-condemnation was created by separating out the parts and distribute them throughout my different identities, so they will react sub-consciously to any stimulant that has me feeling or becoming conscious of the harm I am doing to my Self through this self-imposed condemnation. Once I found this TRUE experience and experienced it fully, meaning to stay with it all and just allowing my Awareness to swim if you will ... in the experience and allow the experience in its totality to reveal to me all that it has within it, the appropriate virtue then revealed its self. Fully experiencing this way, with heightened Awareness, is how we open the space for the correct and appropriate virtue within the experience to reveal its Self.

With training and committed practice, the appropriate time to ask the question of "what virtue is appropriate for this experience?", is known once the experience has been experienced in its entirety. From this deeply experiential, completely open Love space of total Awareness, the correct virtue will reveal itself to you. This is the state of the last step in Ho'oponopono we explored earlier and shows how experiencing with Awareness is Ho'oponopono for the world. The difference for us now with *this* Awareness Ho'oponopono way of Living in-feel in today's level of consciousness, as opposed to when Ho'oponopono originated; is that back then, the virtue was not so much embodied back then, but was brought forth from within ... where it already existed naturally. This was so because the consciousness back then was still intimately connected through the already embodied Spirit to the Spiritual Realm. Back then, we were much less developed as an "I", individual consciousness and were still deeply connected as a collective deeply spiritual consciousness. Today's Consciousness has been separated from Spirit through our developmental evolution into our present "I Consciousness" to become the *total individual* we are today. This is why we now have to spiritualize our human "I Consciousness" again, to intimately reconnect our newly formed individual Soul-Self with its Spirit Nature and the Spiritual realm once more.

The difference between Ho'oponopono and Awareness Embodiment, is that I now have to consciously and intimately embody the virtues into my Soul ... as a state of Soul BEing.

Whereas before the virtue was, if you will, organically brought _out from within us_, now we have to _bring into us_ from our Spirit, the virtue to embody in our Soul's Consciousness. Again, this is done experientially, not by creating an action of the Soul that is the minds interpretation of what the virtue is perceived to be but feeling what the Soul feels like ... AS that virtue ... without connecting or attaching anything to the virtue. True embodiment comes about when you simply experience your human-self AS that virtue. Here is a guide to see if you are super-feeling from Awareness and accessing the correct virtue, or if you are in your Soul's deceptive spiritual identity ... simply imitating virtues.

- An intellectualized virtuous action is always attached to or relates to something. An intellectualized virtue is always separate from you and is something you need to do.

- A _true virtue_ is a state of BEing without attachment or relationship to anything ... it simply IS ... and you are simply BEing it. There is no separation of you and the virtue ... you are both one.

The true and complete embodiment of a virtue happens when I experience my human-self AS that virtue, without any attachment or resistance to any person, place or thing, along with no needs for this virtuous state to do or BE anything.

The virtue that revealed itself to me for my cancer experience, was forgiveness. You see how the Soul Intellectual Consciousness came up with non-attachment as the virtue. This was simply resistance to experiencing the attachment pole of the experience, but the true Spiritual virtue that was revealed from the experience itself, was forgiveness. Can you also see how most of the cognitive systems of belief and mind-based systems of self-development and healing, are really falling way short of the mark of true healing, let alone are they able to spiritualize the Body and Soul of your human-self? When I embodied the virtue of forgiveness, I was not looking to forgive myself for anything or forgive anyone or anything for my experience. My embodiment was to BE forgiveness ... period ... nothing else to be done.

There have of course since that insightful cancer journey, been many other opportunities to embody many more virtues, including more forgiveness as well. I have found that when I look at every human event I am participating in, as another opportunity for me to embody another virtue, Life sends me wondrous gifts of the most in depth insights into our human reality. The ease in which I am able to experience all that Life reveals gets easier and easier, as I feel my consciousness expanding into a much more loving and compassionate Spiritualized human. Ironically, it also has become easier to take full responsibility for far more than I ever had before, and this happens now with happiness and joy, rather than resistant conflict.

There was one time when I was involved with a group of drummers and came to realize how much the Awareness practice had changed the state of my Soul so very much for the better. I was seeing a very different, more Spirit based integrity of things, or rather lack of integrity of things, of dis-integrous things that were happening in the group. Feeling more grounded and courageous enough to voice what I was seeing and feeling, I attracted quite a deal of attack and invalidation from the members. This attack etc. extended out through the social media as well, so the impact toward me was considerable. At one point I noticed that at a previous time in my Life, I would have been in a passionate outrage at what I was perceiving as happening to me. It was actually exhilarating to notice that I wasn't reacting at all to things like lies being said etc. and I was able to simply respond WITHOUT over-emotionalizing and escalating the whole situation. I noticed that my Ho'oponopono through Awareness embodiment, was making things right with self ... with my Higher "I" Self ... in the very moment it was happening, and I didn't need to do the intense consciousness work on it at another time.

I have found that living in Awareness started to become a living meditation for me, as I strived to live in a state of BEing right with self, far more often than the old way of usually BEing in conflict with self ... and others.

You know, if I put my Awareness on a person or event that has lied to me or abandoned me etc., or any area that I retain sadness about and I still feel a charge of *any* kind, then I haven't completed my process of making things right with my human-self. Fact is, I may never complete the process of integration through this Life Walk, but that's the point isn't it? If my Soul at this point in time doesn't as yet have the capacity to embody the FULL state of even just one virtue, then there are many opportunities needed to keep embodying more and more virtues. Without BEing *TRULY* "right with self", forgiveness or Love or whatever the appropriate virtue is for that particular experience, simply can't be truly or fully embodied. I facilitated my own Awareness Embodied Ho'oponopono by embodying both virtues of forgiveness and Love, which effectively neutralized all residual charge between my Self and the other and left a space of quiet calm that has no need for talk about it any longer.

For some, this simplistic healing process is not possible for them. Some people are simply too involved in their illnesses, to identified *as* their state of conflict and dis-harmony from the reactive state between their resistances and attachments. Some people are too blindly identified *as their illness*, to even desire to discharge them or begin living without them. It is perceived as far easier to BE sick, than to own their erroneous thoughts and feelings about their self. For far too many individuals in our human collective of today's materialistic world, the dramatic disconnection between the human-self and Spirit-Self, leaves them floundering in the *human-self-denial* void of their true Spiritual Nature.

True Awareness is an ability of my Spirit-Self, which only becomes accessible, through developing within my Consciousness Soul specifically, a strong and courageous Will.

It is this strong Will that develops in me, the capacity of unwavering commitment to BEing fully <u>responsible</u> ... for ALL of my inner Human-self ... and what that self creates and projects into the outer world.

Ultimately, this inspires my Soul with a courageous Will-ingness to experience anything.

This can be a tall order for most people on our Planet right now, although NOT impossible for nearly every one of us. Once you enter into the realm of TRUE Awareness, once you start to live from TRUE Awareness and not the deceptive mental versions proliferating spirituality through the myriad of spiritual salespeople around now; you will begin to see ALL of the pretenses and self-deceptions you have been operating under. The bonus is that you will also start to feel the <u>forces</u> playing on you that manipulate and inhibit your development into a spiritual human. A difficulty with Awareness for an under-developed Consciousness, is not in being able to bring Awareness into the Conscious self; for that is actually easy and simple; it is in holding Awareness within your human-self and the <u>commitment</u> to living there. This skill and ability is trainable and if practiced diligently, <u>will</u> produce profound results in increased health and wellness of Body Soul and Spirit. There are so many forces and influences impressing their intentions on us all, of which we have VERY little awareness of.

Everything has power over me, as long as it remains out of my Awareness.

Awareness discharges all ties and influences on my BEing, just simply by the light of my Awareness being shone upon them and my Will-ingness to experience them increases exponentially.

The greatest difficulty of all from this, is in having to take the full <u>responsibility</u> for what your Awareness reveals to you. True Awareness *demands* responsibility from your human-self for everything that the light of your Awareness inevitably reveals to you. The good news is that Awareness itself, carries with it the virtues of strength and courage, which are essential to being able to take such responsibility. Full responsibility for your personal human-self naturally and effortlessly comes into play when you start to anchor TRUE Awareness in your Human-self. The full weight of responsibility and consequences for the <u>effect</u> you have on ALL who share and exist in your environment ... is equally taken on also. Most fall away at this point, not because they are *incapable* of taking responsibility for their self, but purely because their weakened Will drops Awareness. Awareness is not a "one pill wonder" solution to anything. With a committed intention to a new level of integrity in the Life of your Human-BEing, it is possible to Live in the immense joy that comes from a humanly embodied Spirit Awareness. This embodied Spirit Awareness has the capability to transport all of Humanity forward, to its re-emergence as a community of Human-Spirit-BEings. The freedom that comes from accepting TRUE Awareness, along with this Higher level of responsibility ... is in-accessible as well as indescribable and even incomprehensible to an under-developed consciousness mind ... yet, it is undeniably liberating and empowering ... to your Soul which becomes free of the mind ... as it becomes Aware ... through the embodiment of your TRUE experiential Spirit-Self.

What could it be like to live in a world where humanity has become free of its mind's drama ... and embodied into Spirit?

What could it BE like to be mindless?

Chapter 8

Mindless

So here we are, nearing the end of your experience of this book and what I hope, you have been able to experience it as a journey through the structure of your Human-BEing with hopefully a sense of its Spirit Nature.

Are you out of your mind ... yet?

You probably noticed that I keep making references to the mind and Soul mind etc. so far through the book. You may be wondering why the title is, "Are you out of your mind yet", yet I keep referring to the mind as something that is still intrinsic in our BEing Human. I have done this to keep your Intellectual Soul connected and amiable with us and stay open to the concepts I've been presenting. To challenge the Intellect too soon and ask it to drop all of its reference points about the mind, without a catch net for it to drop into, can often be too big a jump for some. In this chapter, let's see if we can nudge your Intellectual Soul to unclip its safety harness of preconceived ideas and take a leap of faith with us into a new realm for it of ... mindlessness.

Mindless, and living in a mindless world could be taken so many ways. A perspective from one end of the paradigm could be being out of *your mind crazy*, because you are so identified *as your mind*, that you are trapped in it. A perspective from the other end, is being out of your mind and in a state of BEing-ness. From another perspective, we could say that the world is already mindless, as humanity seems to be operating mindlessly at the moment, doing all sorts of crazy senseless things. Even that statement of "sense-less things" may, I hope, now have a new connotation for you. Hopefully, this new perspective we have been exploring throughout this book on the structure of your human consciousness and its Spirit Nature, will now help you to see the *concept of your mind* from a different viewpoint also. What I want to explore in this chapter is to firstly determine what exactly is the mind that we all talk about. Secondly, I want to then then look at whether; operating from the principles and structure of consciousness we have been exploring throughout this book, this *concept of mind* actually has a truthful place in a truly *experiencing* world.

Some of you may have noticed; maybe frustratingly even, that I haven't seemed to address the issue of mind directly at all, considering this book is titled, "Are you out of your mind ... yet?"

This was not an oversight, but a deliberate intention, because I wanted to first show a structure of your consciousness without it being muddled up in our present-day intellectual *concept of the mind*. Have you noticed how this *concept of mind* is used so often as a generalized label for so many of those parts of self that we quite often don't understand or want to take responsibility for? Statements like, "my mind just wonders off" and "my mind goes crazy" or even my all-time favorite of the spiritual salespeople these days of, "the power of your mind". These are all testimony to either non-ownership or non-understanding of the real forces and principles that manifested these conditions they are talking about. It is far too easy these days to just bundle up what I call "my mind" into a box. It is too easy to take something I don't understand about myself, and then associate all blame for it to my mind. "My mind" is also a great scapegoat for any of my creations I don't want to take responsibility for. How often do you associate conditions to the mind such as; limitations, inadequacies, deficiencies, a lack of focus, a lack of attention, a lack of intention, stress, insomnia, depression, abhorrent behavior, addictions, bad thoughts, too many thoughts, over thinking, not thinking, worry, a lack of understanding, a lack of comprehension, fantasy, delusion, etc., etc., and etc.? From your new perspective of your consciousness, ask your Self, how many of these conditions relate to, or are a result of, a specific part of your whole BEing-Self that you have come to know as your Body Soul and Spirit, and of which we have been exploring throughout this book.

Is my mind "me" ... or is it something I have created to not own "me"?

Why do we call it "my mind" and yet we treat it as something outside of our self that we have to train like a pet, so it doesn't get out of control? Why do we see our mind as being this powerful force separate from our Self that we have to harness to effectively create our life with? Why are we so disempowered by this *concept of mind*, that we are so easily seduced by the spiritual salesmen and women selling their tools for using "the mind" to attract what we desire from life? I find the classic dis-empowering spiritual sales pitch is "to heal your mind-based causes of ill-health". Taking on this belief effectively puts you as a powerless victim to this perceived invasion on your health from this dysfunctional element ... of your Self? I know the author of the book with that title. Having no experiential knowledge of the Soul much less its components, his book of mental machinations with exercises to boot, in truth, trap you in the Intellectual Soul where he originated it all from. Why do we blindly buy into these covert spiritual sales tactics, that sell their secret keys and hidden wisdoms as the only way to heal these so-called *mind-based* illnesses? Is it simply because they *profess* to know the mind? I find *that* one to be the greatest delusion of them all. Their power over you comes from selling you this perception of there being a mystery to this elusive mind ... that *they* have solved. They indoctrinate you with concepts that never completely empower you into *true* Higher "I" Spirit-Self-Awareness, let alone any form of true self-realization that can actually free you from the concept of ... your mind. Here are just some of the Wikipedia definitions of mind, to get a generalized view of what our world consciousness intellectually perceives as ... the mind.

- *The **mind** is a set of cognitive faculties including consciousness, perception, thinking, judgement, and memory.*

- *The mind is the faculty of a human being's reasoning and thoughts. It holds the power of imagination, recognition, and appreciation, and is responsible for processing feelings and emotions, resulting in attitudes and actions.*

- *There is no universally agreed definition of what a mind is and what its distinguishing properties are, although there is a lengthy tradition of inquiries in philosophy, religion, psychology, and cognitive science. The main open question regarding the nature of the mind is the mind–body problem, which investigates the relation of the mind to the physical brain and nervous system. Typical viewpoints include dualism and idealism, which consider the mind somehow separate from physical existence, and physicalism and functionalism, which hold that the mind is roughly identical with the brain or reducible to physical phenomena such as neuronal activity. Another question concerns which types of beings are capable of having minds, for example whether mind is exclusive to humans, possessed also by some or all animals, by all living things, or whether mind can also be a property of some types of man-made machines.*

- *Whatever its nature, it is generally agreed that mind is that which enables a being to have subjective awareness and intentionality towards their environment, to perceive and respond to stimuli with some kind of agency, and to have consciousness, including thinking and feeling.*

- *The concept of mind is understood in many different ways by many different cultural and religious traditions. Some see mind as a property exclusive to humans whereas others ascribe properties of mind to non-living entities (e.g. panpsychism and animism), to animals and to deities. Some of the earliest recorded speculations linked mind (sometimes described as identical with soul or spirit) to theories concerning both life after death, and cosmological and natural order, for example in the doctrines of Zoroaster, the Buddha, Plato, Aristotle, and other ancient Greek, Indian and, later, Islamic and medieval European philosophers.*

- *Important philosophers of mind include Plato, Descartes, Leibniz, Searle, Dennett, Nagel, and Chalmers. Also psychologists such as Freud and James, and computer scientists such as Turing and Putnam developed influential theories about the nature of the mind. The possibility of non-human minds is explored in the field of artificial intelligence, which works closely in relation with cybernetics and information theory to understand the ways in which information processing by non-biological machines is comparable or different to mental phenomena in the human mind.*

Seeing these definitions, we can see how easy it is for the concept of Body Mind and Soul to be accepted and once more, Spirit is pushed further out of our human-self's perception.

I find it disturbingly deceptive to see the statement there of, *"Whatever its nature, it is generally agreed that mind is that which enables a being to have subjective awareness and intentionality towards their environment, to perceive and respond to stimuli with some kind of agency, and to have consciousness, including thinking and feeling."*

This is probably the epitome of how we have boxed up what we choose to not fully understand or worse, choose to not responsibly experience the true nature of within our whole Self. In this statement, is an indoctrinated belief that the mind is some kind of function or maybe even some kind of specific being of sorts separate from Self, that *enables* the Self BEing; that would be you by the way; to *have* Awareness, consciousness, perception, thinking, feeling, willing (intentionality) and sentient capabilities as well. Can you see how this indoctrinated belief of the mind has boxed up all the elements of the structure of your Soul we have been exploring here? Can you see how confusing it becomes to view the structure of your Human-BEing-Self from this *mind-based perspective*; with all these specific elements and functions of your Soul mixed up together. How could you ever address a specific issue or healing within a particular part of your Body, Soul or Spirit, from this mixed up and generalized viewpoint of the *mind* as the cause?

What I find interesting is that this generalized *perception* of the mind has no definitive experiential truth of its existence. All of the accepted and publicized perceptions of the mind I could find, are all formulated by the perceptual limitations of the Intellectual Soul. These concepts are a means to try and explain a structure and function, that the Intellectual Soul is basically incapable of understanding and of course, is unable to actually *experience* directly. On closer and experiential research into the time that this perception and *concept of mind* came into our BEing, you will notice that it was also the time when we started to move into the development of the Consciousness component of our Soul-self. It is only after our human development embodied consciousness, when it started to become conscious of its self, of itself as a Soul-self, that the *concept of mind* came into being. Do you remember your exploration through the components of your Soul in the previous chapters? We looked at the Sentient Soul bringing in the ability to sense the world it exists in as a human, the Intellectual / Perspective Soul bringing in intelligence and perception and now the Consciousness Soul bringing in your ability to be conscious of you as a self, different to the environment it exists in and to be able with the development of the Will forces to think in higher concepts?

What was introduced through the development of the Consciousness Soul, is the true ability to think beyond mere human comprehension.

Again, from the Wikipedia,

- "Thought (also called thinking) – the mental process in which beings form psychological associations and models of the world. Thinking is manipulating information, as when we form concepts, engage in problem solving, reason and make decisions. Thought, the act of thinking, produces thoughts. A thought may be an idea, an image, a sound or even an emotional feeling that arises from the brain".

Logically you may think that thinking is an attribute of the Intellectual Soul, but by experiencing the differences of the actual functions so to speak, of these components, you will find that Intelligence is not really thinking. Intelligence is the capacity to *perceive* things, to rationalize, to *formulate* and piece together through *logic*. I know this looks and sounds like thinking on a specific sensory plane or frequency if you like, but it's not truly thinking. Logic and rationalizations are a form of information arrangement that brings about perceptions, of which trap us in what already exists, in what is dead in respect of thoughts, that are of the present physical world reality, of what already exists. This is Intellectual Soul perceiving that formulates the perceptions of the Intellectual Soul … after it has *perceived* the things it has attention on.

Here again are our Wikipedia definitions;

- Intelligence has been defined in many different ways including one's capacity for logic, abstract thought, understanding, self-awareness, communication, learning, emotional knowledge, memory, planning, creativity and problem solving. It can be more generally described as the ability to perceive information and retain it as knowledge to be applied towards adaptive behaviors within an environment. Intelligence is most widely studied in humans but has also been observed in non-human animals and in plants. Artificial intelligence is intelligence in machines. It is commonly implemented in computer systems using program software. Within the discipline of psychology, various approaches to human intelligence have been adopted. The psychometric approach is especially familiar to the general public, as well as being the most researched and by far the most widely used in practical settings.

AS Wiki says, "Intelligence is an ability to *perceive* information." This is why Rudolph Steiner has termed this particular Soul component as the Intellectual / Perceptive Soul. This is the component of your human-self that *perceives* information. This is where our perceptions come from. This faculty of Soul is not where the higher *thinking* free of logical constraints happens, it's where *perceiving* happens. First, we must perceive information that the Intellectual Soul rationalizes etc., then we can *think* about that information through the ability of our Consciousness Soul and formulate it into concepts and link them together to find relationships between the information we are perceiving.

It is *consciousness* that brings in our true ability to *think* in this true sense, to be able to come up with new ideas and then link them together, to conceptualize, but from a *conscious viewpoint* of the individuality of these ideas and to actually form these links. We create them through *thinking* of ideas consciously and not intellectually from a *specific perspective*, as the Intellectual Soul does. Through thinking, consciousness is able to link and connect perspectives together to bring about an idea or concept that is, *not already manifest*, in this reality. This is what Steiner terms "live thoughts", thoughts that grow and evolve into a final concept not previously perceived of in the existing world reality. The thing to remember is that although we seem to be talking here of these components as separate parts, we must feel in our Soul, that they are most definitely integrated and connected to each other. There is a *relationship* between each and all of our component parts that make up the whole BEing we are. Here is where this higher thinking of your Consciousness Soul applies, to form through living thoughts, the links between these components, to understand the relationship between these components and how they manifest your human reality for you to experience. As we explore here further, BE aware of the forces of your thinking that connect these concepts we are talking about. Stay "in-feel" with your Awareness and let the relationships we are going to explore reveal to you the *forces* they manifest from and their higher intentions.

For example, before we could develop our Intellectual/Perspective Soul component, we had to develop the Sentient Soul sufficiently to be able to sense things from our environment. Intelligent perception of what we are *sensing*, is only possible once we have something from our outer world that we have *sensibly* been able to bring into our Soul, through its functionality of the senses of the Sentient Soul. This is how your Soul brings in and senses the physical world you exist in—through the Sentient Soul. As we developed our Intellectual/Perspective Soul further, it naturally and organically developed our Sentient Soul's forces further as well. This allowed the sensitivity of our *sensing ability* to expand further also, from which, the parameter of what we could sense expanded also, into eventually and ultimately, the first levels of super-sensing the subtle etheric forces of our human-reality. This then gave your Intelligent Perspective component of your Soul the opportunity to develop its ability to perceive and rationalize what is then being more finely sensed even further again.

Once the Intellectual/Perspective Soul component had developed sufficiently to accommodate consciousness, the Consciousness Soul component became active and began to develop, bringing with it our ability to think and conceptualize etc., but most importantly, through this *higher* form of thinking, for the Soul to become conscious as a self ... as an individual separate from its environment. Through being conscious of our self as an individual, we gained the ability to *think* about our *perceptions* of the things we were now *sensing*; to be able to create concepts of these sense perceptions and bring them all together as a single concept. Through these concepts, we became *conscious* of our intelligence and its existence separate from, yet within, our environment. As this level of consciousness developed, it then again naturally and organically further developed our Intellectual Souls ability to *perceive* the subtler and previously un-perceivable elements within our physical and non-physical environment. Gradually, we will begin to sense the more super-sensible elements that make up the fabric within which our sense-able world manifest from. Now, our even more highly sensitive Sentient Soul; which has also developed further through its relationship to the other two components, was sensing both the physical and non-physical world we are existing in. Can you start to see the integrated way our human-self structure of Body and Soul is formed and the potential for it to function as one harmonious entity through the co-creating evolution of each component? Each and every component of our Human-BEing-Self, comprising of the Physical Body, etheric Life Body, Astral Body; which houses the Sentient Soul, Intellectual/Perspective Soul and Consciousness Soul and the greater Ego Body; which houses the Spirit Self, Life Spirit and Spirit Man, all affect each other. If the development of the lower is in-sufficient, it will then become a limitation and hindrance to the development of the one above it and so forth along the line.

The sufficient development of each individual component of my Soul-Self, is essential to the further development of the whole Human-BEing-Self.

So looking at your whole Human-BEing-Self from this interconnected, inter-relationship between all these components of your-self, you may see how boxing it all up into a package called "mind" is really a very dis-empowering distraction from the self-empowered freedom that comes from experientially knowing each component of your-self that makes up the greater BEing—that BEing which is your True-BEing-Self. When you look at all the definitions and descriptions from Wikipedia, you can plainly see that what is described there is simply elements of the different components we have been exploring throughout this book. Perspective is not something that the *mind* has or makes available, it is an attribute of your Intellectual/Perspective Soul. Self-Awareness is not a capacity of Intelligence; it is the end result of the use of the Awareness *attribute* of your Spirit-Self to *experientially* know thy Self—all the components of thy Conscious Human-self as well as its Spirit Nature. Awareness is your Spirit-Self's *attribute*, it's *your* spiritual organ for experiencing, for super-feeling without definition, judgment or descriptions. Consciousness doesn't come from the mind; consciousness is an evolutionary stage of the development of the Soul. In truth, the Soul is not the mind. From the Wiki perspective, the term "mind" is being applied to the conglomerate of our Body Soul and Spirit. The attributes as they are in the definitions we find in Wikipedia and the likes, of which have been assigned to the *concept of mind* by our developing consciousness up to this present day, clearly show a list that spans the collective attributes and abilities of our Body Soul and Spirit combined.

Rudolph Steiner has even stated that "everything is consciousness". Attitudes don't come from the mind processing feelings and emotions, they come from the Intellectual Soul's application of its identities and belief systems. Actions don't come from the mind processing feelings and emotions, they come from the Will, which again is a spiritual capacity of your Consciousness Soul. Ironically, feelings and emotions themselves come from your Intellectual Soul's arsenal of identities and manifest through the Sentient Soul into the etheric body, as a trigger in the physical body. I could go on with the clarifications, but the point I am trying to show is, that all the attributes we are indoctrinated to believe as being attributes of the "mind", are all actual elements of specific components of your Human-BEing-Self, specifically of your Soul and Spirit. They can never be understood or experienced truthfully through the *concept of mind*, because in fact, the mind does not exist ... except as an outdated perspective of a previously under-developed Intellectual Soul rational. Why is it that all of the Enlightened Masters who have come before us, have all shared that the mind is an illusion?

As long as I am chasing an understanding of my Self through a concept of mind, I will never ... be able to truly experientially know my Soul or my Spirit.

I hope you can start to see how the deception of our present "*concept of mind*" has now become a huge limitation to the expansion of your consciousness. How can you truly "know thy self" to the point of full *Self*-Realization, as long as everything about you is packaged into this one mysterious and deceptive mind concept ... particularly when the Enlightened Masters have already told us that it is an illusion? The Masters were right when they said, "the mind is illusion", for the illusion of the mind, is what prevents you from truly owning and experiencing the truth of your True and Highest "I" Spirit-BEing-*Self*. The mind concept is a remnant of the *early* development of the Consciousness Soul, as it became conscious of its human-self, but not yet developed sufficiently to stimulate the lower Soul components of Sentient and Intellectual Soul. Because your human's Sentient Soul's sensory ability was not sensitive enough to detect, to sense these different components of Soul at the time of the beginning of the Consciousness Souls development, your Intellectual/Perspective Soul was unable to perceive the different component parts. It was through the lack of development of these three *states of Soul* ... of the Soul itself, that the newly formed Consciousness Soul could only form a *concept,* of all of these individual parts as a whole, based on their expression through the human reality. It is from this, that our current *concept of mind* was created. Advanced BEing's such as Rudolph Steiner, who has recently brought these higher concepts of the components of Body Soul and Spirit into our human reality for us to experience; through Initiation, has brought into the human reality an *experiential* knowledge of the Higher worlds. His Soul forces of Sentient, Intellectual/Perspective and Consciousness Soul are so highly developed, that he is free of the *concept of mind*. BEing no longer trapped in the concept of mind, *BEing mindless*, he is not just able to now super-sense and perceive and BE conscious of the *super-sensible* elements of our human existence within the Spiritual world, he is now able to *fully experience* them—through his embodiment of the Awareness of his Spirit-Self.

Embodying my Spirit-Self's Awareness into my human Soul-self, eventually frees me from the concept of mind, dramatically increasing the sensitivity of my Sentient Soul.

This in turn, expands the perceptive capabilities of my Intellectual Soul, ultimately increasing my ability to consciously perceive higher concepts of the Spiritual Realms.

Just as this relationship and influence through the Soul forces works from Sentient up to Consciousness Soul, it also works in reverse, from Consciousness Soul, all the way down to the Body itself. This is how we embody *in* our human-self, the virtues of our Spirit-Self we discussed earlier and how we manifest in our human reality. In a healthy human *mindless* system, through the higher thinking from the Consciousness Soul, thought stimulates associated perceptions of the Intellectual Soul, which then get transmuted by the Sentient Soul into sensations passed further into the etheric Life Body, finally manifesting through the physical Body as our human reality. This is why your Sentient Soul is the depository of your passions and desires etc. Rudolph Steiner, via this process, through the embodiment of his experiences of and in the Spiritual

Realm, has grounded them into the etheric Life Body of our Planet, making them now accessible for all of us to *tap into.* This has been done to help develop our own Soul Forces sufficiently, to enable us to experience the component parts of our Soul-self and the spiritual realm—directly for our self. The Christ's impulse has also been grounded into the Astral Body of our planet through this same process. It is through our Astral Body, your complete Soul Body, that it is now possible for anyone to embody this *true* Christ *Impulse* in their life. This is not a religious embodiment, but one of the Christs Spirit impulses—not doctrine. This Christ impulse, along with Steiner's embodied higher concepts of Spirit along with ALL the Ascended and Enlightened Masters that have grounded their concepts and insights here for us to experience for our self, surround us and permeate us all, as *forces of influence* accessible through the etheric Life Body. Much Higher Beings have been orchestrating these and other creative *forces of influence* from the very first conception of the Highest Spiritual concept of human life. The *concept of mind* long ago originated from these very same *forces of influence.*

It is important to certain influential diverting forces, for us to be trapped in this dis-empowerment of being a mind. There are forces that act on the Soul external to its self, and those that act on it from within. The forces within the Soul, your own Soul Forces, are what you are needing to strengthen and develop to a sufficient level to be able to commence the embodied spiritualization of your Soul by your Spirit Self. The forces that influence and act on the Soul from without, are both light and darker forces. The Light forces act on us to support the spiritualization of our human. The darker diverting forces act on us with intent to disconnect us from Spirit and consequently prevent the spiritualization of our human via the Soul. It is important to keep in your Soul the understanding that ALL of these forces of influence, have originated from a higher intention for the evolution of our human through the harmonious integration of our Body Soul and Spirit. The *concept of mind*, as different from the Body and Soul, has come about from the influence of one of these darker diverting forces. This separation is intended to further distance our human-self from our Spirit-Self and as such again ... prevent us from spiritualizing our human-self. However, this separation, is also a very necessary state of BEing that *had to come about,* for us to develop into a truly "I Consciousness". Although *succumbing* to these particular forces brought about our "I Consciousness", as an "I", it is now time for us to *overcome* them. Their purpose has been fulfilled, which now makes them a limitation, a hindrance to bringing our newly formed Higher "I" back to the spiritual realm through the spiritualization of the human Soul-self. These subtle diverting forces act on us as specific influences on our Intellectual Soul through the deception of thought, just as our Consciousness Soul also affects the Intellectual Soul through the thoughts of thinking. A LOT of the misleading and deceptive perceptions being "sold" presently, can be attributed to the influences of thoughts from these diverting forces.

The *concept of mind* conveniently packages up the Soul as different and separate from the mind, but more deceptively, by doing so, it puts a false perception of the Soul as a replacement or substitute for the Spirit. All of this is a deception and great hindrance to the true development and evolution of our human into its full Spiritual Nature. It is the Spirit that is our true higher Self nature. Imagine, if the Soul is depicted as the Spirit element of our BEing, then how can there be any understanding of Spirit, let alone any *true experience* of the true relationship between Body Soul and Spirit? Keeping the

Spirit aspect out of the human equation is a subtle deceptive influence of lower, diverting forces with intentions to prevent the introduction of experiential Awareness and its inevitable spiritualization of the human Soul and Body. There are forces of influence specific to each component of our human self.

When you tell lies for example, there is an effect on your Soul that diminishes your Soul forces. The strength and health of these *Soul forces* are essential for the Soul to be able to embody Spirit. The "diminishing" effect of lies on your Soul forces, becomes an ongoing one, because when you tell a lie, you attach an entity to your Soul that is like a spiritual parasite, of which draws its forces from your Soul. In esoteric terms, this entity is experientially known as a phantom. When you tell the same lie over and over, you build up and strengthen this phantom until it takes a form of its own to such a degree, that you believe it to be an aspect of your-self. At this point, these phantoms take on an illusion as being part of your sub-conscious, of which your Sentient Soul is oblivious. These phantoms are how the darker diverting forces covertly influence you, as they become another access point for the influence of diverting forces throughout your Human-Soul-self.

The work of TRUE Awareness, experientially reveals the forces of which, are the elemental influences upon us all.

Sickness and illness in your human form come from the weakening of these Soul forces. The consequent diverting influences brought upon your Body Soul AND Spirit, create a disconnection between your component parts, rather than a union. These deeper levels of wisdom of TRUE Awareness are what I have tried to share with you throughout this book.

lies are diminishing your Soul forces and leaving you more and more susceptible to deceptive forces that create influences on you, designed to de-spiritualize your human Soul-self. Of course, we never just tell lies to others in our life, do we? We tell them to and of our own self as well. We actually tend to lie to our self far more often than we do to others. Without Awareness of these diverting forces of influence operating through us, we can never truly know our True-Self, let alone develop into an authentic Self.

An authentic Self is Aware and fully immersed in complete ownership of all elements of its TOTAL Self of Body Soul and Spirit.

So, before you can live in a mindless world, you need to look at how you can free yourself from the covert restraints and influences of this indoctrinated *concept of mind,* the one that is so prevalent in our present human reality. To break it down; to free yourself from mind, is to embrace the journey into your Soul and Consciousness with a willingness to experience the component parts and experientially find their relationship and effects on each other. Our present stage of evolution is such that we are now called upon to take the *concepts* of our Consciousness Soul and move them into deliberate experience, through our Spirit-Self's ability to *feel with Awareness*. It is through the development of the Spirit-Self's Awareness, that we will be able to move the human-BEing out of a perceived *state of mind*. From there we can move it into an experiential *mindless state of super-sensing,* not just the forces that make our physical world possible, but the finer forces of our Spirit Nature and the Spiritual Realm that have been influencing the development of the whole Human BEing *and* its environment since its creation.

Freedom from mind, will be the consequence of feeling with Awareness without definition, judgment or description of what I AM feeling.

Through the super-sensing ability of Awareness, you will be able to commence the evolutionary journey toward the full spiritualization of your human-self. Ultimately, this can move it into the cosmic Spirit-Man it must inevitably become. Through feeling with Awareness, you embody into your human Soul-self, your Spirit-Self's intuitive communication via Awareness with the spiritual realm. The inner stress and conflict you experience in your present-day reality, originates from this *lack* of intuitive guidance and communication with your BEing-Self of Spirit.

Reducing inner stress and conflict—creating greater health and wellness in both my inner and outer world, is a natural consequence of grounding the Awareness of my Spirit-BEing-Self into my Human-self.

As I said before, the introduction of a new spiritual component into your human development, naturally stimulates an expansion of the existing components below it. In this case, the introduction of your Spirit-Self is naturally and effortlessly expanding the capabilities of all the component parts of your existing human-self. Just as *thinking conceptually—which links the spiritual realm to your human realm,* became an attribute of your human with the introduction of your Consciousness Soul, it is Awareness that is your new *feeling* attribute to be embodied with the development of your Spirit-Self. A sign that we are at the ready for true Awareness to be embodied, is that Consciousness is now beginning to form concepts of Awareness. Our Sentient Soul is now able to get a higher *sense* of Awareness and our Perspective Soul begins to gain an intelligent perception of it, even though at this stage for some, the Intellectual element perceives it as an attribute of consciousness rather than Spirit. The current level of the Perspective Soul is as yet incapable of perceiving the Spirit, past what is commonly conceived of as the rather limiting and intellectualized religious perspective of Spirit. The more you feel with true Awareness, the more your Sentient Soul's sensitivity increases, which then expands your Intellectual Soul's ability to *perceive* the finer frequencies of your Spirit-Self. It is through this process of evolution of your whole BEing-Human-Self that your

Consciousness Soul becomes *conscious of Spirit*, to ultimately becoming *Consciously Aware*.

There is a lot of talk about Awareness now and being Aware and self-aware and consciously aware etc., but as yet there has been no distinction achieved; apart from intellectually, between being aware and being conscious. With a trained awakened Awareness, you will notice most people mix awareness and consciousness up together. Ironically, this distinction can only be achieved by *experiencing* this difference, through feeling with the TRUE Awareness of your Spirit.

It is through super-sensing that the subtle experiential difference between aware and conscious reveals itself.

Being conscious of something is how you have or gained, a *concept* of that thing and bring it into the physical world your consciousness exists in.

Being Aware of something is how you *feel*, on a much deeper and far more experiential level, the *subtle forces* and *elements*, the spiritual BEing-ness if you will, that is manifesting that thing you are Aware of, in the environment you exist in.

Being Aware reveals the originating or creative forces that are manifesting the thing.

Being conscious of it only reveals the final manifestation of the thing in its form.

There is much confusion; or rather complacency about this distinction at the moment. It is of benefit to certain diverting *forces of non-spiritualization*, that this distinction remains confusing and deceptive. This IS presently the main obstacle to the embodiment of true Awareness. Unsuspectingly, most spiritual salespeople these days are under the influence of these darker diverting forces, as they create great systems of intellectually based exercises and all sorts of dialect's and rhetoric's about Awareness, without any true *experience* within their Soul-self of the distinction between Aware and conscious. The thing to remember, as we discussed earlier, is that accessing your ability of Awareness is so much simpler than all the *secret ways* and *hidden key* technologies that people are trying to sell you these days. Remember that these concepts they are selling, come from a deceptive *concept of mind*, not a clear *experience of Spirit*.

The Awareness potential is inherent in all of us incarnating here now.

So, if we understand that to become mindless, can be as simple as becoming truly Aware, then what are the consequences of living in this state of Awareness ... free of the concept of mind? Awareness is actually the state of Ho'oponopono we talked about earlier, only in this present level of consciousness, the *responsibility* to act on what Awareness reveals, rests solely on the individual. Whereas before in times past, we had the immediate support of higher Spiritual Beings supporting and stimulating the actions necessary to bring about the state of Ho'oponopono, now they have retreated from this up-front guidance. Because of the leap in evolution and the introduction of our Higher "I" Spirit-Self, the Spirits guiding the higher evolution of our collective human consciousness, have stepped back to allow us to become the true creator BEings we have been conceptualizing and of which ... we are destined to BEcome.

The responsibility of becoming mindless, of becoming a TRULY Conscious Aware Human-BEing, is to accept the consequences of ALL of the creative forces I am projecting, both physically and spiritually and both internally and externally.

So, here is the kicker peeps. The bottom line if you will, of living in the world free from the mind ... is living in Awareness. As I said earlier, Awareness is an attribute of the Spirit-Self, the Self that is intimately and intrinsically connected to the spiritual realm, along with all the spiritual *forces* that are inherent in that realm. To be aware of the forces coming from the spiritual realm into my human sphere ... is to be aware of all the external forces of influence that play upon me. Of course, you can imagine how extremely empowering it is to be in this place, because I am now no longer under the *unconscious influence* of these forces. My Awareness of these forces is what simply neutralizes their *influence* upon me, through being able to *experience fully* the *creative forces* that are manifesting these influences. From this place, I can where necessary, *work with* the forces that are in alignment with the higher development toward the spiritualization of my True-Self. At the same time, I am now able to neutralize the forces that are working against my spiritualization ... and even spiritualize them as well.

To be aware of the influences that are coming from within me, means that I can no longer ignore my intentions, thoughts, judgments, projections or lies etc., that emanate from my Soul into the outer world. These forces are what is actually creating the world I experience around me. This is what the Hawaiian's meant by "we are responsible for all that we experience through the environment we live in—of physical *and* spiritual creation". Remember that as each component of our BEing effects each both ways, from lowest to highest and from highest to lowest, then the forces that come *from* us, the projections into our world in the forms of judgment, intention etc., from within our Souls, have a real and potent creational effect on the human environment we all exist in.

I am totally influencing the creation of the environment I exist in.

True freedom is not just the willingness to experience anything, but is that willingness without influence, either internal or external.

Being Aware of all the influences, is the gateway to the path of freedom from influence.

So, this is the existence of living as a mindless BEing. To not just be totally responsible for the consequences of my actions, but to be consciously aware of everything that happens to me, within me and what comes from me .... *prior* to the action I take that manifest in the world I exists in. From this *mindless* state of BEing human, I am on the path to becoming a truly consciously creator BEing. It is inevitable that from this *mindless* Aware state of BEing, I would now only create for a much higher good than if I were not Aware. With Awareness, the consequences of any and all creations, reveal their true and pure Self for review ... before they manifest. From this review and the use of my Will, I am able to TRULY choose what I wish to create ... without influence. Can you get a *feel* for how free it truly is, to be able to live in this personal *mindless state*?

Through Awareness, my Spirit's intuitive sight sees the greater benefits when creations happen for all and not just for self alone. Imagine for a moment, what it would be like to be so consciously Aware, that you no longer react aggressively out of resistance to a viewpoint or judgment projected on you. Instead of living in the *conflict* of reactive resistance to the opposing viewpoint and also attached to your own ridged one, you now seize Life's opportunity presenting itself and you take full ownership of it to the point of embodying the virtue embedded within it. Instead of being resistant and attacking, you are now responding empathically connected and supporting, as you embody the virtues of acceptance and compassion. Wouldn't it be a different existence, if any and all present moments are now seen as opportunities to BE virtuous? To Conscious Awareness, Life's opportunities to be a more virtuous human, naturally and effortlessly reveal themselves, simply through the shinning of your Awareness on them? What would it feel like, to live in this state of TRUE inner-peace; this state that naturally and effortlessly comes from this Aware virtuous embodiment? How different would it feel, to not be trapped in mental denial of the darker side of your human-self; that part that is attached to non-ownership of your life and creates a state of living in a constant subtle and covert conflict? Imagine, no longer having to constantly mentally affirm to your-self, that you are or will be a better person living in peace and harmony, but actually *living* there ... effortlessly virtuous. How do you think your body would respond to being continually bathed in this environment of harmony flowing into it? The result of such harmony would be an empowered co-creative harmonization of all of the component parts of your Body Soul AND Spirit? How would it feel to make decisions based on clear, unfiltered intuition, free of any outside or false internal intellectualized influence? Could the potential from living in these states above, make it possible to actually create a different world than the one you are maybe covertly resisting in this present time? Of course, there are far more benefits to self as a by-product of this way of living, than what I have just listed above, but once you are living there, you then become of far more benefit to others in the world around you.

To live in mindless Awareness, is to flood my Body Soul and Spirit with a constant stream of harmonic health and wellness.

So, from this new concept of mindless-ness, what might it be like to live in this *mindless* state full of your Spirit's Awareness? How would living in this harmonic state of non-resistance affect the world around you? Remember the Rudolph Steiner description of Love, being the resultant condition coming from such complete open-ness, free of all influence and so deeply connected to others and the environment one exists in, that one is able to fully experience ... *as one's Self*, the environment and all those whom exists in it? This Love a natural resultant condition of living in Awareness. Doesn't it make sense now, that the Masters we have known about and the ones that are still with us today, who speak of the illusion of mind and who live as the expression of this Love we have explored; that they may well be the living manifestation of this *mindless state of BEing* we are talking about here? When we hear of self-less acts of courage, compassion and sacrifice to save others, that sometimes invoke super-human efforts resulting in undeniable feats unobtainable in normal human existence; could these simply be moments of mindless-ness? Could the creative power of the mind that the spiritual salespeople keep trying to sell us on, actually just be the free-flowing Life Force that is naturally unleashed when we own and fully experience through Awareness, the true dynamic intercourse between the component parts of our Body Soul and Spirit? Could the real power to *create* in our world be accessed, not through the deception of harnessing the power of an illusion we have been told is our mind, but rather from freeing my-Self up from this delusional *concept of mind* entirely?

Might the greatest power we have to truly create a new world, come from being mindless and full of Spirit, rather than mind-full and void of Spirit?

There are countless quotes of Master's from spirituality to sports, who all testify to the point of excellence coming when they surpass or *overcome the illusion of mind*. Elite marathon runners have shared that there is a point when the mind is no longer present, and an indescribable force takes over. At our present stage of consciousness, you no longer need to carry out extreme physical activities to the point of expelling the concept of mind's influence; to experience what is in fact your Higher "I" Spirit Nature. What if this force is what naturally empowers remarkable achievements ... once the individual becomes mindless? The excitement that rises in me from all of these confirmations of exceptional achievements as a result of becoming mindless, is that now, at this present stage of evolution, we can all access these exceptional states ... simply through the embodiment of our Spirit's Awareness into our human-self. As you gain intimate experience of the specific component parts of your Body Soul and Spirit, you naturally sever the ties to the *mind concept* that chains you to staying a physically limited human-consciousness. This effectively prevents your natural evolution into a new state of Be-in, as a *creator* Human-Spirit-BEing.

A mindless state of BEing, is a super-feeling Aware state of experiential presence with the IS-ness of things.

Will, or rather the lack of it, is a chronic consciousness dis-ease in our humanity right now. This lack of Will is a powerful assist for the diverting forces of non-spiritualization right now. They gain influence because the Will is essential for grounding the Spirit-Self's Awareness into the Soul via the Consciousness Soul component. It is the Will forces within the Consciousness Soul that make thinking in the higher realms possible. This is how we connect to the Spiritual realm and become ... *conscious of Spirit.* It is your Will that; among other things, *holds* your Spirit Self present in your Soul and makes it possible to ground its attribute of Awareness in your Soul. This is what facilitates your Human BEing becoming *Consciously Aware.* Consciously Aware is no longer just *conscious of self* as a separate BEing from its environment. The Aware element added to consciousness, now allows you to be conscious of your Self as a *Spirit Self*, fully *experientially* Aware of the spiritual realm, yet still as an individual from others and the spiritual environment you exist in. This is the first stage of truly spiritualizing your human-self. Activating the Consciousness Soul is essential to opening the door of the Human-Soul, to be able to bring the Spirit-Self into the house of your Soul. Developing the Will forces consciously within the Soul, is how you keep the door open. The higher thinking of concepts outside of existing parameters of the physical senses, is the necessary assistance your Spirit Self gives to your Soul. All new advancements brought into our world through the Masters and geniuses of our time, have come through this grounding of Spiritual input via the higher conceptual thinking of their highly developed Consciousness Souls Will and their Ego Spirit-Self.

None of this happens automatically any longer, which is why we are all at the stage of Will development to activate Awareness into our Consciousness Soul. Once we had developed our Intellectual Soul sufficiently to become an individual, the potential for Consciousness development was introduced into our Soul. We have all heard of the importance of free Will etc. Well it is the Consciousness Soul where this comes from. At the point of the addition of Will through Consciousness, the creator Spiritual Beings who have been helping develop our human to its present *individual* evolutionary level, now *have to* step back and allow us, as being the individuals that we have now become, to take over the responsibility of our *own* evolutionary development into Spirit Consciousness. Think about it. How could you develop your free Will, if you are being assisted all the time? How could you make decisions for your-self, if other Beings are asserting an influence on you to act or BE a certain way? How can you make free-will choices if the environment you live in and are affected by, is being manipulated by outside forces or BEings? On a purely physical level, you can see how dramatic this affects you when you look at the restrictions and limitations placed on you by your society through its governmental controls etc. From this viewpoint, you may see or feel how the development of your Spirit-Self and Consciousness Soul's Will is being sabotaged by the diverting forces influencing us all to take an easy way out, to take the pill, to do less and avoid responsibility or *avoid doing the right thing* etc. It takes a strong Will to overcome these seductive influences. It may well be easy to take the easy way out and instead do the wrong thing, but the consequences are indeed dire spiritually. Although the Light Beings are taking a step back, the darker diverting forces are still in play. They are however, an essential element for us all now, as they create the opportunities for us to develop and strengthen our Soul and Will forces.

A healthy and well-developed Will is necessary to overcome these diverting forces of non-spiritualization.

If you look at our humanities cultural ways now, you may, hopefully see and feel how it is now made up of systems designed to yes, make life easier, but at the same time they are subtly weakening and stagnating our Will forces, when we succumb to Life's challenges, rather than overcome them. Unfortunately, what we perceive as making life easy, is weakening our Will forces. Our society is now primarily based on looking after the self-first, in the easiest and most profitably advantageous way for self only. Even our laws have started to covertly enable deception and corruption, taking power away from the individual and bundling it up in conglomerates and corporations. These systems however, from a consciously Aware perspective, are great opportunities to develop and strengthen your Soul and Will forces. Through our current world reality, time and time again we find situations of dis-empowerment pressing in on us, tempting us to take the easy way out. Every single one of these situations are moments of choice, to either strengthen or weaken your Will forces and to increase your virtuous character or diminish it. The Will is a muscle, a spiritual muscle if you will. As a muscle, even though it may be spiritual, it still operates under similar principles to its physical counterparts in that ... it needs to be worked for it to develop and build up in strength.

Although I say that the Spiritual BEings have taken a step back from our development, Divine Orchestration hasn't gone anywhere. Our Life's *experience* _opportunities_ are still constantly providing us with the correct and relevant Life situations to develop through. Countless times throughout our everyday human events, we have opportunities to strengthen our Will, through the choices we make. When I chose to do my thirty-day fasting's for example, every moment of desire for food became an opportunity to strengthen or weaken my Will forces. From the first moment of making my commitment to my-self to not eat, every hunger pain and consequent mental anguish, became my opportunity to succumb ... or overcome.

To succumb to influence, weakens my Will ... while overcoming influence, strengthens my Will.

At first glance by our Intellectual Soul's rational perspective, we might believe that my body's physical hunger created my Souls mental anguish. However, with experiential Awareness, what was revealed was that my mental anguish manifested chemical sensations of hunger into my physical body. As my journey through those days of deprived physical nourishment continued, I was able to experience that the *suffering* of which I perceived was coming from my body, was actually coming from my Soul and specifically, from my Intellectual Souls "poor-me" identity. What was to become even more fascinating, was that this "poor-me" identity was how hunger sensations were stimulated in my body, whenever Divine Orchestration brought Life situations of lack and dis-empowerment to me. With Awareness and strength of Will; which means a Spirit-Self well-grounded in my Soul through my Consciousness Soul, I was able to "check in" in those perceived moments of hunger and *experience* that my body was not actually hungry at all. Because of Awareness, the first insight of this *lack of hunger* in my body, then inspired the questions and further *experiential* exploration into where this perceived hunger sensation was actually coming from. The next obvious body to explore to find these hunger originations is of course, the Astral Body of the Soul. Once exposed into my Spirit's light of Awareness, my Intellectual Soul very quickly gave up its "poor me" identity as the culprit. As I deep-dived into the depths of my Soul with my Spirits goggles of Awareness, another fascinating insight into the relationship between the Intellectual and Consciousness components of Soul revealed itself.

Firstly, the physical Body doesn't suffer. Suffering is an *emotional* state of conflict if you will, that originates as we discussed earlier, in the Intellectual Soul component. Pain however, is a physical reaction to trauma within the sphere of our physical body. Because our emotional suffering stimulates body sensations through our etheric Life Body by which physical pain manifest, we are deceived to believe that we have emotional *pain*. Yet again, this has been misidentified as something from the *concept of mind*. Again, we come across the deception and confusion created by this *concept of mind*. Maybe we can see here how necessary it is to distinguish the *true* body originations of dis-eases; to be able to facilitate true transformational changes or healings within the correct body. Through this insight into suffering as an origination within the Soul and pain being the physical manifestation of this suffering through the body, another relationship between the Intellectual and Consciousness components of Soul was revealed.

Suffering comes from conflict between my Intellect and Consciousness.

Ironically, the *concept of mind* as it separates and disconnects my Spirit from my Consciousness, effectively chains the *thinking ability* of my Consciousness Soul to the lower realms of my human intellect. Suffering is brought about from this lack of ability to think consciously in or of the spiritual realm. As we discussed earlier, conflict is the resultant dynamic oscillation between resistance and attachment. Suffering is your Souls manifestation of this conflict within its self—within your human-self. Pain is the resultant physical manifestation of your Soul's suffering, due to the conflict that is generated from your oscillation back and forwards between your resistances and attachments to your Life's experiences. Awareness of this dynamic, of these oscillations and differences etc. is not possible as long we are defined through the *concept of mind* or having a mind. This *concept of mind* strategically blocks your ability to become conscious of the specific component parts of Body Soul and Spirit, that make up the Human-Being you exist as.

Your mind is not *yours*. Your mind is an indoctrinated intellectualized concept brought about by an immature Consciousness *faculty* of Soul. A Soul in this condition is trapped in the lower materialistic thoughts of an imbalanced Intellectual *faculty* of Soul. Being identified as *a mind*—your Consciousness is trapped in these lower intellectualized thoughts facilitating rejection by the intellect of any higher concepts of Spirit. This effectively weakens the Will forces in your Soul, further preventing these same Will forces, from being utilized by your Soul to bring your Spirit's *true* Awareness into your Consciousness. Your intellect has no true *idea* or perception of Awareness. It has however created a version for its self contrived of by the lower thoughts of that same intellect confined to and defined by, its *own* <u>concept of mind</u>. Because of this state of affairs, your intellects deceptive rhetorical depiction of Awareness has absolutely no valid *experiential* connection to your Spirit's true *Aware* state of BE-ing.

There is no TRUE Awareness in an Intellectual Consciousness ... without the embodiment of Spirit.

Mindless-ness is a natural resultant experience of your Soul, embodied with Spirit. Anything short of this embodiment, is a human self-deception. All the deceptive power-incentives preached by our current spiritual sales people—who talk of mind and its power or causes but conveniently leave out any discussion concept or practice of Spirit, have a covert agenda to keep you entranced in the *concept of mind*. For them, for you to become mindless, means they no longer have control over your intellect. As you embody your Spirit's Awareness and become *mindlessly intuitively guided*, these salespeople become powerless to manipulate your intellects spiritual identity with their false promises of a life of ease and magnificence that only you (your spiritual identity) deserves. Being mindless through the embodiment of your Spirit's Awareness, frees you from mindlessly being covertly disempowered by the false indoctrinations of persuasive and charismatic spiritual charlatan's. No longer are you duped by their supposedly specialized health and wellbeing practices, that sensually stroke your false smaller ego, effectively keeping you blind to the true self-empowerment of your Spirit. As a truly consciously Aware Human-Being deliberately spiritualizing your human—you are now the personal healer teacher and Guru to your Self; intuitively guided and supported by a loving spiritual realm, completely aligned to your highest good.

So maybe you have an idea or hopefully, an inspiration toward what it is like to live mindlessly in Awareness, and maybe a hint of the inherent responsibility that comes with it. In the next chapter, let's now explore the simplicity of how to live this way and what it would be like to *live in a mindless world*.

Are you out of your mind ... yet?

Chapter 9

Living in a Mindless World

Naturally, to live in a truly mindless world, would require that this world's inhabitants would all have reached a sufficient level of development of their Consciousness Soul and be living through the Awareness of their Spirit-Self. Obviously, this is NOT the state of our present world, but let's play with this concept for a bit and stimulate our Consciousness Souls expansion into higher thinking to conceptualize the ideal of how *living in a mindless world* might be experienced. From this, we could take it further and maybe see where we might be able to apply this ideal into the present world we co-exist in today.

Remember, it is an under-developed or immature Consciousness Soul that becomes victim to the more developed, but maybe imbalanced Intellectual Souls *perspective* of the power of its thoughts. This however is just a perspective of the Intellect, where in fact it is your Consciousness Soul that holds the true power of *higher thinking* within your Soul; power of which facilitates linking you to your Spiritual Self. So, use your Soul forces here to activate and stimulate your Consciousness Soul, noticing the restrictions of your Intellectual Soul's limiting perspectives and intentions when they show up to discount or invalidate. Experience these perspectives fully, then allow your Spirit's Willingness to expand your concepts, to expand your maybe belligerent Perspective/Intellectual Soul out of its self-imposed limiting comfort zone.

Of course, for one to live in a mindless world, one must BE mindless—free of any concept of mind ... right? So, let's briefly recap on our previous chapters, on what it takes to get *out of your mind* and into a state of mind-less-ness. Put simply, mindless is the result of *experiencing* Life with true Awareness, by feeling with your Awareness, but without definition, judgement or description of what it is you are feeling. As you ground true Spirit-Self Awareness more deeply into your Soul, the falseness of the *concept of mind* unravels and naturally reveals itself. True *experiential* knowledge of your *spiritual* connection will now begin to permeate your Soul's consciousness faculty with vivid truth and virtuous living thoughts of the concept of Spirit. The more your Human-Soul embodies your Spirit, the less influenced it is by the denser materialistic forces acting upon it. You start to free yourself from the *false concept of mind*. I feel this is the simple purpose for humankind in this current cycle of evolution; to free the human-self—to become fully conscious of the Soul that is your human-self and free it from the disempowering trap that is the self-deceiving *concept of mind*. It is the *concept of mind* that traps the Soul in its Intellectual faculty, inevitably chaining your Souls Consciousness to the physical world of the senses. This effectively limits your

Consciousness to the materialistic realm of this physical sense world. Consciousness is the component faculty of your human Soul-self which has the capacity to link your Soul to your Spirit. Through this linking and only through this link, is intuitive access to the infinite wisdom of the Cosmos achievable. This includes of course, your physical human reality. It is only through the embodiment of your Spirit-Self that the use of Spirit-Self's Awareness is made possible. To *feel* and *intimately experience* the spiritual *forces* of Life that lie behind the manifestation of your *Soul's human world,* requires the embodiment of your Spirit. By this embodiment, your Soul's Consciousness is drawn out of its enchantment in the Intellectual sense world and enlightened by its Spirit Nature into the Divine super-sensible realm of its *true* existence as a free BEing.

> *It is my Spirit-Self's Awareness that holds the key to unlocking the chains of the sense world; those that bind my Soul's Consciousness to a materialistic Intellect.*

Now understanding or *knowing about* living in Awareness as being the key etc., is all well and good, but how does this equate to truly living in this mindless state in the world consciousness we exist in today? What does it take to live this way? How do you get from being conscious of your human intellectual world, to Consciously Aware of your Spirit-Self's experiential world? How do you successfully live in this world of Creator BEing-ness and Divine creative *forces* and influences—and still function in this current materialistic world of form?

If we understand that to live in a mindless world, requires one to live beyond or free of the *concept of mind,* and to be free of the *concept of mind* comes from living with our Spirits Awareness firmly embodied in our human Soul, then what can that look like as an individual in today's world? Some more materialistic Souls may jump into this concept with the viewpoint that it would be impossible to live this way. They may believe this because one can't extract one's self from the human world workings that we currently exist in. They might say that unless you simply pack up shop and move in to a monastery, it would be impossible to live a spiritual and human life together successfully. They may even reference the likes of the Dalia Lama for example, who although obviously epitomizes an advanced spiritual Being—through their perception—could not build a bridge or farm the land; develop software, be a CEO of a multi-corporation, serve behind a store counter, wash dishes for a living or waiter in a restaurant etc., etc. Their argument may be that to be at that level of Aware Spiritual existence naturally extracts one from the everyday individual occupations that make up humanities function as a society—as a human culture. However, these kinds of viewpoints are merely more covert forms of resistance toward doing what it takes to bring more Spirit-Self into the individuals Soul life. The truth of it all is, that *this IS* the time for bringing it all together, to spiritualize our human existence by combining just these elements of materialistic human culture and Spirit-BEing.

To bring more Spirit-Self into your human Soul's life here on Earth, is how you deepen your experience as a human. Here on this Earth ship transporting us all through this

Cosmic sea of evolution, is where Spirit and human get to embody each other in the one reality. This can only happen here on this planet BEing and it can only come about through you. The result of more Spirit-Self in one's human life, is a life of much deeper and intimate connection with ALL the components of this human existence; both internal and external. It's about gaining a heightened sensory-experience than what you are capable of presently. It is about expanding your sensory capability to the point of becoming super-sensory. This means being super-sensory to the much subtler Cosmic forces that impress influence; both internally and externally, on your state of Being. Quite contrary to the resistant materialistic viewpoints above, a Spiritualized human is much more intimately connected to the everyday human existence, than one who is void of Spirit and materialistically humanized. ALL the drama within our present everyday human existence ... comes directly from a totally humanized Intellectualized Soul. The pain and suffering that is intrinsic in the human reality of today, is a direct result of the evolution of our Being into this present day totally humanized dense Intellectual Consciousness. The delusional self-deception of ending pain and suffering on Earth by addressing it through the Body, Soul and *concept of mind*, is the very trap that now puts one in conflict with one's true Spirit Nature. It is the elements and components of the TRUE Self of Spirit; through which *true* freedom from suffering is obtainable.

As long as conflict and separation continue to exist between the Human-Soul-Body and Spirit Self ... pain and suffering will ensue at the heart of human reality.

Ironically, the compression of suffering is still necessary right now. It is through suffering that we gain the opportunity for expansion from experiential spiritual insight. It's these "Ahh Haa" moments of insight that bring about the necessary transformation of our Soul's capacity; from which makes it possible for us to overcome our presently dense human reality.

So how do we reconcile this conflict and separation between our human and our Spirit? The basic and simple answer is ... experiential ownership. This form of ownership is not the intellectual kind so widely used to covertly *appear* to be taking ownership of one's transgressions etc. When we create a *perception* of an act, before *experiencing* the actual consequences and dynamic of those actions; whether it is a physical or mental action: the action gets trapped in the Soul as an intellectually conscious act. Being intellectually conscious of an act, is what happens when we *know about* something, *without* any real *feeling experience*. Our experience is void of all its subtle effects and influences that come with that true feeling experience of what that act created. Anything less than this *feeling experience* is not ownership ... it is mental *acknowledgment*.

Experiential ownership is when you completely *experience* the transgression, feeling it with your Awareness, *before* <u>acknowledging</u> it and creating an intellectual perception of it. Experiential ownership brings you to an Aware, deeply feeling experience ... before ... consciously creating a perception through thinking about it of what has been done.

I have a stupidly simple exercise in my workshops to distinguish the difference between, "am I feeling what I am describing ... or am I describing what I am feeling?"

This exercise shows the difference between creating a perception intellectually or creating one experientially. This level of ownership brings with it a profoundly deep experiential connection to the consequences of your actions, thoughts and deeds. These consequences aren't just the effect your actions etc. have on you, they are the effect your actions etc. have on others. Experiential ownership through feeling with Awareness, brings with it a profound experience of the other, allowing you to feel as they feel, from the effect of, and as a consequence from, your actions etc. Here now we come to the first insight into the positive potential of *Living in a mindless world*.

Imagine living in a world where you can feel the experiences of another, where you can feel the BEing of your fellow "Earth Walkers". As you embody more Spirit-Self Awareness in your human Soul, you embody your Spirit's inherent *intuitive* capability also. This is what ultimately makes it possible for us all to connect so intimately with others ... through *their* Spirit-Self. From this place, we get to move out of intellectually *knowing about* others from the outside and instead, get to experientially know the other from the inside, from within them. For example, imagine being able to feel the effect on you of a lie from someone else? How would relationships unfold if you could feel a lie when it is told to you? Being told a lie, one naturally does something other than what they would do if they had been told the truth. All lies have an influence of the one being lied to, and that influence is an intended one of the one telling the lie. So simply, if you could feel a lie when it is being told to you, would that truth from feeling, free you from its influence or would it trap you in it? Trapped in the influence of a lie is usually what happens without any knowledge of the lie—along with an equally usual negative result—right? From being able to experience that, imagine also being able to feel the *effect* on your own Soul-self from lies *you* not only tell others, but the ones you tell yourself as well. Do you think the state of our health and wellbeing could be the end result of the highly detrimental effects on our Body and Soul coming from the lies? From this state we naturally become Aware of the self-deceptions we all most likely tell our-self throughout any given day? If you just reacted to that statement and felt an immediate denial of lying to yourself, then you can be sure you do. Don't worry though, because *everyone* does in this present stage of evolution. By living in Awareness, you get to see feel and experience, how you react is actually your red flag. This red flag is waving to you something you resist owning within yourself. By using this super-sensitive Awareness, you become able to see and *feel* the extremely detrimental effects to *your* own health and wellbeing from the "lie phantoms" we spoke of earlier; the ones which come from these lies we are talking about now. Inevitably from this experiential insight of these lies, you may—hopefully—create a new commitment and strength of Will to stop the telling of lies, both to self and others. What might our mindless world begin to look and feel like, if we started to simply stop telling lies to our self and others? What would be the point of lying any more if you knew the other person could *feel* whether you were lying or not?

To know thy self ... is to know God.

Now obviously, this level of ownership, this deep and intimate *feeling ability* that comes with true Spirit-Self Awareness, is naturally going to reveal all manner of covert self-deceptive behaviors and patterns within one's life of human Soul-self. It is through Awareness of these specific aspects of your Soul-self, and all its many materialistic limitations of intellectual perspectives and consciousness etc., that you can truly come to "know thy self". I have often chuckled at the many spiritual identities of today professing their perspective of the human self as an illusion and the need for their special or secret practices for experiencing your TRUE Self. There is no doubt that your TRUE Self is one and the same eternal Spirit-Self that I am talking about also, but the True Self I speak of is the same multifaceted Spirit that Rudolph Steiner talks about also, made up of Spirit Self, Life Spirit and Spirit Man. The other massive difference I speak of is that there is no real separation of Spirit (while we walk this planet's reality) from the Body and Soul self's that make up our physical human cohort for this lifetime. It is through intimately *knowing by experience*, ALL the components and their subtle forces and relationships together; of which bring about their final manifestation as your human-Soul-self: that we can ultimately come to the experiential "I AM". It is this experiential "I AM" that is the true experiencer of the sensor-able and the super-sensor-able realms that we co-exist within. To know thy self, IS to know God the Divine, because we are all creations of this same Divine. *Knowing experientially* the components, forces and relationships etc. that make up your Self, is to come to know the Divine Orchestration that is what we have come to call God. To come here for this present human experience, we have had to forget the intimate experience of God; of which is the Cosmic heritage we all bear.

It is through the full experiential ownership of my human-self, that the window of my Soul opens and lets the light of true Spirit Awareness enlighten my human-Soul-self to ALL of its component parts and characteristics.

Collectively, it is these parts that make me the "I AM" that I "BE" for this lifetime.

There is no true separation between my human and Spirit, except the one I create through resistance to experiential ownership of ALL the components and characteristics of my human-self, especially my Spirit Nature.

It is through a willingness to experience all of your life at this level of experiential ownership, that you can intimately know ALL these components etc., which we have been exploring throughout this book. It is ownership of self, that creates true lasting harmony between your human Soul and Spirit; between your Astral and Ego bodies: from which the *concept of mind* is dissolved and true harmony as the "I AM", can be achieved. When THIS harmony is achieved, the Cosmic forces of creation, of Life its Self, are allowed to flow freely into all of your bodies unobstructed. It is via this free flowing of Life Forces into your etheric body; from which health and wellness become the physical expression. Ironically, it is by this harmonization of Body Soul and Spirit, that the "I AM" that is your true experiential Ego body fully connected to the Spiritual Realm, begins to develop and embody its Life Spirit element. This brings with it the higher Divine Creational Forces of Life itself. This embodiment of the Life Spirit is what transforms the current etheric body as the physical creational force, into a conscious instrument of Cosmic Creational forces. It is at the final developmental stage of Spirit Man, that we achieve mastery over ALL of these spiritual AND physical components, elements and creational forces. From that point, we are then able to manifest at Will, with the Creational Forces of Life Spirit and transform matter, our body and our physical environment. As supported by Rudolph Steiner's spiritual research, this time is still a few thousand years away for humanity, along with obvious further stages of evolution to go through, but ... the potential, the germinal seed for the successful achievement of this God-like state of BEing, lies within us all ... now.

The first barrier for us in this present time, is to develop the appropriate *strength of Will* to do whatever it takes ... to live in a mindless world with Conscious Awareness in experiential ownership of all the component parts of one's Self. This requires of us, a strength of Will capable of standing up to the dense distracting influences of our presently created intellectual materialism. The first piece of experiential ownership may well be to own, that each and every one of us that currently walk this third rock from the sun, have created this intellectual materialism. Inevitably, this brings to your Soul's door, the deception of attachment to the physical sense world. However, the opportunities we have talked of for virtue embodiment, through which we can potentially raise our human consciousness sufficiently to be able to fully embody Spirit, lie hidden within the disguise of our life's present human events. These present-day human events are the physical expression of this intellectual materialism we have created for ourselves.

It is through the light of Awareness and experiential ownership, that the jewels of virtue can be un-earthed and embodied, ultimately enlightening the Soul and enriching ALL of human reality.

So, now that you have this new wisdom; this new knowledge of the components of Self and their harmonious relationships that can potentially transmute you into a truly mindless human Being: how do you get to develop and embody this knowledge, these new states of BEing, into your present everyday life? In so doing, how does that improve the quality of your human BE-ing-ness in this here and now? The answer of course is study and practice. I do not however mean study in the sense of present day education—which has one trying to indoctrinate one's human-self with knowledge, yet never taking it to a truly *living practice* that turns knowledge into wisdom ... as a Life expression ... of you. Ironically, the development of the main requirements to achieve true Awareness and strength of the appropriate Will, is extremely simple. The power in the simplicity however, is in its continual use.

Nothing has power to change ... when it isn't used ... by me.

I have deliberately refrained throughout this book from giving out specific exercises to achieve these states we are discussing ... because they are <u>experiential states</u> of achievement and not possible to be achieved correctly intellectually. The purpose of the stories I have shared with you, has been to connect with your Spirit-Self's *experiential* ability to *feel* the experience of the consciousness within the stories. At the same time, I have tried to keep your Intellectual Soul's perspective in alignment with the consciousness being portrayed within the story also. If you have stayed *in-feel* through the stories and they have made some sense to you, then you can be sure that you have picked up a lot more than what your intellect believes, of the actual experiences that can be gained through specific exercises. Even if you have travelled in and out of *feel* throughout and you have got to this part in the book, then you too can be assured that you have connected your Consciousness to your Spirit far more than you may think. Although it is so stupidly simple for anyone now to access their Spirit-Self Awareness, I have found that without true *Spirit Self Awareness* guiding the initiation of this first <u>conscious experience</u> of the virtue embodiment with one's true Awareness, the whole thing can too easily get intellectualized. Without fail, 100 percent of students I have worked with through my Lomi Conscious Bodyworks, ALL, even after having experienced the real power of their Spirit-Self's Awareness, still slide back into their intellectual *concept of mind* interpretation of the experience. Preliminary work is necessary to strengthen the necessary Soul Forces to complete the virtue embodiment exercises.

There was an incident I had with a specific spiritual-salesman that brought the importance home to me, to not just vomit out the embodiment exercises to the masses through the written word. This particular salesman was an established meditation practitioner and author of several mind-based meditation books for better living etc. We came to meet through a mutual friend who I was living with. He was staying at another friend's rental house to write his second book in a trilogy of his Mind Body Soul concept. Notice that there is no Spirit in his trilogy, which should have been my red flag, but my Spirit had something paramount instore for my Soul to integrate through our relationship together. When we first came together, from putting my Awareness on our connection, I felt there was most definitely a Divine Orchestration happening between us. I felt a kind of, *swept along* influence moving us together. He later revealed to me that after our first meet, he felt a similar thing, but his was steeped in fear of me. As things turned out, I feel it was his spiritual-salesman identity that quivered in its boots at the sense of a Spirit-Self's true Awareness being shone toward it. By the end, it was clear that we both had some substantial Karma to work out.

Karma is an indescribable force of Divine Orchestration that will bring together individuals and circumstances for the parties to work something out from a previous lifetime. This is an incomplete experience that created a residual dis-harmony in the spiritual world and of each individual. The Hawaiian practice of Ho'oponopono is used for this purpose also and originated from an intensely more intimate understanding of the spiritual forces of Karma, then those we interpret it as today. Karma doesn't work it out … you must … together with the other preferably. This was no doubt the opportunity in this life time for both my friend and me.

After meeting a couple of times at my friend's regular meditation group, and after my friend suggested a Lomi Conscious Bodywork session with me may help his book writing; which happened by chance to be about the body: he agreed to a session. On getting up off the table at the end of the first session, he remarked, "I think this is what I came here to write about." He continued, "I haven't been able to put my finger on what this book was meant to be … until now." On hearing this, MY Approval Identity was deeply aroused and so flattered, that my head nearly didn't fit through the doorway on my way out. Not the first time that has happened, but again, thanks to the Divine for Spirit Awareness to see it. On making it conscious, I could deflate my head before breaking down the door. Through this specific meditation organization that we met through and of which he is involved in as a teacher where his supposedly "expertise" in meditation came from: he had a good rhetoric about awareness. I could feel however, he hadn't had the true experience of it yet. I had met several other meditation teachers from this organization also, and although there was a common *good talk* of awareness achieved through their form of meditation, as if the dialog was almost part of the training, it was clear to me, not all of them had truly achieved the living state of true Awareness we have been talking about here. Their Consciousness was no doubt awakened, but as you have learned here, this was not Awareness and their Soul was not embodying their Spirit.

The difference between the states of BEing conscious or Aware, is that BEing truly Aware, naturally invokes responsibility and ownership for ALL of one's Life, along with what is revealed through the conscious use of such Awareness.

Being Conscious only makes things apparent, as something outside of one's self and as such, responsibility and ownership get pushed <u>outside</u> also.

The other red flag with this group is that their whole practice is hinged on a result of Peace and Stillness from the meditation. You see, they are still trying to get away from the experiences that their human-self is creating and of which Life is constantly and purposefully providing for them. Supposedly, their meditation is to induce a state of peace and stillness to offset it. I can't help feeling however that most of them often use their meditation to distract their-self out of their Life's experience opportunities to embody more virtues. This state of peace etc. however, never included finding a virtue that might transform the Soul and its experiences, rather than just get rid of them. This practice rarely inspired one to embody full ownership of all their components of self that are creating their experiences, along with the inherent higher characteristics of Spirit that go with it. As I stepped my newly acquired best friend spiritual salesman through the Awareness exercises, he experienced the true power for healing and transformation. For the first time, he experienced the power of transformation that comes from the embodiment of the virtues that come through true Awareness of Spirit. He was stunned to say the least, but reticent to take ownership of his self-deception around his pretenses about Awareness. Rather reluctantly I felt, he eventually shared with me that he sees now, the difference between what he thought was Awareness through his meditation practices and the true experience he was now having through the experience embodiment work.

The following few months entailed an intense collaboration for his book. Now however, his book now included the Awareness concepts and techniques I use for my Conscious Bodywork. This became for me, a fantastic case study on the limitations our *concept of mind* places on our ability to truly experience Spirit BEing. Remember I said this salesperson was writing a trilogy of Mind Body and Soul? His first book was on Mind, the second of which was on the Body, which was the one we worked together on to incorporate the specific techniques and concepts of this work I am sharing with you all now. As supposedly experienced and enlightened as this salesman would make out to be, you my reader, have probably by reading this book *experientially*, through feeling your way through the stories and get to this place in the book, had more experiential integration of these concepts and components of Soul etc. than he gained from our whole time together over the following year. Remember, his first book was on Mind, so his *concept of mind* with all his exercises to unlock it or quieten it etc., etc., was the chain to the intellect that prevented him from allowing the *truly experiential truth* of Spirit-Self to be embodied in his Soul. At one point, he even said that we must change the wording to not include any reference or talk of Spirit in the book," because it will alienate some readers and existing students of his works." His refusal to give any credit or reference to Spirit, was testimony to the degree of disconnect and rejection he was living in ... toward his own Spirit.

Although he had let me read the proof before print and final edit; which revealed some glaring mental interpretations that I obviously disagreed with, the book went to print and his mental version void of Spirit prevailed. We did talk every couple of weeks, and explored a lot more of the concepts etc., however, I had a sense that all was not as it appeared to be. I have a deep obligation to my work and what Spirit has revealed to me, so although I could feel that everything wasn't as he said it was, I still wanted to help get the truth of Spirit out there through us combining for this work. He put on a good show toward this end but, I could feel other agendas for self were obviously operating. Here is one of the attributes I mentioned above, of living mindlessly and being able to feel the others space and not just their lies, but their agendas etc. as well. As he asked me to participate via video call to the class in his first Body workshop, I thought he was still open to moving to the depth of experiential ownership that true Awareness asks of us, so I agreed to continue together.

The persuasive power of a spiritual-salesman, lies within their ability to seduce the spiritual-identity within my Intellectual Soul, effectively trapping me in my intellect.

This effectively blocks my Spirit-Self's intuitive Awareness from exposing the hidden agendas that are running their rhetoric.

Yes ... I was seduced ... for a time. Again, this is how the *concept of mind* is used to confuse rather than clarify. This was how my Spirit enlightened my Soul to the misuse of the intellect. I had to *experience* the seduction first, to be able to integrate the difference between the virtue of spiritual integrity in actions, as opposed to the deceptions of our Intellectual Soul's spiritual salesman identity in actions.

A few months later and he announced his next Body workshop in London and I felt this kind of Cosmic shift slap me on the back, knocking me forward. I knew I had to be on that course to try and set the standard of the Awareness work right. From reading his published book, I could feel the subtle and covert mental slant he had put in the words, taking people out of Awareness and pulling them back into his mental versions of intellectualized consciousness exercises. His avoidance of alignment conversations with me about compensation and lack of sitting with me to do deeper Awareness exercises of self-ownership, were red flags to beware for sure. Every time however, Spirit would interject with the overwhelming feel of "the right thing to do for the students", so I booked my ticket and made my accommodation commitments. I felt a twinge in his space when I surprised him with, "I'm coming." My insight was that if I can help he and his students get a true experiential embodiment of Awareness, then he will see the power of Spirit and be inspired to take further ownership of his spiritual salesman identity. I was banking on this higher experience to inspire him to look deeper with me for the empowerment of his students and set them free from his systems. Instead, his spiritual identity upped its game. He shared that he had found a new business model from another financially successful spiritual-salesman he knew. Once he explained his new model, I could see that it would turn his existing system of indoctrinating his students and coaches, into a system that locks them into his materials, books, CD's etc. He was especially excited in describing how this model will turn it all into a million-dollar business. When I asked him what he would do with that million dollars. After what I suspected was a hesitation to try and say the right thing to me, he said he would put it back into the system to make more product for the students etc. Of course, the huge self-deception in that reply, was that it was *the products* that were already trapping the students and coaches in their intellect. This simply meant that more product would just equate to more indoctrinated dis-empowerment to the people, attracting and seducing more Intellectual Souls and of course, bringing him more money.

Yes, this was a massive red flag. Now this had me question my own motives for being involved in this deception and how would this equate for me to uphold the integrity of the Awareness Embodiment work. I always felt a responsibility for this work, because it had been entrusted to me. Through living the work, through experiencing fully and bringing my resistance and attachments together with my Awareness, the virtue of "doing the right thing" was revealed and embodied and I went to London anyhow. Through my involvement in his community website of his students and coaches, it turned out we inspired many students old and new and this course ended up being his biggest enrolment to date. I had thought that the alignment meeting we had the night before the workshop had gone very well, as he seemed to accept my suggestions for the Awareness exercises I had developed from my own workshops. The intention for the exercises was to ensure the student gets well-grounded Spirit Awareness in their Soul, before doing his mentalized healing techniques with the embodiment exercise's we had put in his book. Again, I was seduced, as the next morning he states that he is going to do it "by the book" he had written, and he discarded all my Awareness exercises.

My spiritual-identity was ropable by this callous self-centered invalidation, which triggered up my pouting-identity as we set up the room for the students. In that moment, yet again shinning my Spirit-Self Awareness on this identity, my resistance and attachments revealed what was making it all about me, again pushing the students highest good out the window of the two-story building we were in. Some further experiential ownership and an embodied virtue of *surrender to Spirit* and within minutes, I was back once more, present for the integrity of the work and benefit to the students. At every opportunity that showed up to clarify or rectify his mental versions throughout the course, without invalidation toward him, Spirit would slap my Soul into action and an embodied experience within the students prevailed. After the two days of this dance between Soul and Spirit, the course ended up a massive success. Everyone had a good result, most had great successes, and some had Soul altering experiences. At the end when everyone had left, we sat down, and he said to me, "what just happened?" He shared that he had never had a course like that before and I pointed out that, being able to keep Spirit present in the Soul for most of the time throughout the course, produces this kind of result, the result of which is a truly spiritualized human. I pointed out that this was a great example of the importance for true Spirit Awareness embodied in the Soul and the difference in this power as opposed to a mental version. I was excited for him, as I felt he had finally had a true experience and glimpse of his Soul embodied with Spirit, without it being some religious indoctrination.

Over the following few months, the inspiration from this course would have us connect a lot more and talk of future courses together. Although I was excited to finally be delivering this work to many more people than I could do through my Lomi practice, my Awareness continually revealed elements of mis-alignment with him. A continual sense of his hidden agendas became more pressing as we went on. Still, we weren't doing any experience work together, which my Spirit was insisting had to be made as a consistent practice for us both together. It would be through this consistent weekly practice that Spirit could stay embodied in Soul and higher guidance could prevail. It was this higher guidance of Spirit that was necessary for our actions and decisions to remain in alignment with the highest good for all. Without this higher Spirit guidance, it was inevitable that the lower mental self-indulgent guidance of the analytical Intellectual Soul would infiltrate his life of Soul once more. As months flowed on and my numerous requests for experience sessions together were continually swept under his carpet of, "too busy a schedule" and "not enough time", I felt deep disappointment from his dis-integrous intentions weighing on me, like a heavy wet woolen winters coat.

My *attachments* to continuing courses with him began creating the inevitable conflict within me, as its associated *resistance* to selling my Soul and becoming yet another spiritual salesman like my newly acquired friend, grew within me. Another moment for Aware experiential ownership to reveal the truth and for me to bring the attachment and resistance together. From this, the experience I was living in but not seeing of "it's all about me", revealed itself. I experienced this deeply with my Awareness, but of course, without definitions, judgments or descriptions and my own spiritual salesman identity within me showed its colors. It was this identity I found that was the motivational force creating my "all about me" experience. Although I was fascinated by this and the subtlety of this powerful motivational force from this identity, I was deeply saddened as I realized that my spiritual salesman friend was living in the self-deception of his own "all about me" identity. I asked Life's opportunity in this moment, for the appropriate Spirit-Self virtue to embody. The answer was again, surrender. With a quick virtue embodiment resulting in a now surrendering Soul, I became free of the subtle internal influence of attachment and resistance to self. Free higher thinking began its intuitive guidance for me once more. From this higher guidance and the intimate experience of my own spiritual salesman, I realized that if my new friend didn't do any experiential work around his own spiritual salesman identity, then there would be no way our relationship could work. The integrity of the Awareness and experience work couldn't be upheld and guided by Spirit without this ongoing work in ownership of our identities.

Attachment and resistance are the subtle and covert internal influences; from which all human conflict originates.

When un-owned internally, this conflict finds it's expression as a personal projection into the external world and manifest physically as all forms of disharmony, separation, wars, etc.

Inevitably, this conflict manifested in the world of our relationship as distrust and avoidance. The closing event for us came when finally, some nine months after we did our first initial fateful session on my table, we finally did a session on all the specific points of mis-alignment and integrity issues I had been talking about. I had so often told him that this work needs to be lived to be taught correctly. I explained that living it will demand of him a level of commitment to his deepest self-ownership that would challenge him beyond anything he may have already experienced. That fateful session took over an hour and reminded me of the many times as a parent, I had to bring my teen age daughters to ownership of their lies or self-deceptions. The duck-and-weave of his avoidance identity fueled by his spiritual identity trapped in his *concept of mind*, extremely artful. It was however no match for the light of Spirit Awareness embodied in a spiritualized Soul. It appeared no doubt these identities had been running his whole life. Through the openness of Love between our Spirit's, he eventually popped into the self-realization of his own spiritual salesman identity, the one he had been denying most of his life. The fabric of our relationship reality vibrated anew, like it had never done before. There was silence, there was true stillness and connection in our individual and relationship space in that brief moment of his self-realization. We ended our session lovingly, with what I thought, was a renewed commitment to continue the experience work further on this identity. We scheduled our next session for two weeks and signed off.

I felt renewed in faith for our work to continue, even though my partner and my good friend; both intuitive, warned me that it was not enough and that he would revert to his "all about me" life again. This would happen because he wasn't yet … living the practice. Unfortunately, they were both right. Two weeks passed, and more busy excuses flowed from him with still no alignment discussions on payments, compensations or more Awareness sessions. I realized that, although he had most definitely had a realization *about* his spiritual salesman, he hadn't yet moved to the full *experiential ownership* we have talked about here. He had recognized this identity but not yert owned it and the consequences of its actions. There was not yet any ownership of what he, through this spiritual identity, had been creating. I knew that, without further deeper experience session with him truly living in Awareness, this level of ownership was not going to be reached. It was time to do the right thing … by Spirit. Spirit had slapped me more than once about this and so, I broke off our relationship and any further chance of working together again. Ironically, but not surprising to me, he has never responded to my separation or questioned any element of the experience we had in that last revealing session.

My purpose for you in this story, is to show how no matter how spiritually advanced we may *think* we are; especially if we have created new systems of teaching for others, what we are doing is mostly void of Spirit. I am not saying this as a wrong thing or negative energy or any of the other "New Age" labels of resistant and judgmental actions that float around today. I say this as a clear understanding of the importance and role of this level of Intellectual Consciousness we have achieved now, and of the limitation to evolve further that this very same level now also places on us all. At the peak of our Intellectual Souls development, that same intellect then becomes a tremendous hindrance for our humanity continuing to evolve into the truly Human Spirit that we are each Divinely intended to be. Divine Intelligence has been granted us, so we may develop our Conscious intellect. This is of paramount necessity for our "I Consciousness" to develop sufficiently and manifest in this present materialistic paradigm. This "I Consciousness" is also as yet, void of Spirit; which is where we are at right now, as this is the only way that an "I" *can be* separate from its Divine Origination. The logical Intellectual Soul component has created a spiritual identity as its substitute. In our ancient past, when we were still just a Soul, before we were granted the Ego Spirit Body and its associated "I AM", humanity as a group collective, had a direct connection and communication with Spirit Beings and the Spiritual realm. For the "I" to come into BEing, this spiritual connection etc., had to be severed, and consequently for most people, the Soul became void of any Spirit connection, so it could develop "individuality".

Our <u>spiritual identities</u> are remnant creations of our Soul from that ancient time, but it is a mere copy, a thin and false image of Spirit, like your reflection in the mirror is not the true BEing that is looking at it.

The Enlightened Masters who have come before us, shone their light of Spirit Awareness as a lamp in the Cosmic darkness for us to see ahead back to the spiritual realm. Nearly all of them have shared that this spiritual identity, or spiritual ego, is the last deception, the last self-illusion one must come to own and discharge, before true enlightenment will be Graced. This spiritual identity of the Intellect is an alchemical deceiver. It can only masterfully *replicate* <u>knowledge</u> of the spiritual world rhetorically, within its intellectual domain. It cannot however embody in the Soul, the *experiential wisdom and power* to transform the "I Consciousness". Only the true Spirit-Self that waits patiently within our Spirits Ego Body, can bring in this power of wisdom and facilitate the transformation of our consciousness. The *concept of mind* originated from a spirit-less Soul identity, as its intellectual concept of what Spirit is and as a substitute for it.

Because our evolution has brought us to this present stage of now having a Spirit Ego Body; the body that houses the "I AM" that we talk about here, means every one of us … without exceptions … has a spiritual identity. This "spiritual ego" however, doesn't reside in the Spirit's Ego Body, it resides in the Intellectual Souls identity arsenal. It is THIS spiritual-identity that the master's talk about as being the last hurdle to true Self-Realization and Awareness. Experiencing the illusion of this humanly limited spiritual-identity, is the only way to cross the threshold to your eternal Higher Spirit BEing-Self. The only difference between yours and mine and every other spiritual identity on this Earth Mother Gaia, is the level of its development. Some are very lowly developed, which are the more tribal collective group Souls and their spiritual identity is trapped in the past. Others are highly developed, which manifest as the true spiritual seekers of the world. The truth is that the more highly developed *spiritual identity* of the *seeker*, is more developed than a lot of the perceived *spiritual salespeople* Souls I have talked about throughout this book. The spiritual seeker has evolved past needing to persuade, convince and convert. The spiritual salespeople need this, as they try to justify their own interpretations and avoid the actual experience and true Spirit embodiment. The spiritual seeker is now greatly open to revelations of Spirit, and reverently strives for the true experience of Spirit that can be embodied in the Soul, as a living reality.

The spiritual seeker strives to have the experience of Spirit, embodied in their Soul.

The spiritual salespeople teach only what their Intellectual Souls "spiritual identity" has comprehended and interpreted … of what others have experienced.

They do this to avoid true ownership of their false identities, simply to keep it all about their self and avoid embodying Spirit in their own Soul.

At this point in our evolution, neither of these identities are wrong. Each is a unique and potentially transformative experience. One is becoming truly free of influence as they develop their Consciousness Soul's Will forces to take true ownership of ALL that they are as Body Soul and Spirit. In turn, they embody more and more Spirit-Self and its inherent Awareness. The other is trapped in the inner influences of their spiritual identity, until they can become *conscious* of the lack of freedom they actually exist in as a consequence of their Intellectual Soul and *lack* of Will from a still under-developed Consciousness Soul. If you have had a react to my use of the label spiritual salesman now or throughout this book, then it is simply because your spiritual identity is reacting to being found out and exposed. If you are reacting to the label, then with Awareness feel the resistance force that is stimulating the react. If you are reacting, it is because you don't like something about it ... right? Feel with your Awareness the "not like" force and notice what it creates in your space. If you find the force of resistance, then you can be sure there is an associated force of attachment that goes with it. If you resist the label spiritual salesman, then what is it you are attached to that is connected to that resistance? For example, are you attached to your spiritual identity? Just allow yourself to experience these two opposing forces and notice, when you bring them together as one experience, what *that* experience is. Just experience whatever that is without defining, describing or judging it and just be curious and interested in it. See if you can feel the identity that is creating this and be interested in that identity to get to know its character etc. It is healthy to be intimate with your spiritual identity. This is how you can harmonize with it and neutralize its covert power of influence on you. This will then reveal the true virtue that is needing to be embodied.

Because my friend from the story above exists in the intellectual realm and is so influenced and blinded by his spiritual identity, he had formulated an intellectual concept of the original true Spirit experience from that first session he did with me. This is where his Intellectual Soul had created a *perspective* of my work and mis-interpreted the true Spirit Awareness experience ... but without truly having the full experience. From this intellectualized perspective, he derived an interpretation that fitted within his spiritual identities pre-existing concepts. Once he had formed this concept, it was then embodied in his Soul, which prevented any further expansion of that concept through his Consciousness Soul. This effectively prevented his Spirit from being allowed to enter his Soul again, which also prevented his Soul from receiving any higher thinking or insightful input from the Spiritual Realm. Can you see the strategy of this spiritual identity? With this intellectual *concept* of the experience firmly in place, his *concept of mind* could interpret, manipulate, mis-construe and mis-translate everything I was trying to share with him, in any way that suited the self-indulgent hidden agendas of this identity. This is also why he wouldn't do more than two original sessions with me. It was in the second session done through skype some nine months after the first, that the veil of deception of this identity began to crumble and be exposed. Each time you truly embody your Spirit-Self Awareness, the veil of deceptions from your identities start to be revealed and your opportunity to discharge them is presented to you. If you keep doing the Awareness practice and *live* in-feel through Awareness, you can expose all of your identities, which sets you free from their influence. This is also what frees you from the *concept of mind*. My spiritual salesman friend couldn't afford to keep doing them with me, because he could already start to see his self-deceptions and felt it was easier to avoid, as he had been doing most of his life, then to own them. He is a part of a massive family of avoiders like this on our planet right now.

It is because of this spiritual salesman identity of my friend, that what I shared with him of the Awareness exercises and particularly the embodiment exercises I use in my Conscious Bodyworks sessions had lost its power with him. They lost the power and wisdom of the Spirits experience when he put them into words of his intellectualized choosing. As I read his book, I could feel the *concept of mind* influence, drag my Souls intellectual component forward and push my Spirit-Self to the side. When I experienced it as a reader without embodied Awareness, I could feel my spiritual identity seduced and subtly influenced to not just push Spirit aside, but to open the back door of the bus and kicked it out for the rest of the journey through the book. One of the reasons for going to the course in London, was to see and feel the effect of his written mental versions on the students and of course where necessary and possible, see if I could correct it for them. Some were too far entrenched in his doctrine, while others were open for Spirit. Of course, the world reflects our self, back to us, both denied and accepted parts of self. His coaches (teachers) were at a similar stage of spiritual identity development as he, so a lot of the coaches struggled to embody Spirit fully also.

By the end of the course however, it was clear to me that the vomiting of my Awareness exercises in book form, or to him directly now, was not appropriate or respectful to the Spirit of the material or the individual student's highest good. Also, it became obvious from the follow up we did in the three months after the course, that there were not enough Spirit grounding exercises for the individuals to move it all into a rhythmic living practice for them. Having said all of this however, I have decided to include some startup Awareness, Willing, thinking and feeling exercises for you all at the end of this book. This is so you can carry on from what you have learned here … if you choose … with the further expansion of your Soul and embodiment of your Spirit.

Without a consistent rhythmic living practice, the spiritual identity
quickly takes back control and the Spirit is very covertly kicked out the
back of the bus again.

To make real and substantial transformational change toward living in a mindless world, a consistent and persistent introduction of the new system etc. needs to be carried out with a highly committed strength of Will. This strong Will is one that will diligently follow through for specific times, times which are relative to the specific body one is trying to change.

For the physical body-self to integrate a specific change of living and for that change to be implemented as a new living practice, that specific change must be carried out for a minimum of 30 days. This time frame of course, is dependent on the individual's strength of Will and Soul Forces. What this means is, in the case of a dietary change for example, you need to keep up the change of diet for at least 30 days for the body to accept the change and respond to it as a now normal part of its rhythmic system. When I did my first 30 day fast, I was astounded to find that at the end of the 30 days, there was almost no body need for food at all. Also, I developed my 30-day reset cleanse for breaking my bodies food habits and addictions, which was not a total fast but, it did involve partial fasting of those foods that I wanted to drop and cleanse from my body.

This then enabled my Body to very easily take on the new appropriate food source without any great deal at all.

For the human Soul-self's Astral Body to integrate a specific change, one must unequivocally commit to that change and that change must be carried out for an absolute minimum of 60-90 days. This commitment must have far more diligence than what's required for the Body change. For the Astral Body change, diligent Awareness and ownership of the Soul-self's subtle and covert emotional deceptions coming from the Intellectual Soul, is a key to success. Remember, the Soul is your human-self, the transient temporary person that you are for *this* lifetime, with all your fluctuating beliefs and individual characteristics. It is these human elements that lie within your Soul's Astral body, that you set out to change, when you make resolutions for example. You may find this surprising, but, when for example you resolve to stop smoking, or any addiction really, you are setting out to change a habit of Soul ... not one of the Body. When I ran my "Smoking Addiction Clinic", it was the clients that *didn't* follow the consciousness exercises designed to curb their Sentient Souls stresses, who always failed and returned to smoking. I used a low-level laser to quickly shift the body attractions, which it did within two weeks for most. What I noticed however, was that if the individual didn't follow the Soul exercises diligently for the whole first 60 days at least, then the body triggers would come back around the third or fourth week. As the Souls conflict from resistances and attachments grew within them and were not experienced with Awareness fully to the point of discharge, they would then begin to stressfully influence the body again. At this point the client would again turn to the sedative trigger influence of the tobacco's nicotine. If they carried the exercises out for the whole first 30 days, then the body would be completely comfortable without falling back to the sedative triggers of the nicotine from the cigarettes. This would complete the bodies shift, but the Soul's shift required carrying out the exercises to at least the end of the 90 days. In truth, all Soul exercises need to be carried out for the rest of our life, for there to be any true shift of Soul, one that will bear spiritual fruit and carry into the next incarnation. At the 90 day point however, the Body and Soul are both shifted and more harmonized, free of the triggers that lead to smoking, or whatever addiction you were dealing with.

Remember, addictions are habits of Soul ... not habits of Body.

The Will is definitely strengthened by doing the exercise, but it is rhythmically carrying out the process that actually strengthens the Will, not so much the exercise itself. However, this concerted commitment and diligent Awareness to all the subtle influences on the Soul, requires an extraordinary strength of Will to carry you through the 90 days and beyond. The extra Will is necessary to keep the Spirit Awareness heightened and tuned to the deceptions of the Souls identities illusions. If you fail at your resolution, don't condemn yourself, but take strength from it, by knowing that it is simply because as yet, you don't have a sufficiently developed Consciousness Soul with its inherent Will forces. This doesn't mean you never will for this life, after all, that is what you are here to develop at this time in evolution. This just means you need to workout at your "Will

Gym" some more and build up that muscle. Failure is simply a red flag from your Spirit to your Soul, trying to let you know that you need to do more work. Apart from the couple of exercises I have included in the last chapter of this book, you develop your Consciousness Soul by becoming more conscious, expanding your perceptions, taking ownership of the subtle traits of self you resist most, reading more spirit-based books that expand your thinking out of your physical reality, etc., etc. This is what living in a mindless world is and requires of you.

Developing your Will is doing things you don't want to do ... even though you know they will be difficult and are good and right for you. This could look like becoming more conscious, taking ownership of those subtle traits you resist most about yourself, and reading more spirit-based books that expand your thinking outside of your physical reality, etc., etc.

Failure doesn't and never will, mean that you should stop. Why, continuing is a Will exercise in itself. It is the Will after all that creates forward movement in both physical and spiritual realities and ultimately, what determines all success. To be fully conscious of these Soul triggers, is why it is so important to develop your Consciousness Soul. Remember though, it is the Will force of the developed Consciousness Soul, that gives us the power to ground the Spirit-Self's Awareness in the Soul.

BEing conscious of the subtle triggers is not enough to discharge them. It is the power of my Spirit-Awareness that makes me capable of experiencing the forces of influence and ultimately, discharge them.

It is the *completion of the experience* that discharges the forces of influence lying within every experience and it is the strength of Will that allows you to ride that experience bronco to its virtuous corral.

The necessary time required to create a shift in your Spirit's Ego body, is a whole other story and not one to be concerned on at this point in our evolution. Your Spirit's requirement for a shift to happen, isn't defined by days months or years, but by committed intention and ultimately ... lifetimes. Just as the Body is influenced by the Soul, the Soul is influenced by the Spirit, but the relationship between Soul and Spirit is vastly different to the relationship between the Body and Soul. Your Soul is the "middle-man", the "go-between" if you will, and it has two relationships happening at the same time. Your Souls relationship to your Body, is one that exists within the *finite* parameter of your physical material reality and is defined to a large degree by the material laws within that Body reality. Your Souls relationship to your Spirit, exists within the *infinite* parameters of the Spiritual Realm, and is defined by the Divine Laws of that Cosmic reality. Although the Body is influenced by the Soul as to how and what it manifests in this physical reality, the body however, does not determine the Soul's evolutionary advancements. Your Souls evolutionary development is determined by the Soul Spirit relationship itself, by you the Human BEing, through your active development and use of the forces of *thinking feeling and willing* that come from—as we have discussed—their relevant Soul components within the Astral Body. Ironically, the Souls development, or the development of the component parts of the Soul specifically, aren't developed by what we <u>do</u> in this human lifetime, they are developed by what we <u>BE</u> *throughout* this lifetime.

Doing comes from BEing ... never the other way around.

From this, you can see that *living in a mindless world* isn't something you do ... it's a way you BE in the world. What you do, comes directly from who or what you BE. If your BEing a spiritual person, then your actions will be spiritually inclined toward a bigger picture than just self. If your BEing is a materialistic person, then your actions will be materialistically aligned with materiality and will be ALL about self. Spiritually inclined and materialistically inclined are both states of BEing, and they create how and what you do in this world. The BEing that you are ... determines how you express your-self in this world. For example, a liar and pretender are the *doing expressions* of one who is drowning in their BEing state of self-deception and avoidance of ownership. The saying that, "we are defined by what we do in the world", is a truth from a materialistic perspective, but it can't be considered a spiritual truth, because it doesn't consider in any way, that you are a BEing, a Spirit BEing Human that brings about that doing state.

So, the Souls development or evolution is determined by how you BE in your life here. It is the fruits of your Soul's life of BEing Human through this lifetime, that you, the True and Higher Spirit-Self, takes with you into the Spiritual Realm after death has taken both Body and Soul. If your Soul has been fertilized with life giving virtues and grown in healthy beds of conscious ownership and service to the greater good, then your fruits will be spiritually bountiful and expand the potential of your Soul and Spirit for your next life.

Also remember, that when you expand the life within your Spirit, when you evolve your Spirit by expanding its capacity for higher existence, you automatically expand the Spiritual Realm's capacity to the same degree. The Spiritual Realm is completely dependent on the evolution of YOUR Spirit, for the Spiritual Realms expansion and evolution also. So, when you develop your human Soul-self to be more virtuous, it is the fruits of those virtuous human experiences, such as wisdom, intuition, compassion etc., that your Spirit reaps and takes with it back to the Spiritual Realm, where you make the Spiritual Realm more virtuous also. It doesn't happen every time you are virtuous here in this lifetime, it happens at the end of this lifetime when you go back to the Spiritual Realm with the fruits from your living a virtuous human life. It doesn't happen because you were virtuous once, thrice or even a hundred times. It gets transferred into a shift of your Spirit, only when you "LIVE" your life of Soul that way. Remember, we never get more than we can handle within this lifetime. This means that the first time you embody a virtue of let's say compassion, doesn't mean that you get the full parameter, the complete virtue of compassion granted to you. The Soul must be strengthened, its forces and capabilities need to be enhanced and expanded to be able to handle greater and greater parameters of virtue, until ultimately, you are ready to receive the full and complete Divine Force of compassion. Therefore, life continually throws the same or similar experiences at you, so you get maximum exposure and opportunities to embody as much of the full parameter of the virtue as possible throughout your limited life here. It is the fruits of this virtuous Soul life here and now, that the Spirit embodies as higher attributes and capacities. It is these capacities and abilities of which your Spirit can then take back into the Spiritual world and from which, the Spiritual Realm evolves also. We could architype this ideal as "living in a mindless world".

Now the other end of this paradigm, is that you live a spiritless life, a life of material fixation, a life of all about self and not expanding your thoughts feelings and willing's outside of this physical reality, a life cut off from any concept and connection to any form of Spiritual existence. A lot of people think that "being in service to others" and making things OK for people etc is a virtuous life. This can most defini9tely be true, but if I have attached to the doing any intended gain to self ... then it is still selfish, not selfless. From this then, the Spiritual Realm also suffers the same disconnect etc., and just as your Soul is diminished in its capacities and abilities, so too the Spiritual Realm is diminished. What's worse, is that when you die and leave this human existence, without any connection or concept or perception of the Spiritual Realm, you will have no Awareness of it when you arrive there. Yes, you will most definitely arrive there, as everyone does at some point get to the Soul Realm. However, when you have no Awareness here of the Spiritual Realm, then when you die, you are unable to enter it to create, setup, formulate, or organize your next lifetime here. Before the Spirit Realm, there is the realm called Kamaloka, the Soul Realm. In a nutshell, this is where you, your human Soul-self goes until you have released your Soul from its physical human attachment. Your Soul becomes attached to the physical human world through the senses of the human world. If for example, your happiness throughout your life here was only derived from external physical activity, from the heightening of only your physical senses of sight, sound, taste, smell and touch etc., then you will be highly attached to those sensory experiences. These sensory attachments only exist within this human materialist environment. When you go to Karmaloka, you are void of all sensory input. We have to free our-self from these attachments our self ... deliberately and consciously.

Once released from these attachments, your Soul is able to impart the fruits of your Souls life here, to your Spirit. The passing of the fruits of your human life experiences can't get passed on to your Spirit until your Soul has discharged all attachment to its material existence as a Human Soul. It is your Spirit BEing that determines, organizes, defines, sets up, coordinates and charts the flow of your next life. You make connections and agreements with other Spirit Self's to meet and play out each other's Karmic propensities through your Souls next life, so you can learn more, use the fruits of your previous life and in this new life get more opportunities for virtuous developments and implementations. Without this phase of the Souls transfer of the fruits of its human experiences and developments, then your Spirit is stuck in a state of limbo so to speak, unable to move forward or back to correct anything. Consequently, the Spiritual Realm will experience this same limbo effect.

We are each individually responsible for the evolution or devolution of both this Physical and the Spiritual Realms.

So, therefore the "*concept of mind*" and its false perspective of *Body Mind and Soul* as humankind's makeup, are so detrimental to Humanities true evolution. Both perspectives of *concept of mind* and *Body Mind and Soul*, covertly trap us in a perception that there is no Spirit, and as such, there can be no real Spiritual Realm. Compounding this is the fact that a Spiritless Soul is incapable of seeing any proof for the Spiritual Realm either. Needing physical proof is yet another attachment to the physical world, which again is another enormous hurdle to get over in Kamaloka. Can you see how these subtle deceptive influences work in favor of those diverting Beings of influence wishing to keep us earth bound, materialistic and void of real Spirit influence? If this path toward blind rejection of the Spiritual Realm were to continue, it will effectively destroy the Spiritual Realms ability for us to reincarnate. Imagine, if Souls are stuck in Kamaloka, then they can't reincarnate as human again. If the Soul can't reincarnate into a human body, then your Spirit can't incarnate through the Soul either. Your Spirit is dependent on the Soul and visa-versa, for it to be able to experience the physical world reality of space and time. Your Spirit can not incarnate directly into a physical body. Having said all of this however, we must be careful to NOT swing this pendulum of perception too far the opposite way and create a Soul Life that rejects the physical human world. We are at our time now, to bring them both together, to spiritualize the physical human reality, to walk as the Buddha wisdom tells us, "to walk the middle way". The Buddha was the first preparation for this "middle way" and left us with the insight toward it. Being able to *see* this middle way in concept, sets the platform for us to now embody the "Christ Impulse". This Impulse is what strengthens the Soul to not just see the Spiritual Realm but gives us empowering abilities to begin to embody the Spiritual Realm into our human's Soul Life. The embodiment via this truly self-empowering Impulse, moves the middle way out of concept and into a true experience of a Human ... Spirit ... BEing. THIS embodiment is the only way that we may truly spiritualize Humanities future evolution ... ensuring it functions for the good of ALL.

What will it take for humanity to see the light of its true Spirit-Self? The answer is to simply live in a mindless world free off the concept of mind. How is it, that it is only when we come to the point of extinction, that our TRUE Spirit kicks in; which is by the way what constitutes what we term humanity? Why is it only under threat of existence that we drop the selfishness-of-self and become a united humanity again, there for each other? I recently saw the movie called "Sully" with Tom Hanks about the airliner that went down in the Hudson River. This stimulated in me, how ridiculous it is that yet again our human has to come to the brink of extinction to drop the self-pretense of its own importance and come face-to-face with the fact that, although it is important to BE a Self, the human-self is actually what isn't important. It is the Spirit-Self that holds importance for us all right now. Why does man have to be taken to the point of extinction, to become self-less enough to care for another without need for gain to self? This fact alone seriously shows how disconnected and un-Aware humanity has become from its TRUE nature, from its Spirit Nature.

We are ALL human ... we are all the same ... we just appear and act differently. This however, is what it is meant to BE. It is just the blind, highly materialized human-self that can't see the same-ness of our fellow man. It is the Spirit of Man, our Spirit Self that experiences the same-ness of us all, the IS-ness of our Spirit-Self's TRUE Human Nature. Have we pushed Spirit so far out the back door of the bus, that we have lost ALL sight and experience of our TRUE Authentic Experiential Self? Even if this is true ... it IS most definitely reversible ... if YOU choose to do the work.

Whenever I contribute a shift in Body Soul or Spirit, to ANYTHING outside of my-Self, I diminish my ability and power to create further shifts in my-Self ... by my- Self.

I become, but a pale reflection of my True Authentic Self.

In the next chapter, I wish to give you some basic *"Living Exercises"*, so you can start developing your Soul forces deliberately. These exercises can accelerate your grounding of Awareness and activate more of your Soul's forces very quickly. If you stick to them diligently for the required minimum 90-day Soul shift, then you will most definitely notice a subtle change in your perspective of not just *your* Life's events, but the world events around you also. Although this new perspective will most definitely bring you more wellness healing and happiness, be very clear with yourself right from the beginning that, happiness etc., are NOT the goals of the exercises. To gain Peace or Stillness is NOT the intention for doing the exercises, and Bliss CANOT be the expected experiential result. Although ALL of these experiential states have been achieved at various times from these practices ... absolutely NONE of them are the end game or finish line. When these states are achieved within the Soul, it is by Grace from the Spiritual Realm, as acknowledgement of your achievement of a certain integration within the Soul. They come about as an expression within you, at a point of harmonization between your Body Soul and Spirit, with both the Spiritual and physical worlds. In my experience, I would say that these are your true moments of *mindless-ness*.

To not attach to these states and continue to *live* these exercise practices simply for the experiences they produce or more importantly, for the advancement of the Spiritual Realm and Humanities evolution; they will empower a continued harmonization of your Higher "I". The result from this non-attached practice is ... *"living in a mindless world"*.

Chapter 10

The Living Exercises

In this chapter, I wish to give you some basic exercises to live by and start developing your Soul forces ... deliberately. Although the exercises are designed to facilitate the development of your Soul's forces, understand that the exercises themselves hold NO power that will develop those forces for you. In truth, there is nothing outside of one's self that can truly develop one's consciousness power. The true power to develop your forces, lie in the forces *you use* and activate from within you ... by *doing* the exercises and BEing intimately involved in all the processes that it takes to bring the result about. It is imperative the student of any esoteric training, intimately understand that it is NOT the *exercises* that hold the power to bring about development of the students Soul forces. It is the <u>self</u>-activization of the inner forces when *doing* the exercises, that brings about the development of those very same Soul forces. These Soul forces are like your physical muscles but are instead ... spiritual muscles. When worked correctly; just like your physical muscles, these spiritual muscles will strengthen and some eventually, develop into spiritual organs. The exercises are simply a direct means to stimulate the appropriate *activity* ... the activity which uses the intended forces you are wishing to develop. Once you have gained enough experiential realization of the necessary Soul *activity*, and increased your ability to activate them deliberately, then you will no longer need the exercise and can make *the activity* itself a continuous living one. From the moment you make this a *continuous living activity* in you, you have entered into a deliberate living practice of Soul Force development.

As I pointed out in the previous chapter—giving up your power to exercises to create shifts within yourself, diminishes your ability to make those shifts yourself ... without using any exercise. Every time you use ANY consciousness esoteric exercise and credit the shift you experience while using it to the exercise itself, you have missed the empowerment of yourself to stimulate or activate *the activity*. Just by *using* the *activity*, the correct Soul forces are activated; from which, the shift naturally comes about.

Do you remember my story of my American "ferryman" wife, who made it possible for me to come to the USA? Remember through that relationship I came here to live "in-feel" and work together in the consciousness development organization whose premise was and still is, that our beliefs create our experiences? Well, a large factor of that marriage breaking up, was because of the exercises of that organization and its covertly indoctrinated perception that *the exercises,* hold power to transform. My then wife was and still is an ardent advocate and teacher of this organizations belief system, along with its thirty plus exercises. In any new relationship, there are always going to be issues, but one steeped in consciousness work with a focus on conscious self-ownership, well that relationship is inevitably going to see more issues than what might be termed normal. So, whenever we had ANY relationship issues, we would jump on the consciousness exercise treadmill, to process yet another emotion, wrong comment (that obviously had some hidden agenda behind it ... apparently), negatively perceived belief, or anything that created a disturbance in either of our spaces—both individually and collectively.

Now I am an overwhelmingly staunch supporter of self-ownership, but the Divine Orchestration and Spirit-Self's intuitive Awareness, revealed to me the dis-empowerment that comes from putting your power in exercises ... to gain a *false sense of ownership*. Rather than actually taking true ownership of self, and as Ho'oponopono gives us ... *make things right with Self first,* the choice was always to do another exercise process ... together. Ironically however, the issues we have in Life are NEVER really about the other.

I am never a victim to life or anyone else, unless I make my-self so, in which case however ... it's still not about them, because it is "I" not them, who made myself a victim.

There was a moment in these daily workouts on our consciousness exercise treadmills, where my Spirit Awareness revealed that we were spending more time processing life through these exercises, than we were truly experiencing our Self's in it. I noticed a growing covert pattern that we were also processing the same thing we had often processed the day or two days before. Something was off. My Soul was crying out. My Spirits red flags were waving frantically, and the Divine Orchestration was relentlessly bringing the same experiences into my space, over and over again. Ironically, the belief perspective of this organizations teachings was, that if Life repeats itself, then we had not fully integrated something, or we hadn't yet fully owned the element within our self that was creating this situation. Now, although this most definitely can be true in some circumstances, the truth of this specific situation was in the revelation that, the power to fully experience life's events, to deal with the experience triggered within an event, didn't lie in the use of an appropriate exercise of this or any other organization. The *experience* within this particular event, was the dis-empowerment of one's self to truly own one's life actions, in the moment it happens ... because there was always an exercise *needing* to be done, to supposedly expose and integrate this ownership.

Remember I said earlier in this book journey, that the power in ownership lies within your Awareness to expose what needs to be owned and integrated? From this premise, we can see that there is no exercise needed to expose any element of self to be integrated. There is only the necessary *activity* of Awareness needed, to expose any and ALL elements of self, of the active forces that come from both human Soul and Spirit Self's. An exercise is only helpful when there is NO Awareness. With well-grounded Awareness ... all can and will naturally and effortlessly be revealed. Ironically however, only what is relative in *that* present moment ... will be revealed. Rudolph Steiner talks about this as the essential and non-essential elements of thinking. Through the over-use and dependence on exercises to process our drama, my consciousness wife and I were more often trying to deal with a lot of non-essential thinking. All that this did was simply create more drama, which we then had to process further with more exercises. The correct development and use of *true* Awareness, reveals the distinction between the essential and non-essential ... in brilliant Spirit-color clarity. From this empowered clarity, it is easy to just work with the essential and leave the non-essential alone. The non-essential are only necessary to bring about our human events but are NOT essential to the development of Soul and Spirit. Ironically, the essential doesn't need any processing or exercises to be integrated and is most often discharged simply through owning and experiencing it fully.

So, the point I am trying to make here, is that in doing these exercises, be sure to do them with Awareness, along with no attachment to the exercise itself. Understand also that the exercises I am giving you, are to help you *activate* your Awareness, so that you may strengthen your ability to ground it in your Soul. Be consciously Aware of the *activity* the exercise is stimulating and with your Awareness, notice the *forces* being used by that activity. This simple activity of *noticing* will integrate far more than doing a bunch of exercises to find a result that you are happy with.

So, what is the work you can do right now, or at least start to do? What can you do to start dissolving the chains of your "*concept of mind*"? How can you start to truly feel the love of your Spirit, solidly grounded in your Soul, filling it with true Awareness? How can you become free from influence? What can you do to start living in *your* mindless world; one that will send a powerful and empowering influence for change throughout this entire human reality? Let's together, see if we can put a new strengthening, rhythmic Soul practice in this world, one that may ultimately bring Humanity together, through the harmonization of Body Soul and ... Spirit.

BE the mindless world ... you wish to see in the world.

Remember that famous wisdom from Mahatma Gandhi. "**You** must be the **change, you** want to **see in the world.**"? Well, this IS what we ... you ... need to do. Sorry ... I meant, need to BE. To BE this change, to live in a *mindless world*—you need to BE the mindless world you wish to see in the world around you. Granted, a mindless world may be a really BIG change from where the world is right now, but it will never change into one until we start making it one ... within our human-self. You first need to practice diligently what it takes to shift your Soul Consciousness out of its existing "*concept of mind*" reality. The way to achieve this is to raise your Soul forces of thinking, feeling and especially Willing, to new elevated levels. This does not mean using the gazillion New Age techniques, apparatuses, chemistry adjustments, specialized meditation CD's, mind resonance, mind detox, herbal extracts, and the seemingly endless inventory of the spiritual supermarket saturating todays self-development marketplace. Every week there seems to be someone coming out with yet another new hidden steps, ancient wisdom or secret to what ... make your life better or give you the life of happiness you deserve ... apparently. All the while these supermarkets covertly indoctrinate you with the belief your present life; the one that is actually orchestrated by Divine Intention for your *highest* good ... is not adequate or sufficient. What's worse is, they are often using techniques from practices of an old past evolution, which carried a higher design for *that* past time—but not for this present time.

These past techniques and exercises were powerfully effective for their time, because they were meant to *bind* the human Soul into the body. At that time, humanity was not yet fully grounded in its present fully materialized "separate I" form of human consciousness. Those practices of old were brought to humanity at that time, for the purpose of embodying the Soul in the physical form. We have already evolved pass this spiritual requirement and our Souls have now become too densely embodied in our materialistic reality. We are now at the extraordinary evolutionary time of freeing the Soul from the Body-self's chains to its physicality and embody the Spirit now in the Soul and Body. The *concept of mind* is now, our present-day chain.

Lisa Romero wrote in her book, "Developing the Self: Through the Inner Work Path in the Light of Anthroposophy" and says it wonderfully:

~Many people practicing ancient meditative techniques, such as yoga, experience feeling connected, peaceful and centered. This is undoubtedly a true experience. We can even gain deep insights into the development of the bodily sheaths by binding the soul into the body in a less subjective way. The consciousness can experience the forces behind the physical sheaths, gaining insight into the past. This is a very different experience than holding the clarity of the "Awakened I" in relationship to the living spiritual world in the present. Returning the consciousness to the body returns the consciousness to old states of awareness. Powerful, calming, and centering, some of these ancient exercises relieve us of our personal struggles, yet keep us dependent on the body. The level now being asked of us is freedom from any transitory self, developing sense-free perception to live as soul in a non-sense perceptible world. Many people are using ancient techniques such as mindfulness practices like watching the breath to manage the chaos of their speeding lives. This could be an indication of the collective weakness in the modern soul because, although this technique can bring calming and centering, it rarely brings soul strength, or the tools required for our future stages of being. In the consciousness soul age, we need our practice to directly strengthen the soul to meet the adversaries we are to face, currently. We need strength that can meet the inner and outer worlds; this is not the same task as it was thousands of years ago. Strength is needed to face what needs to be transformed now, both in ourselves and in the world around us. ~

What I would like to share with you in this chapter ... is NOT what lies on the shelves of the spiritual supermarkets of today. Neither are the exercises here, secret practices from some ancient handbook of our spiritual yester-year—although the essence of those ancient's intentions does come through within the exercise. Now, you don't have to change your life completely to raise and develop your Soul Forces. However, raising and developing your Soul Forces as a living practice, will most definitely change your life, through the harmonization of your Body Soul and Spirit Self's. Ironically, entering these practices with intentions to change YOUR life or make YOUR life better, will quickly become the limitation to it truly becoming better. The hidden influence here, the hidden hindrance, is that you would be doing it for self-gain out of resistance to the experience you are trying to avoid. This is just another subtle and covert form of materialistic goal setting and again, it is part of the spiritual practices of old. Some time ago, I studied a research once done, on the profound and amazing healings that come from prayer with Our Lady of Lourdes. The research showed that a success rate of about 20% was achieved from prayers that were made for self—whereas prayers made for others achieved a success rate of over 80%. This clearly shows that we are not here for self alone, but for the benefit of ALL. It also shows that when we *do* in this world for the benefit of others ahead of self, then we activate very subtle yet greater unseen forces, both within us and from outside of us, that work in alignment with our higher good intentions.

There is no separation in the Spirit Realm. Separation is a creation of this, our human world, derived wholly from our individual rejection of our own Spirit from our human existence. The Spiritual Realm is however, dramatically affected by everyone of us here. Look to a bigger goal than just self. Meditate on and become intimate with the fact that our collective Humanities evolution and that of the Spiritual Realms, are completely interwoven and dependent on each other. To break it down further, realize that it's all dependent on *your* evolution—on *your* ability to spiritualize *your* human Soul. Understand intimately, that evolving through this life time has a far greater benefit to all those who exist in the Spiritual Realm, than it does to just your human-self. Experientially come to know the effect of your Soul trapped in Kamaloka, void of any spiritual sense, as well as void of any capability for human sense satisfaction. BE willing to feel the ripple effect of what we discussed in the previous chapter, of what effect that will cause in the Spiritual Realm. Think and feel into the ultimate result of this stuck effect, on your Spirit and Soul's ability to re-incarnate and continue to grow and evolve. Feel how you will also be responsible for the devolution of those loved ones around you in the here and now of this lifetime. This is what the Hawaiian Aloha philosophy means when it tells us that "we are responsible for ALL who exists in our environment." This means in our *spiritual environment* also of course. What detrimental effect does this all have on both worlds of human and Spirit? By aligning with the Higher Realm intentions rather than the materialist intentions for self, we bring in the forces of those Higher Realms, into alignment and support of our actions ... of both Body, Soul and Spirit. In the case of this chapter, you will empower your-Self with the higher spiritual forces to use within these exercises. It is these Higher Forces that can now empower you further, to develop a more advanced spiritualized human-self in greater service to a bigger picture for humanity than you can humanly conceive of.

Don't worry about making your life better, because a better life will be the natural consequence of practicing these exercises with the intention to make other people's lives better.

These exercises are not going to introduce or implant new attributes or characteristics or skills into you. I will not deceive you that the exercises hold special powers to instill in you something you don't have. The purpose of the exercises is to simply bring out what you already have, to bring them out into your Awareness ... where *you* can develop them further, right up to their full potential for this life. We came here with every spiritual organ and muscle we need for this life. You already have the Soul forces of thinking feeling and willing, along with all the Awareness you need for this life time. We don't need to bring new traits in and in truth ... we can't. The pre-design you created for this life time was very specific and all that is required is to bring your existing forces and abilities—which are the harvested fruits from your previous life—to the surface and develop them further by simply using them in specific ways ... throughout this *whole* life time. Once brought to the surface, you may then develop them further and be able to use the power that lies within their full potential.

A quote from Rudolph Steiner's lectures on "Happiness" shows us that as we evolve, so must the development exercises we need to use, to bring those newly evolved fruits of our previous life to the surface in this life.

> ~ We must also consider that humanity is continually evolving through succeeding epochs, giving rise to ever new and developing experiences; that our soul experiences different things in different eras of humanity's evolution. According to these changing experiences, therefore, our feelings about life, our whole sense of things also changes. To find inner peace and contentment within the rushing current of life, a person today needs a different relationship to the world from the one the human soul could have in former times. Spiritual science shows us that a certain sum of powers, a kind of treasury, a source of spiritual life, resides today in human souls. These powers seek to emerge, rather than to stay concealed in the soul: they seek to appear in human consciousness so that we feel them to be not just an inner urge, an inner imperative, but something we can incorporate into our thinking, our world of ideas. How exactly does spiritual science speak to humankind today? It does not seek to bear messages from alien realms of existence, from strange foreign lands as it were, but it speaks in a way that tries only to tell each soul what already resides deep within it. The spiritual researcher is, basically, convinced that there is something present in each and every soul, that he tries only to clothe in outward concepts and ideas, and that therefore he says nothing to people other than what they already bear within them. The whole of spiritual science, when the spiritual enquirer presents it to humankind in the right way, seeks to offer only what already rests in the deep stratum of each and every human soul. Therefore, this science of the spirit, is only a prompting to every soul to draw forth what resides within it. A whole sum of powers rests in these depths of the human soul; and only when these are drawn up into our awareness do they show what acts within us, what inwardly pervades and lives in our soul. The human being is truly richer, fuller, than he often thinks. There is a remarkable law governing our relationship with knowledge and perception of the world and, when we know it, it can give us deep insights into many enigmas of the human soul. ~ Rudolph Steiner.

So, the exercises I am sharing here, are for you to use to bring forward the *activity* of specific Soul Forces into your *Awareness*. Once they are in your Awareness, you may then develop them. You already have these forces and activities lying deep within you. The exercises will help you to remember what you already know and have learned from your past lives here, so that now you can use them deliberately and grow new fruits from the tree of *YOUR* life's experiential source. Just as there are many facets to your Soul's dimension, there are also many *truly* esoteric exercises designed to shine the light of your Awareness on each of those facets within your Soul. There is however no point or benefit in doing exercises to heal early childhood trauma, if you first don't have the Awareness to unearth the *truth in the event*. This truth lies in the clarity of Sentient Soul feeling, to distinguish what is truly yours and what is other's projections on you. A higher thinking ability of Intellectual/Perspective Soul is necessary to bring in a greater spiritual perspective and rationality of the event. A much greater strength of Will of the Consciousness Soul is required to embody the virtue of courage necessary, to go the distance of holding Spirit Awareness throughout the whole Soul journey of the event. Please don't look to go into these exercises intention of healing and getting rid of all sorts of "life trauma". This will only create a massive limiting wall of expectations that will inevitably sabotage the success of your continual development. Remember, these exercises are specific to develop your Soul Forces. Once these forces of Awareness, Thinking, Feeling and Willing have been developed further and you are truly living within these forces ... THEN, there are deeper techniques I touched on earlier in this book, of which will allow you to use these forces in specific ways. From this use, you can then discharge the life-traumas you have been storing within you. By using these deeper techniques with your now strengthened Soul Forces, you will be able to effectively and quickly, move to the virtue embodiment practice. It is here that you nurture and grow your virtuous fruits; from which you can then improve this life and begin the harvest for your next life. Remember also as we discussed earlier, that until you can ground and use Awareness correctly; to distinguish which self of Body Soul or Spirit the life-trauma exists in, then a true *healing discharge* can never be sustainably achieved.

So, here is an instance where simple is more powerful. The simplicity in truth is, that there are only four forces or attributes that you initially need to focus on to automatically strengthen your Soul Forces and start dissolving the deceptions of your covert "*concept of mind*" reality. It IS as simple as that to begin creating and living in *YOUR* mindless world.

These four are:

1. Awareness

2. Feeling

3. Thinking

4. Willing

As we have already explored, feeling thinking and willing are Soul Forces. Developing them with Awareness will create a shift of Soul in the form of:

1. Awareness is a Force of Spirit. Developing Spirit's Awareness in the Soul will create a Soul shift in the form of a heightened sensitivity to the *forces* of influence, both external and internal, as well those higher and lower ones also. Awareness brings a far greater sensitivity to the *differences* between the components of Soul and as such, a source of empowerment to make changes, to bring them together and harmonize them all. It is only through true Awareness that we are able to truly embody the *virtues* of Spirit within our Soul. Truth is, that without Awareness, you can't intimately know the individual components or practice the correct exercise with the correct component.

2. Your Consciousness Soul will become more grounded in this world, as you become more conscious of the hidden Spirit within all things and able to stay focused with better attention through the use of a much stronger Will force. This strengthened Will force is the linchpin that holds *all* of the components together and is pivotal to grounding Spirit Awareness into the Soul.

3. Your Intellectual/Perspective Soul will become more intelligent, able to extrapolate, contemplate and most importantly, perceive at a much higher and expanded level. You will find the quality of your thinking dramatically improve. An elevated state of this component of Soul, brings about an increase in your ability to now *perceive,* what was previously unperceivable, and understand what was previously incomprehensible.

4. Your Sentient Soul will become more highly tuned and super-sensitive to all of your bodies and their relationship to the outer world. This facilitates a much deeper connection between the physical and Spiritual worlds we exist in. This heightened *feeling* sensitivity also enables your Soul to differentiate finer and higher frequencies etc. It is through the higher development of your Sentient Soul's sensitivity, that ultimately facilitates the Soul to have true spiritual experiences within it and its human reality.

There are even more benefits achievable through these practices that develop our Soul's forces and with time and diligent study and practice they will come to you. These exercises below will give you the solid base that all other attributes and abilities can grow from. Some of these a lot of you will already have and these living practices will bring those qualities of your Soul-self to Awareness and you will be able to accelerate your development of them.

The Exercises

1. **Awareness Exercise:** *To notice the difference of things.*

As we covered in the previous chapters, Awareness is a super-sensitivity faculty of your Spirit-Self and as such, it is difficult to accurately put in words what the faculty truly produces. As we stated earlier, *experiencing* is feeling with Awareness, but without definition, judgment or description of what you are experiencing. The *non-definition* of what is being experienced is applied here, so that we don't lose anything of the experience through mental interpretations of what Awareness is revealing to us. It is Awareness that allows things to reveal their self, their true nature, their forces so to speak, that normally cannot be seen, perceived or experienced through the Souls attributes of attention etc. Attention will only see what already exists in material reality and is defined ... where Awareness, feels and *experiences* what is un-defined along with the deeper levels of what is defined ... but also what exists in the non-linear Spiritual Realm. Our experience is deepened and all-encompassing, when we are first able, through the proper use of Awareness, to allow the full experience to permeate our whole ... Spirit and Soul. It is essential to allow the experience to permeate all three components of Sentient, Intellectual and Consciousness Soul ... before allowing the necessary *judgment* of the experience to be formed by the Intellectual Soul. Remember, it is in the act of the Intellectual Soul placing a judgment on the experience, that moves the imprint of the experience from its Spirit-Self origination, to its Soul-self relationship with our personal human reality. I am re-explaining this so that you deeply understand the importance to not judge, define or describe your experience within this first exercise.

The exercise:

I recommend this exercise be done in your own quiet space at first, rather than in your everyday moments. Done this way, it is then an exploration into clarity of your Awareness ability, so you may gain an experiential understanding and command of it within you.

1. To simply notice the differences between things, but to NOT ... define, describe or judge what that difference is. To notice something is not defining it. The *activity of noticing* happens first, then a definition is formed by the Intellectual Soul in its process of judgement. Noticing is just a *sense* of the difference ... that there IS a difference. This is very subtle. This is done to get a feeling-sense of the difference—or rather, to get a super-feeling-sense of the difference ... to feel the difference rather than see it and to not define what that difference is. Your *"concept of mind"* thinking, will automatically jump to its existing defining function. There is no need or benefit to try and stop this. In fact, trying to stop it, will only empower it to persist. Instead, use this Awareness of the shift to think, to deepen the exercise and see if you can

notice the difference to feeling with definitions ... and feeling without definitions. Remember, just notice the difference ... and once you have it ... then notice something else.

2.   Notice the difference between a leaf and a branch, between a stone and a leaf, between a flower and the air, between a sign on the side of the road and the road itself. Do this on as many things as you can, for any period throughout your day. Make a commitment however to do _at least_ 5-10 different things in a row. If you think about it, there isn't anything that is identical in our world, so it's not likely you could ever run out of things to notice differences between.

To do this exercise for a 10-15-minute duration at least twice a day, is affective.

To do this exercise twice a day for a month is powerful.

To do this exercise for a matter of minutes as many times as you can throughout your whole waking day ... is transformative.

To live this exercise ... is empowering and freeing beyond words.

The Living Awareness Exercise:

Once you have a more experiential integration of your Awareness _activity_ from the exercises above, and greater command of its deliberate activation, then there is a way to do the exercise as an ever-present-moment ... living practice.

- This living exercise is to normalize the use of your Awareness in any and every moment of your waking life. While standing in line at the supermarket, notice the difference between anything and everything. There is no shortage of different things in supermarkets. As you walk passed the shelves, just pick items and notice the difference. While you are talking to someone, maintain Awareness of the differences around you and the other person ... while continuing to _keep your attention_ on the other and what they are saying. Remain _present_ in the conversation AND of differences around you ... at the same time. There is no doubt that this IS a higher level of skill (and stronger Will) required to achieve this state of true presence, so don't be discouraged if you struggle or fail when you start out. It is inevitable to fail many times throughout your whole life of this exercise. The power in the exercise is in coming back to the activity and then holding yourself in it longer and longer. Just notice what happens and what gets triggered and then go back to it. Of course, if you find you can't stay present with the other enough, then move all your Awareness to them and feel totally present with them first, before going to other things around you. I find just jumping off for short moments in these situations is extremely helpful to staying present with the other on a much deeper level. This living exercise can be done ANYWHERE at all-times. Sitting in your car at the traffic lights, waiting to see the doctor, buying your coffee from Starbucks, hosing your plants in the yard, etc., etc., etc. There TRULY is NEVER a time you cannot be Aware or EVER be overly Aware.

This exercise is about differences ... period. It doesn't matter nor make any difference at this point by what you choose to notice. Remember, it is the *activity* we are stimulating, not the elements or aspects used within the exercise itself. The things you notice are the elements. Noticing with your Awareness is the activity. Don't let your Intellectual Soul define *that* as the only activity. The activity here is super-sensing by using your Spirit-Self's Awareness, not your Souls astral attention activity of Sentient, Intellectual/Perspective and Consciousness. There are more hidden aspects to this activity than just the two I mentioned here, and the *activity* itself of noticing with your Awareness, will ultimately reveal other elements and forces involved. Be attentive to your Awareness of *all* the differences that show up, but don't get pulled into any of them.

Ironically, the use of Awareness naturally stimulates the Souls activities of all of its three components, but this exercise is designed to isolate your Spirit's Awareness *activity* separate from these Soul activities. Remember earlier I said the exercise is designed to bring the activity forward into the light of your Awareness, where you can then develop those forces etc. further? This is about you becoming Aware of your Awareness activity. By not judging, describing or defining, you are isolating Awareness from your intellectual faculties. From this isolation, you are then able to develop it individually from the Soul activities. What this means then, is that once you get an impression, a super-feeling-sense of a difference ... you move on to the next thing. Catch your Sentient and Intellectual Soul-self's when they want to collaborate and create a "WOW moment" of any of it, but don't get trapped in it. The "WOW!" is the judgment of the experience ... not the true super-sensible experience. Simply be amusingly interested in how those wows etc. were stimulated ... and then go back to the exercise and pick something else. Again, notice the difference between the "WOW" moment, and the feeling with your Awareness of the moment you just popped out of.

Eventually, and you may find this surprisingly quickly, you will be able to simply activate Awareness without having to notice differences. Having said that, this is an exercise we should never stop doing for the rest of this life. It is after all "stupidly simple" and takes very little time and can be easily interwoven into one's whole day. However, understand that we only ever get what we are capable of handling. As you develop the strength in your other Soul Forces, then you will also be able to handle a greater parameter of Awareness in your Soul-self. Imagine what would happen for example, if you went to the gym and picked up a 250-pound weight straight of the bat, before you had done any appropriate preparatory work to build up the back muscles required to be able to handle the stress that weight would put on your spine. Now imagine if all of a sudden you became Aware of ALL the forces that exist, of all the BEings of both Light and Dark, of all the thoughts that fly around the Astral realm ready to pounce like a tiger on any open un-Aware Intellect. A form of madness and Soul sickness has inflicted many who have not done the appropriate preparations of Soul, before accelerating their spiritual development. Don't be in a rush, be patient. Embody *that* virtuous state of BEing that IS Awareness, and you may be surprised at the speed of your advancement.

All future exercises below need to be undertaken ... with Awareness. Use this Living Awareness exercise as the base for everything you undertake.

2. Feeling Exercise: *To be Aware and control of your feelings and ability to feel.*

There is a great misconceived indoctrination in Humanity, that feelings are weak and should be suppressed and even in some trainings ... eliminated. In my context here, control of feelings is not stopping or suppressing or getting rid of bad *feelings* etc. If you *feel* into this with Awareness, you will find that there is great power and truth in that— there is more control of feelings by simply being present and non-attached to them ... but not detached from them. As we discussed earlier, *feelings* reside in the domain of your Sentient Soul; through which the Soul; via the Intellectual Soul—can emotionalize its relationship to the world it exists in. Now although our *feelings* do reside in our Sentient Soul, because it IS the feeling/sensing component of our Soul; you may remember that through our earlier exploration of the activity or ability *to feel*, that *feeling*, and *feelings* are not the same. The sentient quality of the Soul is its ability *to feel*, to sense things. *Feelings* ... are then associated or assigned by the Intellectual Soul to what was felt or experienced; through which the experience is then emotionalized. This Feeling Exercise is to develop your ability *to feel* more deeply, with more sensitivity for sure, but to also be more Aware of the difference between *feelings* and your ability *to feel*, so you can then control your created feelings and not cloud your *activity of <u>feeling</u>* ... with those emotionalized feelings.

You are probably sensing a close similarity here to the Awareness exercise above, which has you *feeling with your Awareness*, but without any judgements, descriptions or definitions. You may also notice that the judgement, description and definitions all relate to the Intellectual components of Soul we are talking about here. If you have ... then you are most definitely right on all accounts. The *activity* of your Spirit-Self to *feel with Awareness* however, is truly what gives us the ability to *experience* this human life; through which, via Spirit, we bring our experiences into our Soul. The truth is though, that the Sentient-Soul's *activity of feeling or sensing*, is an ability of Soul, from which, we can intimately bring the outer world reality into our Soul. The Feeling Exercise here, is designed to bring both Spirit and Soul abilities together. As this happens, they both then compliment and expand together. This IS, to the greatest degree, the first true vestige of spiritualization of your Human-Soul-self.

Remember we talked of how the Spirit-Self will transform the Astral Soul Body, the Life-Spirit will transform the Etheric Body and Spirit-Man will ultimately transform the physical body? Well, embodying Spirit-Self Awareness in the Soul through the Sentient-Soul specifically, is the first transformative influence of Spirit in Soul. We are talking about developing your Souls Sentient quality and raising it to a higher-level of Spirit super-sensitivity. In the exercise of noticing differences, you are purely activating the *activity* of Awareness. In this *feeling exercise*, you are embodying or rather, you are *integrating* that Awareness *activity of Spirit* into your Souls sentient ability to feel and sense. Presently, for the Soul *to feel*, judgements descriptions and definitions from the Intellectual Soul make what it feels, or more correctly senses from the external material world, conscious within the Soul itself. The transformation of the Sentient ability of your Soul by the addition of your Spirits Awareness, will ultimately as a devoted living practice, develop the Souls *feeling* ability to the level of super-sensing. This means that your Soul will then be able to—without the necessity for any definitions judgements or descriptions—to intimately experience the inner spiritual forces—those forces that manifest the outer external material world it currently exists in and relates to. This will not just be a conscious experience any longer, it will then become a TRULY Consciously Aware experience ... beyond any present intellectual Soul experience.

The Exercises:

a) To feel with Awareness, but without judgement definition or description. Where before with the Awareness exercise, you were just *noticing differences*, with this exercise you are not just "noticing" ... you are now *feeling* the difference. With Awareness, allow yourself to feel those feelings you resist the most. Don't judge or define etc., these feelings, but just feel what they actually feel like, without any other emotionalized *feelings* attached to the feeling-experience. For example: feel what sadness feels like ... without attaching a sad moment or existing memory to it. Just feel what the raw and pure feeling of sadness ... *feels* like. There is nothing to do with any of these *feelings* you bring to the surface. You are just feeling what they truly feel like ... as the pure feeling that it is. Do this with many and all of the feelings you hold within your Sentient Body. If you start to get emotional about the experience of the feeling, then again with Awareness, feel the difference between the emotional feeling and the pure feeling. As soon as you have that difference, then move on to another feeling. For example, from sadness to anger to joy to happy to doubtful to courage to compassion etc.

b) Now with Awareness again, see if you can *feel* the difference between your active ability *to feel* ... and what *feelings* feel like. You may notice with your Aware feeling, that there is a different quality of one to the other. Be interested in these differences for a while. It is true that to do this now, you are to some extent, defining these differences, but here you are NOT defining them intellectually ... you are defining them experientially. *Feel* the difference between those two types of defining's. It is essential to keep working with this until you have a clear experiential difference between intellectually and experientially defining.

The Living Feeling Exercise:

- With constant and diligent Awareness, deliberately feel every emotional feeling that is triggered throughout your everyday experiences ... in the moment they are happening. BE interested in how and what each *feeling* is stimulated by and *feel* the effect through your Sentient Soul body when they arise within you. Once you notice these feelings, then determine the essential to non-essential *feelings* associated with the present moment experience you are in. For example, an essential feeling would be one that is totally related to the present moment you are in and has no reference to any other experience you may have already had. A non-essential may be one that has an attachment to a childhood memory, or previous encounter with an individual, or even the same individual. If it is with the same individual, by feeling/experiencing the influence on you and your reaction; notice how the past *feelings* are clouding and affecting your present moment experience. *FEEL* for the slightest influences on your present moment BEing. Once you locate these influences, then by *feeling with your Awareness*, experience them fully, until you can *feel* yourself fully present again, free of influence. This does not mean drown in the *feelings* about that person etc., nor does it mean pushing the feeling out or down to get rid of it. Remember the very first "feeling exercise" here of experiencing the *pure feeling* and not the *emotionalized* one created by your Intellectual Soul. Remember once more, the primary purpose of everything created ... is to be experienced fully. Once something has been experienced fully, its primary purpose has been completed and it will naturally discharge its creative force back to its source; which in this case ... is you.

Awareness Feeling Meditation

This meditation is best done sitting upright in a comfortable chair.

- Sitting upright, become intimately present with yourself by doing the Awareness Exercise of differences for a few minutes. Looking around from object to object, notice the *difference* between them. Feel what the difference is without defining, describing or judging what that difference is. Do this for just a few minutes only.

- Relax and become present with yourself in this present moment. Notice what is happening within your inner world self and *feel* any influences within. There is nothing to do with any of this. Just be interested, yet non-attached and experience it all fully. BE Aware and *feel* what you feel like, in this present moment. Do this for just a few minutes.

- Now become Aware of your body, get a sense of it without putting your attention on it. Without forming any definitions, judgements, descriptions or pictures of your body, just simply get a super-sense of your body and feel what it feels like.

- Become Aware of the skin covering your body and see if you can feel the difference between your body and the skin covering it. No details necessary ... just a feel of what the difference is between them. Feel the difference between the skin and everything else within it. Get a *feeling sense* of the skin as the outer edge of the body.

- Get a sense of and feel the *space* your body occupies ... from the skin inward. Be interested in this space and what it feels like as a totality, without defining or separating any parts within it. Feel it from the edges inward.

- Now, notice the space outside of the space your Body occupies, and be interested in it with your Awareness, yet without attention toward it. Notice and *feel with your Awareness,* the difference between the space outside your Body and the space within your Body. Just *feel the difference* between the spaces.

- Now move ALL your Awareness into the space outside your Body space and feel what that space feels like. Be interested in what this *space* feels like and let your Awareness feel its way through this space until you get a sense of the outer edge of *this* space. Just get a sense of this edge without defining it. Just notice where the *Aware feeling* of this space seems to change, fade or stop.

- Once you have found the edge of this space, let your Awareness feel its way around the edge in all directions until you get a feeling sense of the space that this space occupies from its edges inward. Use your Awareness and not your attention for this. This means you are not looking for the space, you are feeling for it to just have a sense of it without attention on it. Having found this, just BE presently Aware and *feel* what this space *feels* like from the edges inward.

- Now notice the space outside the edges of this space you are now feeling. See if you can notice and get a *feeling sense* of the difference between these two spaces ... the one previous and this present one you're now feeling. It will be subtle but *feel* for the difference in how they feel ... no matter how slight that difference is.

- Once you find the difference between these spaces, then gently move ALL of your Awareness into that next space ... and intimately *feel* what that space feels like. Let your Awareness feel its way through this space until you become Aware of the edges to this new space also, where the feeling seems to fade change or stop. Let your Awareness feel its way in all directions and dimensions until it finds all the edges of this space ... and feel the space or form that it occupies.

- Now feeling the space and form this space occupies ... again, feel it from the edges inward ... without definition, judgment, description or picture.

- Completion: When ready, open your eyes and maintain the high level of feeling in your state of *Present Aware Super Sensitivity* (P.A.S.S.) without effort. Just allow your Awareness to stay wide and gentle, present and feeling. Continue to feel the space of the objects you now see around you ... without getting attached to any feeling or thing you now experience.

These steps can be continued until you run out of spaces and edges, or you feel complete. Effortlessly maintain your new level of Awareness from your state of P.A.S.S. existence, by simply continuing to feel the space the object occupies, rather than the object itself. It is subtle, but this is THE most powerful moment of integration of your Spirit Awareness into your Soul. As with all meditations, maintaining your open Aware space and remaining in your state of *Present Aware Super Sensitivity* (P.A.S.S.) once you open your eyes, will help tremendously to integrate Awareness into your Soul's human activities.

3. Thinking Exercise: *Control of the activity of thinking*

It is commonly understood, that thoughts are the end result of thinking. However, when I looked up *thinking* in a dictionary, all I could find was one definition that stated, "to think is the creation of a thought". Now I am not saying that this is wrong in any way, for there is no doubt that thoughts come from thinking, but when explored with Awareness, the *activity* of thinking is revealed as something quite different to simply the intellectual creation of a thought. I find it fascinating that most people think, that all the thoughts one has, all come from their own thinking process. With Awareness, it is easily recognized that more often than not, thoughts are popping into one's head without any thinking about that thought at all. This is often another instance where the *concept of mind* is brought in to assign an attribute of the mind to something that can't be fully explained or experienced intellectually. Without Awareness, it is wrongly assumed that this deceiving creation of thoughts, is an origination of one's mind and that it is the mind that creates all thoughts. Without Awareness, there is no cognition that the thought just popped in without any true thinking happening at all.

How many times have you said, or maybe heard, "my mind won't shut up with so many thoughts"? What about, "I can't think straight, because I have too many thoughts going through my mind." There are so many other examples to be had. The point I am trying to make is; just because one has thoughts, it is incorrectly assumed that ALL those thoughts, are the result of one's own thinking. The truth of this is, that not all the thoughts that roll through one's head, are the result of one's own thinking. Within Anthroposophical understanding, it is understood that every thought ever produced still exist, even if the producer of that thought has passed over to the spiritual realm. These existing thoughts are stored so to speak, in the elemental sphere of the astral realm. Have you ever noticed how often a thought will just pop into your head without any thinking at all? These are the ones floating about in the elemental sphere and they are there for the taking, for all to have access to. In meditation, the adage that we must quiet the mind to meditate, is based on the *belief*, that thoughts and thinking come from the same place. Again, because generally there's no Aware experience of where these two elements originate from, then they get bundled up once more into the *concept of mind.* Yet again attributed as another process of the mind. In ancient Hawaiian philosophy, it is understood that thoughts are just ethereal elements, until they have been emotionalized by an individual, who then transforms that elemental thought into a thought-form. It is this thought-form that then becomes grounded in our material reality of form by the individual, where it can then create an influence to manifest physicality.

Through true Awareness is it possible to distinguish where these thought elements originate from—and out of which component of Soul they become substantiated.

What is revealed through Awareness is that thinking is an activity of the Intellectual Soul component that forms thoughts. These thoughts are then emotionalized by the Sentient Soul component and once emotionalized, then reside within it. Thinking is an intellectual *activity* of the Intellectual Soul; through which ideas, concepts and even those existing thoughts in the elemental sphere, can be formulated into a form, a structure if you will. These final forms or structures are what the actual thought is. Thinking is an *activity* of Intelligence; by which the Intellectual component of your Soul can create ideas etc., as well as rationalizations about things. The thinking creation of ideas etc., becomes a thought-form, once it has been emotionalized by the Sentient Soul component. These formulated concepts, ideas etc., are emotionalized by the designation of either an attachment or resistant sentient feeling/emotion, being assigned to the thought through judgement. This is how a thought becomes a thought-form within one's Soul, via the co-creation of the Sentient and Intellectual Soul components. Our beliefs are created this way.

So, with the likes of meditation for example, if you are trying to stop the thoughts from *coming in*, then you are not going to be successful if you are addressing it through your Intellectual Soul, because it is the Sentient Soul that needs to be experienced to quieten it down, to stop it emotionalizing thoughts. The existing thoughts from the Astral's elemental realm, just seem to continually "pop in", enter the Soul through the Sentient Soul's emotionalizing of that realms existing thoughts. If it is the "flow of thoughts" that you're wanting to stop, then the Sentient-Soul needs to be experienced fully to be quietened, not the Intellectual-Soul. Likewise, if it is the "thinking" itself that you're wanting to stop, then the Intellectual Soul needs to be experienced fully to be quietened, not the Sentient Soul. Remember, the primary purpose of everything created is to be experienced fully, and when it has been, its purpose is complete, and it will automatically discharge its creative charge. Here again is another example of the power of the Awareness exercise and the importance of grounding your Spirit Awareness in your Soul.

This however, although it is most definitely *thinking* ... is not *Pure Thinking*. The thinking of the Intellectual Soul is almost like an automatic thinking activity associated with the rationalizing, extrapolating and logical ability of your Intellectual Soul. This form of thinking can only ever form ideas etc., from thoughts that already exist within our human reality, within the elemental realm of ALL thoughts. This form of thinking and its consequent thought forms created, can NEVER be truthfully associated with "New Thought". These thought-forms are simply the re-arrangement of existing thoughts etc., plucked from the elemental realm, yet creatively put into a new construct. Again, this happens automatically, yet deceptively creative, but ONLY through the processes of the Intellectual Soul component. There is no true *conscious deliberateness* in this process. There is no truly Conscious thinking activity in the creation of these thought-forms. In a real sense, we could say that the degree of development of one's Intellectual Soul, determines the *amount* of thoughts one is able to collect, construct and formulate, into what is then perceived as intelligent, or even deceptively ingenious concepts.

Pure Thinking however, can only come about when the Consciousness Souls activity of Will, is engaged in the thinking process. It is the Will force of the Consciousness Soul that shifts our concepts and ideas from dead-thoughts to live-thoughts, from creations of existing thoughts, to truly New-Thought-Forms. It is in the activation of the Consciousness Souls Will-Force, that we may now direct the Intellectual Souls thinking process, to access the higher and truly "New" thoughts of the Spiritual Realm. All true New-Thought ONLY exists in the Spiritual Realm. To access these evolutionary and revolutionary new-thoughts from the Spiritual Realm, requires the development and employment of our Consciousness ... specifically of our Consciousness Souls Will-Forces to direct our Intellectual Souls thinking ability away from the collection of thoughts out of the elemental realm and connect it to the Spiritual Realms stream of Higher-New-Thought-Forms.

Rudolph Steiner gives us more insight into this in one of his lectures on education in 1922.

> *Assume that you are capable of it, that you can think in such a way that your thoughts are only an inner flow of thoughts. What I called "pure thinking" in my "Intuitive Thinking as a Spiritual Path" was certainly not well named when judged by outer cultural conditions. For Eduard von Hartmann† said to me, "There is no such thing; one can only think with the aid of external observation." And all I could say in reply was; "One only has to try it, and one will learn and finally be able really to do it." Thus, take it as a hypothesis that you could have thoughts in a flow of pure thought. Then there begins for you the moment when you have led thinking to a point where it need not be called thinking any longer, because in a twinkling—in the twinkling of a thought—it has become something different. This rightly-named pure thinking has become pure will, for it is willing through and through. If you have advanced so far in your life of soul that you have freed thinking from outer perception, it has become at the same time pure will. You hover with your soul, so to speak, in a pure course of thought. But this pure course of thought is a course of will. The pure thinking or the striving for the practicing of pure thought begins to be not only a thought exercise but also a will exercise, and indeed such a will exercise that works right into the center of the human being. For you will make the following remarkable observation. It is only now, for the first time, that you can speak of thinking as it is in ordinary life, as an activity of the head. Before this, you really have no right to speak of thinking as an activity of the head, for you know this only as external fact from physiology, anatomy, and so on. But now you feel inwardly that you are no longer thinking so high up, you begin for the first time to think with the heart. You actually interweave your thought with the breathing process. You actually set going what the yoga exercises have striven for artificially. You notice that, as thinking becomes more and more an activity of the will, it wrenches itself free first from the breast and then from the whole human body. It is as though you were to draw forth this thinking from the last fiber of your big toe! And if with inner participation you study what has appeared with many imperfections—for I make no claims about my Intuitive Thinking as a Spiritual Path—if you let it work upon you and feel what this pure thinking is, you will experience that a new person is born within you who can bring out of the spirit an unfolding of the will.*

"Becoming the Archangel Michael's Companions" Steiner Books, Collected Works.

It is the actual *activity of pure thinking* that we want to develop here, through our thinking exercise. Truth is, by developing our *thinking activity*, along with the development of the Feeling, Willing and Awareness, the quality of the thoughts produced from this raised level of thinking, improves dramatically as well. This comes about because, by not resisting or rejecting thinking, and bringing it under your own *conscious* control of your Will, you remove the lower influences on it that trap you in materialistic thinking, in the dead-thoughts of the elemental realm. Ironically, it is through pure-thinking that you are able to intimately connect the worlds above … and below. Without control of your thinking however, without *Pure-Will-full-Thinking,* you are open to the thought influences of the darker forces of the materialistic Beings that are here creating our physical world for us. These Ahrimanic Beings, influence us directly *through* thought, injecting materialistic thoughts we then emotionalize and associate with … as our own. These Beings of influence are the ones that create the materialist viewpoints we see operating so selfishly around our world now. The materialist perspective of life as a human are not a result of your Spirit-Self, nor even your Human-Soul-self, but are a direct result of an Intellectual Soul *under the influence* of the materialistic BEing of Form. The first achievement of the Thinking Exercise is to help you take back control of your thinking and free you from this materialistic BEing's influence. This influence is what creates the non-essential thinking I mentioned earlier, or in Anthroposophical terms, the dead-thoughts that keep us materialistically bound. Live-thoughts can grow, expand and morph into something new. They are filled with life and growth forces. Through the combination of Awareness with this state of pure-thinking, we can raise and strengthen the ability of our Intellectual Soul to perceive these *live-thoughts* and bring them into our human reality. This is how we can develop the Intellectual/Perspective Soul to become capable of receiving, or rather perceiving, the higher living frequency of the truly *creative new thoughts* of the spiritual realm. From there, we can then ground them in this human reality. Ultimately, through the higher development of our thinking ability in harmony with the other attributes of Awareness, Feeling and Willing, we will be able through this higher level of pure-thinking—to transmute dead thoughts into living ones. Through what will ultimately become your spiritualized Intelligence, you will be able to combine dead thoughts into a new living thought-form. From this ability, we will be moving human evolution into its next phase of development.

The Exercise:

a) Pick any object that exists in our world. Think about this object and all the possibilities of how this object came into being. BE *Aware* throughout this whole thinking process and diligently catch and notice when the thinking turns to non-essential with respect to the object. For example, say you are thinking about a pensile. An essential thought might be one that is directly related to the pensile and its origin as a tree and all the transformations that might have taken that tree through to become a pensile. Essential thinking might also include thinking about the machine itself that cuts down the tree or the machine that shaves it down to a pensile etc. Although the machine is definitely connected with the creation of the pensile, it is not how the machine was built that is essential to the pensile itself. Essential is only connected with the pensile itself. Non-essential thinking would be connected with everything else, like a favorite pensil you had or using a pensil to draw or write etc. Once you notice the non-essential creep in, then with your Awareness, feel/experience the difference between the non-essential to the essential ... but be aware to not define it. As usual, just feel the difference, then with your Will, control your thinking and go back to thinking only the essentials. With Awareness again, while still thinking about the pensile, feel what this *thinking process* feels like. Notice what this form of thinking, what this *activity of thinking* feels like ... without definition, judgment or description.

Do this part a) continuously for a minimum of 10 minutes.

b)   Now, think about something that *doesn't* already exist in our present reality. For this part, you will need to invoke your imaginative capability also. At this point, it is ok to create something out of elements of our world that already exist, but you're doing it to create an object that doesn't exist. For example, you could create the likes of a tank with helicopter blades and see it flying. Do you get the idea? Rudolph Steiner gives us a particular meditation, which involves thinking about a black cross with a ring of 12 red roses at its central cross point. This particular image however, is a spiritual one with wisdoms embedded in the symbols of cross and red rose configuration. The form of this meditation—which we will cover later in this chapter—can evoke revelation from the spiritual realm. The point of this part of our thinking exercise however, is to control the *line of thinking* again and deliberately stimulate the *activity of thinking*. This form of activity of thinking however, is developing your ability to allow the thinking to evolve and grow and expand via live thoughts, but to not lose the original concept. Of course, you are doing this with Awareness also, to notice any non-essential dead thoughts trying to fill in the gaps so to speak. Again though, you are *controlling the flow* of creative essential thinking and at the same time notice what this form of thinking feels like. At various times, see if you can notice the difference if any, between the two different forms of thinking, but once noticed, then go immediately back to the controlled Willful-Thinking. Can you see how you are using your Awareness throughout this exercise to notice differences between these thinking modes and the forces activated by each?

Do this part b) continuously for a minimum of 10 minutes.

There is a developmental process that happens from doing these parts a & b, so doing it just once is not necessarily going to produce the required development. Create a rhythmic cycle of practice for yourself by doing these short 10-minute sessions in the morning and evening each day for the first 30 days. You can of course do these more often than that if you wish. Insights will begin to show up each week, but transformation will become apparent between 30 to 60 days.

The Living Thinking Exercise:

- As a living exercise, you are going to hold vigilant Awareness throughout every-moment of your waking day. This Awareness is on the thoughts that stream through you in every moment—to determine the essential from the non-essential. If you have done parts a) and b) diligently, in the quiet of your own space and got to the point of being able to notice the differences between your dead and live thoughts, then you may be pleasantly shocked at how easily you can distinguish them while in the rush of influences from your everyday activities. The living exercise empowers your ability to control thinking and maintain a heightened quality of thinking throughout your waking life. Ironically, this higher developed thinking, reduces the uncontrollable thinking of the old, *concept of mind* materialistic thinking. Now, you will notice that your Intellectual Soul will begin to perceive far more intuitive thought than ever before. With this intuitive thought, inspiration from the spiritual realm on all manner of things, both physical and spiritual, now has a newly formed conduit into your BEing.

Thinking Meditation

I know this almost sounds like a contradiction to what many believe meditating is all about, but in fact, *thinking* in meditation, is what true spiritual science is about. From what we have just covered however, you may see now that it is true *pure-thinking* that is required … not the random lower thinking of the intellect alone. Rudolph Steiner is quite specific about the correct use of not just thinking, but the higher form of pure-thinking you have just been doing through the above exercises. Although you can pick any topic with this form of meditation, for this "Thinking Meditation", let the first topic be "the activity of thinking" itself. Remember, the topic is "thinking" and not "thoughts". Thinking about thoughts would be the non-essential, where thinking about thinking, would be the essential.

Pick a quiet spot for yourself with a comfortable chair for sitting upright.

- Sitting upright, become intimately present with yourself by doing the Awareness Exercise for a few minutes. Looking around from object to object, notice the difference between them. When you feel you are BEing Awareness and can recognize the difference between Awareness and attention, then move to the next part.

- Now using your Soul's Will forces, hold all of the thinking activity of your Intellectual Soul on the topic of thinking. Let this thinking flow, as you explore what the *activity of thinking* is and how it affects you. Don't feel restricted in your thinking … about thinking. Look at it from as many perspectives as you can. Be diligent with your Awareness on essential to non-essentials, as you dive deep into the Universe of thinking.

- If you feel like you have explored ALL perspectives of thinking, then just relax and feel the space you occupy, then ask your Self, "what other perspective is there of thinking." Once the question is asked, BE still in Awareness and open to another perspective showing up ... then explore and think about that one also.

- After thinking about this topic for approximately ten to fifteen minutes; using again your Will forces, just stop thinking and BE in silent Awareness. Be diligent to not attach to any thoughts that may try to come into you. With your Awareness wide open and still, use your Will to BE free of all thinking. If the dead thoughts of the Elemental sphere show up, then just allow them to flow through without thinking about them, while maintaining your Aware state of non-thinking.

- Maintain this non-thinking Aware state for another five minutes or so before opening your eyes. With eyes now open, maintain your state of Awareness as you softly gaze upon and go about the world around you.

As I mentioned earlier, the activity of thinking has the potential to connect us with other spiritual realms. With this form of meditation, the first part of thinking is connecting to the topic by bringing in through pure-thinking, everything that can be perceived of the topic—in this case being thinking. The latter step of silent Awareness without thinking, is opening your Soul's space for wisdoms on the topic from the spiritual realm to enter and reveal their-self via your Spirit-Self's Awareness. This meditation can be used for any topic you desire clarity on from the higher perspectives of Spirit. Again, this is a developmental meditation practice, so don't just do it once and because your intellect may judge that nothing seemed to come of it, you should give it up. BE patient, and diligent ... embody those virtues and continue with the same meditation topic for at least a week, more if you feel so moved. Embody the virtue of "allowing" and allow the Spiritual Realm to connect with you. Remember, this is the first time you are creating this connection deliberately and as yet, it may still be weak and clouded or veiled in non-essentials. Allow it all, the skill, ability, forces etc., to develop first. Understand and accept that your Soul-Forces may not be sufficiently developed yet to facilitate clear and strong communications. We are Graced with results only after we have committed consistent effort and intention to "live the practice". The Divine doesn't reward one-time-wonders.

4. **Willing Exercises:** *Developing the Will of the Consciousness Soul and its deliberate use.*

As we discussed earlier, the lack of Will forces is a chronic sickness of Soul for our present humanity. If you feel challenged by that statement and see yourself as having a good command of your Will, because you often complete projects and so forth, then notice what your *truthful* answer to the following questions is. Do you do anything without thinking about it and consciously direct the action first or even while you are doing it? There is an old Buddhist exercise to bring the body under greater control of the Will, by not making any move or gesture, without first *deciding* to make the gesture, and then not start it until you *deliberately* direct it with your Will. Doing this exercise is a great indicator of where you may be with being able to use your true Will deliberately.

By todays illusion of our *concept of mind*, the "asserted force" used in making something come about, is misconstrued as the true power of Will from our Consciousness Soul. This Will is the true power that *creates* and *manifest*. Remember, the Will is an ability of your Consciousness Soul, so its deliberate use, would come from using it ... consciously. Unfortunately, this rarely happens for a very large proportion of our planets population. Will is what creates ... not just actions and movement, but manifests form. ALL creation ... comes about from an act of Will ... all be it Divine Universal Will. Our Consciousness Soul's Will is the very same, yet it is through our Consciousness that we are given the ability and right to direct Divine Will and use it to create our human realities. Life confirms for us that ... although we all do most definitely have Will, Life can show us the level or strength or stage of development that this Will is at. It is a spiritual vison through Awareness however, which can bring to light *where* Will exists and *what* is needed to develop it further.

In looking for the intellectual definition of Will, it was interesting that at the top of the list it said that Will is a part of the mind. Again, we see that *concept of mind* showing up to take credit for another super-sensory attribute that no one knows where it comes from or how to develop it or use it correctly. Going on the research of the current definitions and descriptions of all these elements we have been discussing, it wouldn't seem too far-fetched to just wipe all recognition of Soul and Spirit altogether and let's just say that we are made up of simply Body and Mind. So fortunate Humanity is, that we have entered the Consciousness Soul age. Fortunate are we, to now have the "I" of Spirit-Self to shine its light of Awareness on the higher truth of the actual individual components—those that make up our Human BEing.

> *My Will is literally, the spiritual glue of Consciousness.*

Your Will is a force of your Consciousness Soul, which motivates and moves things into creative action. Mistakenly, we may take that as meaning movement of limbs, or undertaking or completing projects in the physical world. This is most definitely true, however the real power of the Will resides within the Soul, not in the Body, even though it is Will that most definitely moves Body. Will is a force of Soul, without which, man would not be able to progress any further along his evolutionary path. It is your Will that directs and holds attention, Awareness, thinking, virtues, all the senses, concentration and so much more. It is through the Will that your Soul can bring in the fruits of the spiritual realm and it is the fully developed Will that will eventually transform us into true free creator Beings in the Cosmos. Rudolph Steiner talks of the Universal Will that is the force in everything that creates and moves and transforms. He also shares that everything IS consciousness, so we can see the connection between consciousness and the force that is ... Will.

Take a moment and feel what it takes to "BE conscious" of your right arm. Notice your attention being directed toward your arm and notice what you feel like as you are now BEing *conscious*. It is subtle, but with Awareness again, see if you can feel the *force* that is your Will directing and holding your attention. It is this force of your Soul we are desperately needing to develop, that comes from your Consciousness component of Soul. It is the Will that is the game-breaker for grounding your Spirit-Self's Awareness into your Soul. This is the force necessary to discharge the *concept of mind* from your Intelligence. There are many forms of Will exercises that can develop it and you may have noticed that all of the exercises we have gone through above, ALL incorporate and need the Will to one degree or another. In fact, every time you do any of the above exercises, you are also using and developing your Will throughout them all. However, like the other exercises above, the Will exercises below are designed to isolate the Will, so you can bring the *activity* of the *force* that is the Will, into your Awareness. From there you may gain an intimately experiential knowing of it. It is this intimate *experiential knowing* that gives you the power to then deliberately use your Will. Although Will is a most powerful force, it is extremely soft and subtle, so a heightened level of Awareness is necessary to truly identify it correctly.

The Exercise:

Basic Exercise

- Sitting upright, become intimately present with yourself by doing the Awareness Exercise for a few minutes. Looking around from object to object, notice the *difference* between them. *Feel* what the difference is without defining, describing or judging what that difference is. Do this for just a few minutes only.

- With eyes and Awareness now wide open and still, look at a physical object near to you. Be interested in this item, but not thinking about it, yet putting all your attention on this item and hold it there.

- While maintaining attention on the item and keeping it in view, with your Awareness, try to feel the *force* that is holding your attention and vision on the object. Just get a sense of it without defining or describing or getting caught up in it in any way. With Awareness, feel what it feels like to *hold* attention on the object. Feel the force that is holding the attention.

- Now notice when your attention fades off the object. When it does, feel the difference between attention on and attention off the object. Once you have felt the difference without definition, description or judgment of it, using your Awareness and Will ... direct your attention back onto the object again.

- Continue to do this for 10 minutes. Every time your attention wanders, 1st feel the difference, 2nd bring your attention back using your Will ... and feel the difference again.

Advanced Exercise

- Sitting upright, become intimately present with yourself by doing the Awareness Exercise for a few minutes. Looking around from object to object, notice the *difference* between them. Feel what the difference is without defining, describing or judging what that difference is. Do this for just a few minutes only.

- With Awareness, retrace your life's experiences from the present moment *backwards,* until 10 minutes is up. Retrace this with as much detail as possible of every moment from your present backwards.

- Be diligently Aware of when your attention drifts off your life's events and wanders into detail of aspects of the people etc., that are in the events. There is nothing wrong with this happening, for when Awareness is shone on our events, it is not uncommon for aspects and details to show up that we may have skipped over in our everyday participation. Once noticed however, with Aware Will, gently bring your attention back to the retracing of your days life from your present moment where you originally started from.

- Continue to do this for 10 minutes using your Will to stay on task and your Awareness to notice differences throughout.

The Living Will Exercise.

Although we have set a time of 10 minutes for these exercises and it is recommended that you do this morning and evening like the thinking exercises, there is far more power to develop your Will force if you do this continually throughout your day. This Living Will Exercise is as simple as diligently with your Awareness, notice when your attention wanders from whatever you are doing in any given moment and ... *deliberately* bring it back on task and *feel* the difference with your Awareness. Once you have noticed your attention shift off task etc., the power in this living practice lies in always ...

1st. notice with your Awareness, what your present immediate experience feels like when you are off task.

2nd. deliberately feel with your Awareness the *force* that is your Will and then gently use it to direct your attention back on task.

3rd. notice with your Awareness what being on task feels like in the present moment.

The truth of this practice is that it is done completely within seconds ... but it is recommended to do it continuously throughout your day.

The Will Meditation

In a true sense, this is not just a Will meditation, but incorporates all the attributes of Awareness, Feeling Thinking and Willing of your Soul and Spirit-Self. Its benefit is two-fold, in respect that obviously it takes a lot of Will to use all of your attributes together, so obviously you get the opportunity to use your Will to a greater degree than normally, but it also has a powerful aligning effect on your Physical, Soul and Spirit bodies, by bringing them all together in unity and harmony as well. This state of harmonic unity is actually the TRUE state in which real healing can occur.

This meditation is an extension of the previous Will exercise of tracing your day backwards from your present moment. The difference here however, is that you are going to incorporate much more deeply, ALL of the other component attributes of Awareness, Feeling, Thinking and Willing throughout the whole meditation. The other difference here is that, as you retrace your day's events, this time you are going to *fully experience* them as well. This means that you are not just scrolling through the physical events of your day, but you are going to recall the *experience* that was stimulated by each of those event moments also. This means for example; that if your event moment was driving to the store, you will also recall the frustrating *experience* you had from the other person who cut you off, or the anguish and impatient *experience* you had while—according to your perception, you were sitting at the traffic lights too long, etc., etc. You see, this is an *experiential retrace* rather than a *physical* event retrace; of which the earlier *exercise* above is.

I further recommend you do each of the steps in this meditation individually first, so you can have a real *experience* of the actual step in its entirety, separate from the others. Having embodied the experience of each individual step, it will be easier to remember each when you put them in sequence for the complete meditation. The whole meditation shouldn't take more than 20-30 minutes. You however, you decide the final time you take.

Meditation Steps

a) Sitting upright, become intimately present with yourself by doing the Awareness Exercise for a few minutes. Looking around from object to object, notice the *difference* between them. Feel what the difference is without defining, describing or judging what that difference is. Do this for just a few minutes only.

b) Close your eyes and using your Will, direct your Awareness to your body and feel what your body feels like. Get a sense of the skin covering the body as the outer edge of it and feeling the difference between the skin and everything inside the skin. Feel what the body feels like, from its edges inward.

c) Now notice the space outside the edges of the body and notice the difference between that space and the body. Once you have a sense of that difference, then, using your Will deliberately, move all your "Awareness" into the space surrounding your body, and *feel* what that space feels like ... experience it.

d) With Awareness, experience your way through this space until you feel the edges of this space and then ... feel/experience this space from the edges inward.

e) Now experience "the space YOU occupy" and notice the difference between the space you occupy and the space your body occupies ... without definition, judgement or description of that difference. Simply BE Aware of the difference then continue to experience the space YOU occupy.

f) Now recall your present days experiences/events ... from the present moment backwards. Fully experience/feel with Awareness each event moment as you progress backwards from the present moment. Do this for 10-15 minutes.

g) Now using your Will deliberately, for just a few minutes, BE the observer without attaching to anything. BE the open space that the Spiritual Realm can reveal its Self into.

h) Before you open your eyes, BE Aware of the state of Awareness you are in, in this moment. Now open your eyes and maintain this state of Awareness, as you become present now with your immediate environment. Continue to be present and notice the differences of everything within your immediate physical environment.

i) BE Aware of your Will Force now directing your Awareness. Now allow your Awareness to expand beyond your immediate visible physical environment, continuing to *notice/get a sense of,* the differences outside of your visible environment. Allow these differences to reveal their-self to you … rather than looking for them. Just feel what they feel like as they reveal their-self … and move on.

j) Now, continue to LIVE throughout your day in this state of … Present Aware Super Sensitivity. (P.A.S.S.)

- To do this meditation once a week for 30 days can give you an experience of the meditation and its subtle, yet powerful effect on all three of your subtle bodies.

- To do this meditation once a day for 30 days, can transform the state of your health and wellness to a degree that may shock you.

- To do this meditation in conjunction with the other exercises and meditations above, will accelerate the development your Soul-Spiritual forces exponentially beyond belief.

Allow yourself to receive and embody the gifts that this simple meditation can give you, by initially committing to do this every day for 30 days. Create a new rhythmic routine that works for your lifestyle with this meditation included in it … and simply commit to it. Your life will naturally and effortlessly improve on many subtle levels, but you will also begin to notice that those in your environment will experience changes also. Your relationship with them improves, as a direct result of your commitment to living in your new state of Present Aware Super Sensitivity (P.A.S.S.) existence. They will experience subtle shifts in their own space when they are with you as well. The state of our existence—each and every one of us—has an effect on the state of each other's … without exceptions. Whether that affect is a positive or negative one is solely determined by your-self and the state of BEing that you exist in. Even before you have fully experienced the effects from this meditation, I'm sure you could already sense what a massively positive affect you are going to have on those you love and the friends you keep, from you living in a P.A.S.S. existence. Imagine the potential shift that could be achieved in Humanities consciousness, when there is a high percentage of our population living in a P.A.S.S. existence. That shift starts with you.

Conclusion

With every ending ... there is always a beginning.

When we look at our material existence and we see events etc., seemingly end, we tend to take this as proof that our human nature through its changing modes, is in a state of endings and beginnings also. The ultimate of this false perception is that we believe we are only here as physical humans for a limited lifetime. In truth, it is only the *external* physical nature of actions and motions created within our Earth reality, that we perceive as having endings and beginnings. The true nature of the Human Being is that it actually never ends and never begins, even though we have the process of death and re-birth. Although a particular finite life of physical experience is most definitely finished when our physical vehicle for this Earth-walk has been returned to the Earth, our truly spiritually *BEing* existence as a human; which is our true and infinite Soul-Spirit Nature, continues to exist and in fact never ends, but simply transforms to something other than what it was for this finite lifetime. My point in bringing this up is, that there is never any end from one existence to another, from operating a certain way and then a week, month, year or decade later, you are operating a different way or perceiving things differently.

The fact is that yes, you have changed, but you haven't completely stopped doing what you had done previously. You have in fact transformed what you were doing before and are now just doing it differently. Even though it may *appear* to be completely different, there are still elements in your new actions that are remnants of your old. The real difference is that you have actually added more actions, different perceptions and viewpoints etc., that change the way you were, to a seemingly new way of BEing. You see, an end of a Doing, only comes about in the physical material world reality, but the change in Being, is a continual evolutionary transformation brought about through the addition of more and more knowledge of Self, more attributes, characteristics, energies or frequencies if you like, perspectives and viewpoints, abilities and intentions. All of these simply change the way you BE in the greater Divine fabric that ALL Life exist within. The key piece here though, is that it is a *transformation* and not an ending and beginning of a new you.

Knowledge is Power.

Self-knowledge holds the power for me to transform my-Self.

Within the Soul's heartbeat of every human Being, lies this insatiable thirst for knowledge. Most important of all knowledge however, is our internal compulsion for self-knowledge—to intimately and completely know our human-self and to experience the freedom that comes from its acquisition. We may pretend to others that all this "stuff" about self and Soul and Spirit and consciousness etc., all mean little to us, but look at all the subtle ways you are continually trying to change all manner of aspects of your-self, to improve your life and state of Being. The spiritual salespeople and the supermarkets they create to sell their *self-development wares*, all exists because of the subtle internal pulse of every human Being's Soul to improve itself and at a deeper level, embody its Human-Spirit-Self. No matter the denial and invalidations the materialistic thinkers of our world would have you believe; even deep with them as well, this driving pulse of Soul yearns to marry Human and Spirit together again. This inner pulse continues to silently beat and caressingly felt, when you allow your-self to look past the physical and with Awareness, *feel* the un-seeable. Through this self-realization will be revealed that this pulse of Love; of Love for knowledge which can simplify the complexities that lie within Self-knowledge, is in fact coming from your own True Nature.

Rudolph Steiner has an insight for us in his lecture on Happiness.

> *It is perfectly understandable that people in our time, naturally inclined to materialistic thinking, will find it absurd and paradoxical when spiritual enquiry states that the human being is more than external science acknowledges, that we are more than biology, physiology and psychology admit, the latter founded likewise on external facts. Spiritual enquiries lead to the assertion that we are in fact composed of a complex of aspects of which the physical, material body is only one, while the others—only perceptible to spiritual enquiry as I said— live in an invisible, supersensible realm, and from there work and act upon us. It is perfectly natural that people today ridicule such an idea, that they rail against the idea that we have besides the physical body; which serves us in the sense world when we act outwardly and perceive things in that world, also subtler bodies, subtler aspects of human nature. Spiritual science tells us that we have, apart from our physical body, an 'etheric body', which is 'subtler' in comparison to the grosser physical body; and that these two aspects of human nature are the ones that remain in the physical realm when we immerse ourselves in the unconscious state of sleep. It further tells us of higher aspects, more spiritual constituents, which we call the astral body and the I, and states that these, pass over into a world of spirit when we fall asleep. Spiritual science shows that these higher aspects of human nature, resting in an unconscious realm during sleep, are in fact the real, active agencies that ensoul and give strength to the physical and etheric bodies when we awaken from sleep again. The inability of modern science to acknowledge these higher aspects of human nature resembles a person's failure to accept that air exists because he cannot see it or touch it.*

"Happiness" by Rudolph Steiner.

Life experienced only through your physical senses is a life of always combating external influences from the world you live in. This is a victim existence, continually coming under the influence of some other force than your own. To come to know the forces that impose these influences, and more importantly to know where they originate from, what their source is, will free you from their influence. To experientially know the forces that reside within your inner world of Soul and Spirit, can unleash immense power and wisdom not achievable through your physical senses alone. In reference to what Rudolph Steiner says above; just because you can't see these forces and influences etc., and just because you can't see your Soul and Spirit in physical form with your physical human senses yet … doesn't mean they don't exists. It is a materialistic fool trapped in the influence of external forces that says, "I only believe what I can see and prove with my mind." Seeing and proving are limited by the definitions you already have, and the biggest limitation is the *concept of mind* created by your Intellectual Soul. In truth, it wasn't even your Intellectual Soul that created these limitations of the concept of mind … it came from others. These thoughts etc., already exist from someone else, from a past humanities intellect and your Intellectual Soul has simply and blindly accepted them in from the Elemental realm of the Collective Astral. Proof can only ever prove what is already known by and exists because of the Intellectual Soul. Your Intellectual Soul component of you, has now become the boundary to you, of knowledge of your worlds existence. This has come about because it is incapable of finding the complete truth, because it is your Souls organ of *perception* … not *conscious experience.*

Perception is an ability to see the seeable … Conscious Experience is the ability to embody and feel the un-seeable.

Truth, of the unseen world of Soul and Spirit, lies within the abilities of your Consciousness Soul and its marriage to Spirit Awareness. Because we have turned another page in Human evolution, by having already developed our Intellectual Soul, we have ALL now entered the Consciousness Soul stage. From this evolutionary page turning milestone, through which you are now able to become conscious of the unseen—the "I" of your Spirit-Self can now join the consciousness of your human-Soul-self. Collectively, this alone gives all of us, the potential to become conscious of our Spirit and the spiritual realm we all exists in, in a truly experiential way. It is this *experience* that holds the power to become a true creator of your human existence—to be free from influence and truly Self-determining in your life. In the marrying of your Soul and Spirit, of your Spirit-Self "I" with your Soul Consciousness, you are creating a new existence of true "I Consciousness"—making you now capable of accessing and directing the greater creational spiritual forces that all life exists because of.

YOU are now, in this present day and age, potentially capable of self-manifesting real health and wellness in the human life you are NOW living through. This is not by just gaining self-knowledge but using this knowledge to become Self-Realized.

Self-Realization comes from the experiential embodiment of self-knowledge.

By putting this knowledge, what you have gained here through this book study into a practice; the living practice set out above, with the correct tools and exercises that are designed to develop the appropriate Soul development within you, you have the potential to be able to bring *yourself* to this state of Self-Realized P.A.S.S. existence.

It is time for you to P.A.S.S. through life.

As I stated earlier, Self-Knowledge holds the Power for one to transform one's self. The transformation I wish for you all from the knowledge within these pages is one of freedom. This means freedom from external influence that comes through an empowered willingness to fully experience anything, as you live in your P.A.S.S. state, of Present Aware Super Sensitivity and find the true Power that is … your Spirit.

The Living Exercises and Meditations given here can accelerate your journey into Higher Self-Knowledge, if undertaken with loving patience and commitment to *truly know thy Self*, for the betterment of all Humankind.

- The Exercises will bring into your Awareness the aspects of your components of Soul you have learned about throughout the earlier pages. These exercises can help you find the seed of P.A.S.S. existence that resides within you, waiting to be germinated.

- The Living Exercises will bring your new experiential Awareness of the components of Soul and BEing Human, to life within your human reality of everyday life. These exercises will help you develop the skills needed to *live* your P.A.S.S. existence within your everyday human life.

- The meditations will embody your Spirit into your human-Soul-self, opening up the world of your Spirit to your Human as a continual living experience. This is what I call "I Harmony" … a state of harmonic co-creation between the Body Soul and Spirit. Within this realm of creating, P.A.S.S. creates a constant state of Self-Realized Being.

So, this is not an ending or a beginning, but if you are willing, it can be the start of a new intimate journey into your own ever self-evolving personalized Self-Realization—a realization into the complex wholeness of the complete Human *BE*-ing that you truly are.

My commitment is to support you on this journey through the highs and lows, the ecstatic and heavy, the expanded and contracted and all the other levels and modes of new experiences that await you. I especially want to support you through the resistances and attachments that will inevitably show up as you deep-dive into your Souls components. Remember that this is to a greater degree, the start line, not the finish line. So, when you hit these moments of resistance, attachment, doubt and fear, discouragement and disappointment and any other testing points where it appears to be easier to succumb rather than overcome, remind yourself lovingly, that freedom comes from overcoming, and entrapment comes from succumbing.

Also know that I am here with you, as we have been together throughout this book journey, and I am available to you through the medias of email and website when you need.

Email: iharmonysolutions@gmail.com

Website: www.iharmonysolutions.com

I look forward to the time when we all come together in P.A.S.S. on an iharmony workshop, and support each other to go to the next level of discharging past patterns, embodying virtues and deepen our state of P.A.S.S.

May you have the courage to experience your-Self fully ... the Love to embrace your-Self openly and wholeheartedly ... and the willingness to do whatever it takes to develop and embody the power to P.A.S.S. through your life's journey ahead, spiritualizing your human along the way.

I am here with and for you.

Are you out of your mind ... yet?

27661633R00158

Made in the USA
Lexington, KY
06 January 2019